Dec.
Test 5+6
Sutter vocab.
&
idioms

ACTIVE GERMAN

W. P. Lehmann
Chairman
Department of Germanic Languages
THE UNIVERSITY OF TEXAS

Helmut Rehder
Professor of Germanic Languages
THE UNIVERSITY OF TEXAS

George Schulz-Behrend
Associate Professor of Germanic Languages
THE UNIVERSITY OF TEXAS

AN ELE

ACTIVE

MENTARY GRAMMAR

GERMAN

HOLT, RINEHART AND WINSTON, INC. NEW YORK

PREFACE

Active German is founded upon the premise that any language is made up of recurrent patterns. The linguist's task is to distinguish these patterns; the language teacher's, to present them most effectively. Beginning with the first lesson, therefore, we have used, in both the reading texts and the exercises, patterns that occur frequently, that illustrate the essentials of German grammar, and that include a high proportion of the words most frequently used in contemporary German. In selecting words we have occasionally departed from the somewhat outdated frequency lists; for example, we have preferred such words as *Telefon* to words whose rank in frequency lists no longer corresponds to current usage, such as *Dienstmädchen*.

Although language teachers and linguists must make use of the experience of their predecessors in preparing textbooks, a text must forfeit its claim to pedagogical excellence unless it presents realistic materials. By employing an American setting for the stories that comprise the reading texts of the lessons, we have brought the situation and vocabulary close to the life of the students, although we have deprived them of the smattering of information which they might have obtained from simple texts about Germany.

Instructors will succeed best in their teaching with *Active German* if they have their students repeat the German sentences aloud until they have memorized them, or nearly so. Choral work is very effective for economical teaching: and students will master German most readily if they repeat the German materials presented in the texts until they have them completely under their control. Selected materials, such as the brief conversations and specific exercises, can also be recorded for use in language laboratories.

By memorizing the German materials in class work and home study, students will learn grammar and syntax as well as the vocabulary. The word lists and grammar sections can then be used primarily for review. The German exercises will extend to new contexts the vocabulary and grammar learned in the German selections. We have designed exercises dealing with various grammatical difficulties, so that students can learn their grammar through these alone, with no great study of grammatical explanations. The English-into-German sentences and the free conversations provide a final review of each lesson.

Active German is designed for the typical introductory course. It contains ample basic reading material and exercises for a complete five-hour, one-semester course or for the three-hour, full-year course. The exercises have been held to the minimum required for a suitable program; we assume that instructors will supplement them with others of their own devising.

Although every instructor has his own techniques of teaching, it may be helpful to describe how *Active German* has been used by the authors through a number of semesters.

In the first period devoted to a lesson, we read, sentence by sentence, the German texts at the beginning of that lesson, requiring the class to repeat each sentence in chorus and then individually as time permits. During this reading we establish the meaning of each sentence, either giving it ourselves or asking students to do so. We also discuss briefly the passages that illustrate grammatical points dealt with in that lesson. The student is then equipped to go home, master the text, and through it begin to master the vocabulary and grammar of the lesson.

In the second period we review the text, then present exercises dealing with points of grammar. If, for example, we are teaching Lesson 2, we start work on Exercise A. This exercise concentrates entirely on forming accusatives of nouns; through it, we teach the forms of articles and nouns in the accusative and the use of the accusative for the direct object. Exercise B is similar but deals only with personal pronouns. Exercise C deals with **ein**-words and nouns. By reviewing these three exercises, changing the objects to the plural, we teach the accusative plural forms. We may complete only part of an exercise in class, assigning the rest as homework. Each exercise is focused on one grammatical point, and all are designed to suggest additional drills. When desirable, other substitutions than those suggested in the lesson can be put into the exercise frames; for example, in Exercise C in Lesson 1 the instructor might teach additional **ein**-words (a pencil, your pencil) or additional nouns (my paper, my story). As the vocabulary of the students increases, such expansion of the exercises becomes considerably easier and is useful for review.

After two periods given to one lesson, students are in control of the text matter, vocabulary, and grammar, and we expect them to begin to use these freely. We then make use of the questions, again adding to them, particularly in later parts of the course. Well along in the course we also use such exercises as Exercise F of Lesson 6 to teach the formation of correct simple sentences; these exercises provide a pattern for students to follow but require them to produce new sentences.

In the fourth period given to a lesson we complete the exercises, checking vocabulary and grammar, and translate some or all of the English-to-German sentences orally before assigning them to be written out at home.

The fifth period on a lesson is devoted to correction of the English-to-German sentences, to use of the Free Conversation exercises, and to work on the Brief Conversations. During later stages of the course we use a simple reader to introduce our students to a different style.

Our way of using *Active German* is determined by our apportionment of class hours to the introductory course. Most of our classes meet five hours a week, earning four credits; hence there is no home assignment for two of the class meetings each week. A smaller number of our students are on a schedule of three meetings a week. For this schedule we use *Active German* throughout the year, adding more reading material. Other programs will suggest other ways of using the book. But in any program, a minimum of time should be spent on formal grammar and discussions in English. Students can learn grammatical terms from the Preface to the Student; the grammar itself they can best learn from forming German sentences, referring as necessary to the grammar sections of each lesson and to the Appendix. Any presentation should be based on the three steps in learning a language:

> acquiring native patterns;
> learning to vary these patterns;
> using them freely in new contexts.

There has recently been much discussion of how languages may be learned most simply—whether by reading alone or by oral study plus reading. Common sense suggests that whatever the student's aim, it is most effective and most economical of time to use *all* the learning processes that are available. In working orally, students use their aural and motor faculties in addition to the visual and thus learn much more effectively than through simple reading and translation. Hence the importance of oral repetition in class, and, for economy of time, of repetition in chorus. Homework should also be oral. Accuracy of learning can be checked by oral review with the instructor or with the help of recordings. We suggest these learning procedures even for those students whose aim is only to achieve the ability to read technical texts; for these texts, too, are composed of the common patterns, and the more thoroughly the patterns are learned, the simpler the student will find advanced readings.

Most students who fail languages do so within the first three weeks of the semester. Accordingly, instructors will produce the best results by insisting on thorough preparation from the first and by giving frequent quizzes.

We have tried to avoid presenting German as though it were a collection of paradigms and, further, to avoid treating it as a puzzle. As we believe that grammatical materials must be selected as carefully as vocabularies have been in the past, we have attempted to present the most frequently encountered grammatical patterns as well as the items of vocabulary that are used most often. To the patterns presented here, the more complex ones which occur mainly in colloquial, technical, or literary German can readily be added in subsequent work.

The approach to a new language as a puzzle has been largely responsible for the myth that foreign languages are impossibly difficult for Americans. Fortunately this myth is vanishing as more effective language-teaching methods are introduced and as greater numbers of Americans are coming in contact with peoples who use more than one language.

Language teaching in America is further handicapped by a naive (and paradoxical) perfectionism among students and the general public. Underestimating certain difficulties of language learning, American students expect to attain as much proficiency in a second language as in the first. People who use several languages, on the other hand, are aware that it is very difficult to master more than the first language on which they spent most of their youthful intellectual energies, and they therefore aim for the greatest possible proficiency, not for perfection: they are not discouraged by difficulties of accent, grammar, or style that are almost impossible to overcome. If learning a second language brings home to us the complexity of our own and the control our language exerts over our thinking and expression, the hours devoted to it are well spent.

We are grateful to our colleagues for numerous suggestions, particularly to Leroy Shaw, Stanley Werbow, and Leslie Willson.

W. P. L.
H. R.
G. S-B.

Austin, Texas
February 1958

PREFACE TO THE STUDENT

WE HAVE LEARNED our own language by speaking it, by making whole sentences and varying these to suit different situations. You will most readily learn German in the same way—by mastering the reading texts of each lesson and by constructing the various sentences suggested in the exercises. The vocabulary and grammar sections are merely secondary aids; they help you to sum up what you have learned in the texts and exercises. To shorten the grammar sections, we have needed to use technical terms: many of these you have met before, but the most common ones are reviewed below to refresh your memory.

Language may be analyzed from various points of view. We may identify individual forms; these we call **parts of speech,** such as nouns and verbs. We may also identify elements of sentences; these are units of **syntax,** such as subjects and predicates. Each type of analysis has its uses. In a sentence such as "The oldest man in the village knew the answer," *man, village,* and *answer* are nouns; and making the identification is useful in teaching someone how to inflect nouns, *e.g.,* how to form plurals. (To **inflect** means to modify, chiefly by adding endings.) In the

XII   PREFACE TO THE STUDENT

sentence given above, *The oldest man in the village* is the subject; this identification is useful when we teach someone how to form English sentences, for *he* could also be the subject of this sentence. We identify parts of speech on the basis of the inflections they take; units of syntax are identified on the basis of their role in sentences.

Parts of Speech

Nouns are words which are inflected for number, case, and, in German, gender. *Professor* 'professor' is a noun, because it may refer to one individual and have **singular number** (abbreviated Sg); it may refer to more than one individual and have **plural number** (abbreviated Pl), *e.g.*, *Professoren* 'professors.' *Professor* may have no ending and be in the **nominative case** (abbreviated N or nom.). It may have an **-s** ending and be in the **genitive case** (abbreviated G or gen.), which in English we call the **possessive case**; *e.g.*, *Professors* 'professor's.' In German there are two additional cases, which are to be recognized chiefly by their articles: the **accusative case** (abbreviated A or acc.), which in English we call the **objective case,** *e.g.*, *den Professor* 'the professor'; and the **dative case** (abbreviated D or dat.), *e.g.*, *dem Professor* '[to] the professor.' English has distinctive forms of the accusative or objective case, *e.g.*, *me* from *I*, but not of the dative case. By **gender** we mean that nouns fall into certain classes depending on their present-day form or their form in an earlier stage of development of the language. English nouns have no gender, but when a yachtsman says: "Doesn't she sail smoothly?" he is assigning feminine gender to his yacht. All German nouns are either of **masculine gender** (he-words), **feminine gender** (she-words) or **neuter gender** (it-words). As you see from the use of *she* for a yacht, grammatical gender has very little to do with sex.

Nouns are often preceded by **articles:** *der, die, das* 'the' is the **definite article;** *ein, eine, ein* 'a, an' the **indefinite article.**

Pronouns are inflected for number and case. There are various types. **Personal pronouns** generally refer to people, *e.g.*, *ich* 'I,' *er, sie, es* 'he, she, it.' **Interrogative pronouns** introduce questions, *e.g.*, *wer* 'who,' *was* 'what.' **Demonstrative pronouns** are used to point out people or things, *e.g.*, *Das sagte ich nicht.* 'That I didn't say.' (You must be prepared to see words which look the same used as different parts of speech, as English *that* is used in: "Give me that book" [demonstrative adjective]; "Give me that" [demonstrative pronoun]; "The car that I saw" [relative pronoun].) **Relative pronouns** introduce clauses which relate to something mentioned earlier, *e.g.*, *Dies ist das Buch, das sie mir gab.* 'This is the book that she gave me.'

Adjectives generally stand before nouns and may be inflected for use as **comparatives** and **superlatives**, *e.g.*, *schnell, schneller, schnellste* 'quick, quicker, quickest.' (One must distinguish carefully between adjectives and pronouns; *my* is a **possessive adjective,** *mine* a **possessive pronoun.**)

Adverbs modify verbs and generally are derived from adjectives, as is *quickly* in "She came quickly."

The two most frequently encountered types of **numerals** are cardinals and ordinals. **Cardinals** take the place of nouns or adjectives, *e.g.,. Hier sind zwei (Bücher).* 'Here are two (books).' **Ordinals** are used to indicate numerical order and are generally adjectives, *e.g.*, *Dies ist das zweite Buch.* 'This is the second book.'

Prepositions are used before nouns, *e.g.*, *in* 'in,' *mit* 'with,' *zu* 'to.'

Conjunctions connect words or clauses, *e.g.*, *und* 'and,' *aber* 'but,' *daß* 'that,' *wenn* 'if.'

Verbs are inflected for number, person, and tense. Different forms may be used in the **singlar number** and in the **plural number**: *e.g.*, *er sieht* 'he sees'; *sie sehen* 'they see.' The form may vary with the **person** involved: the **first person,** *e.g.*, *ich sehe* 'I see'; the **second person,** *e.g.*, *Sie sehen* 'you see'; the **third person,** *e.g.*, *er sieht* 'he sees.' The verb form may vary with the time of the action and be in the **present tense** (abbreviated Pres), *e.g., er sieht* 'he sees'; in the **past tense,** *e.g., er sah* 'he saw'; in the **present perfect tense** (abbreviated Pres Perf), *e.g., er hat gesehen* 'he has seen'; in the **past perfect tense,** *e.g., er hatte gesehen* 'he had seen'; in the **future tense,** *e.g., er wird sehen* 'he will see'; or in the **future perfect tense,** *e.g., er wird gesehen haben* 'he will have seen.' (Tenses, although they are inflections for time, must not be directly connected with literal time; in English, for example, we use the present tense to indicate future time in "He is going tomorrow.")

Verbs may also be inflected for **mood,** but there is comparatively little such inflection in English. There are certain special forms to indicate contingency, possibility, or doubt, as in "If he were your friend, he wouldn't say such things." Such forms are said to be in the **subjunctive mood** (abbreviated Subj); forms to indicate a straightforward attitude or statement towards an action are in the **indicative mood** (abbreviated Indic). Separate forms, **imperatives,** may also be used to indicate commands, *e.g., Geben Sie es mir!* 'Give it to me.'

Verbs may also be inflected for **voice,** either **active voice** or **passive voice.** In the active voice, emphasis is put on the individual performing an action, *e.g.,* "She saw you there." In the passive voice, emphasis is put on the action, *e.g.,* "You were seen [by her] there."

Forms that are inflected for tense may be called **finite** verb forms, *e.g., am, is, are.* Forms that are not inflected for tense are **infinitives,** *e.g., be,* or **participles** (abbreviated Ptc), *e.g., being, been.*

Auxiliaries are verbs whose primary function is to help in the construction of verbal forms consisting of two or more elements, such as the German *habe* in *Ich habe sie gesehen* and the English *have* in *I have seen her.* If the auxiliary generally indicates a mode of action or an attitude towards an action, it is called a **modal auxiliary,** *e.g.,* German *kann* in *Ich kann gehen* and English *can* in *I can go.*

In building vocabulary it is often helpful to pick out the part of a word which carries its essential meaning. The essential part of English words like *introduce, educate, deduction* is *-duc-*, which means 'lead.' The essential part of German *einführen* 'introduce,' *Führung* 'direction,' and related words is *-führ-*. This part is called the **stem**. Any part before the stem is called a **prefix**, *e.g., ein-, intro-*. Any part after the stem is called a **suffix**, *e.g., -ung, -tion*.

Sentence Structure, or Syntax

Simple sentences may be made up of **subject** and **predicate,** *e.g., Er sprach* 'he spoke'; of subject, predicate (verb) and **object,** *e.g., Er nahm es* 'he took it'; of subject, predicate (verb), object, and **adverbial elements,** *e.g., Er nahm es gestern* 'he took it yesterday.' Objects may be **direct objects,** *e.g., das Buch* 'the book' in *Er hat mir das Buch gegeben* 'he gave me the book' or **indirect objects,** *e.g., mir* 'me' in that sentence. Verbs that are followed by direct objects are called **transitive verbs,** *e.g., geben* 'give'; verbs that are not followed by direct objects are called **intransitive verbs,** *e.g., gehen* 'go.'

Sentences may consist of more than one **clause,** *e.g., Als er ankam, gab er mir das Buch.* 'When he arrived, he gave me the book.' Clauses which may stand alone are called **independent clauses,** *e.g., He gave me the book.* Clauses which must be accompanied by another clause are **dependent clauses,** *e.g., when he arrived.* Most dependent clauses are introduced by conjunctions or by relative pronouns.

Sentences, particularly quotations and questions, may be cast in either **direct** or **indirect** discourse. If in direct discourse, the words of the speaker are repeated as they were originally spoken, *e.g., Ich fragte: "Hat er es Ihnen gegeben?"* 'I asked, "Did he give it to you?" ' If the discourse is indirect, the words of the original speaker may be modified, *e.g., Ich fragte, ob er es Ihnen gegeben habe.* 'I asked whether he had given it to you.'

Merely learning the technical terms used in grammars does not assure mastery of a language: many people speak perfectly without being able to analyze and label the words of their speech. But for educated speakers, acquisition of a new language and mastery over one's own may be facilitated by learning the technical terminology.

As we have indicated in the Preface, it is most economical of time for you to study orally as much as possible. If you do your work aloud, you are using your ears, your facial muscles, and your eyes to help you learn the language; if you read silently, you are using only your eyes. Obviously you will do better by employing as many faculties as possible.

Remember, too, that language learning is cumulative. This means, for example, that your work in the sixth week is based on all the work of the first five. Don't let the simplicity of the first lesson deceive you. If you prefer to work hard during the Christmas recess rather than at the start of a course and throughout the term, reserve this type of study for your other courses. Unless you start working on your foreign language at once, you may soon be lost.

The chief aim of foreign-language instruction is to widen the possibilities of communication. Learning German will make another culture accessible to you; it will also expand your understanding of your own culture.

Here is a list of expressions which you will hear from your instructor:

Schlagen Sie bitte das Buch auf! *'Please open your books.'*
Lesen Sie, bitte! *'Please read.'*
Auf Deutsch, bitte! *'In German, please.'*
Wie heißen Sie? *'What is your name?'*
Wie heißt das auf Deutsch? *'What is that called in German?'*
Wie heißt das auf Englisch? *'What is that called in English?'*

Machen Sie bitte das Buch zu! *'Please close your books.'*

Gehen Sie an die Tafel! *'Go to the blackboard.'*

Schreiben Sie an die Tafel! *'Write on the board.'*

Gehen Sie bitte an Ihren Platz! *'Please go to your seats.'*

Übersetzen Sie, bitte! *'Please translate.'*

Wie buchstabiert man . . . ? *'How do you spell . . . ?'*

Fahren Sie fort! *'Continue.'*

Alle zusammen, bitte! *'All together, please.'*

Bitte, schließen Sie die Tür! *'Please close the door.'*

Danke sehr. *'Thank you very much.'*

Bitte sehr. *'You're welcome.'*

Guten Morgen! *'Good morning.'*

Guten Tag! *'Hello.'*

Guten Abend! *'Good evening.'*

Auf Wiedersehen! *'Good-bye.'*

Das ist alles. *'That is all.'*

CONTENTS

Was studieren Sie ?

NOUNS AND GENDERS

THE NOMINATIVE CASE

THE PRESENT TENSE

WORD ORDER OF SIMPLE SENTENCES

THE GERMAN CONSONANTS

TEXT

Read the following sentences aloud and work out their meaning with the aid of the vocabulary. Then go over them repeatedly in German, without translating them.

FRITZ MOELLER *is waiting for* INGE PFEIFFER *so that they may go together to their German class. As he waits for her to show up, his friend* HANS FISCHER *passes by.*

FRITZ: Guten Morgen, Hans! Wie geht's?
HANS: Danke, gut. — Was tun Sie jetzt?

Lesson 1

FRITZ: Ich habe jetzt Stunde, meine Deutschstunde.   Und Sie?
HANS: Ich bin jetzt frei.   Um zehn Uhr habe ich Physik.
5 FRITZ: Da kommt Inge. — Guten Morgen, Inge!
INGE: Guten Morgen, Fritz!   Ist es noch zu früh?
FRITZ: Ja, wir haben noch drei Minuten.   Frau König ist noch
nicht hier. — Inge, dies ist mein Freund, Hans Fischer.
INGE: Sehr angenehm!   Studieren Sie auch Deutsch, Herr
10 Fischer?
HANS: Nein, ich studiere Physik.   Wir haben keine Lehrerin;
wir haben einen Lehrer.   Unser Professor ist schon alt und
grau.
FRITZ: Unsere Lehrerin ist jung und schön!   Sie heißt Frau
15 König.
HANS: In meiner Klasse sind keine Mädchen.
FRITZ: In unserer Klasse sind vier oder fünf Mädchen!   Sie
sind alle schön — aber nicht so schön wie Inge!
INGE: Fritz Moeller! — Was tun Sie in der Klasse?   Lernen
20 Sie etwas oder träumen Sie nur?
FRITZ: O, wir hören und sprechen jetzt nur Deutsch.   Frau
König sagt: „Ich habe ein Buch — er hat ein Buch — sie hat
ein Buch — wir alle haben ein Buch."
INGE: Und dann sagt sie: „Das Buch ist rot.   Das Papier im
25 Buch ist weiß."
FRITZ: Ja, und dann sagt sie: „Der Bleistift ist billig. — Das
Buch ist teuer. — Das ist das Fenster. — Dort ist die Tür.
Sind Sie schon alt?"
INGE: „Nein, wir sind noch jung. — Wie heißen Sie?"
30 FRITZ: „Ich heiße Fritz Moeller. — Und wie heißen Sie?"
HANS: Mein Name ist Fischer und ich bin aus Detroit.
INGE: Da ist Frau König, und jetzt haben wir Stunde.   Kom-
men Sie in die Klasse, Herr Moeller!
FRITZ: Auf Wiedersehen, Hans!
35 HANS: Auf Wiedersehen!

th = s t̲
j = y̲

IDIOMS AND VOCABULARY

Auf Wiedersehen!   Good-bye.
Guten Morgen!   Good morning.
noch nicht   not yet
Sehr angenehm!   Pleased to meet you.
so (schön) wie   as (pretty) as
um zehn Uhr   at ten o'clock
Wie geht's? Wie geht es?   How are you?

aber   but, however
all   all
alt   old
auch   also, too, even
aus   out of, from, of
billig   cheap
der Bleistift   pencil
das Buch   book
da   there, then, in that case
danke   thanks
dann   then
das [*demonst. pron.*]   that
deutsch [*adj.*]   German
[das] Deutsch   German language
die Deutschstunde   German class
dies   this
dort   there
drei   three
ein, eine, ein   a, an; one
etwas   some(thing), somewhat
das Fenster   window
die Frau   woman; wife; Mrs.

das Fräulein   young lady; Miss
frei   free
der Freund   friend
früh   early
fünf   five
grau   gray
gut   good; well; O.K.
haben   have
heißen   be called
der Herr   gentleman; master; Mr.
hier   here
hören   hear
in   in, into
im   in the
ja   yes; to be sure; indeed
jetzt = nun   now
jung   young
kein, keine, kein   not a, not any, no
die Klasse   class
kommen   come
der Lehrer   teacher [*man*]
die Lehrerin   teacher [*woman*]

lernen learn
das Mädchen girl
mein, meine, mein; meiner
  my [**ein**-*word*]
die Minute minute
der Name name
nein no
nicht not
noch yet, still
nun now
nur only
oder or
das Papier paper
die Physik physics
die Physikstunde physics
  class
der Professor professor
rot red
sagen say
schon already
schön pretty

sein be
so so, thus, then
sprechen speak
er spricht he speaks
studieren study
die Stunde hour; class
teuer expensive
träumen dream, daydream
tun do
die Tür door
und and
unser, unsere, unser; un-
  serer our [**ein**-*word*]
vier four
was what
weiß white
wie as, like, how
wo where
zehn ten
zu too; to

GRAMMAR

1.1 Nouns and genders In German, all nouns are capitalized.
For additional rules of capitalization, see Appendix 1.7.*

1.1,1 Every noun belongs to one of three gender[†] groups.
The best way to learn noun genders is to memorize the definite
article that accompanies each noun. In German, genders and

---

  * References to the Appendix will be made, as here, by citing section
and subsection numbers.
  † Technical terms have been defined in the Preface to the Student.
If such words as "gender" are unclear, please look them up in that
preface.

cases are indicated by the articles or adjectives that precede nouns, generally by **der**-words or **ein**-words. It is highly important for the understanding of German materials to memorize thoroughly the forms of **der**-words and **ein**-words.

1.1,2 The definite article 'the' is: *der, die, das*

> **der** for nouns of masculine gender: **der Bleistift**
> **die** for nouns of feminine gender: **die Klasse**
> **das** for nouns of neuter gender: **das Fenster**

Words that may replace **der, die, das** will be referred to as **der**-words.

1.1,3 The indefinite article 'a, an' is: *ein, eine, ein*

> **ein** for nouns of masculine gender: **ein Bleistift**
> **eine** for nouns of feminine gender: **eine Klasse**
> **ein** for nouns of neuter gender: **ein Fenster**

Inflected like **ein** are **kein** 'not a, no' and the possessive adjectives:

mein	my
sein	his; its
ihr	her; their
Ihr	your
unser	our

We will refer to words so inflected as **ein**-words.

kein (mein, unser) Bleistift	no (my, our) pencil
keine (seine, ihre) Klasse	no (his, her) class
kein (Ihr, ihr) Fenster	no (your, her) window

Do not confuse possessive adjectives with pronouns. In English *my* is an adjective, *mine* a pronoun; compare *This is my pencil* with *This pencil is mine*. The German **ein**-words are like *my*, but have varying endings which depend on the following nouns.

1.1,4 Generally speaking, nouns that designate males are masculine, *e.g.*, **der Professor**, and those that designate females are feminine: **die Frau**. But the gender of nouns that designate things varies: **das Papier**, but **der Bleistift, die Stunde.**

The gender of some nouns is determined by their form. All nouns ending in **-chen** and **-lein** are neuter, regardless of sex: **das Fräulein** 'the young lady,' **das Mädchen** 'the girl.'

1.1,5 Reference to a masculine noun is made with **er**; to a feminine noun, with **sie**; to a neuter noun, with **es**.

> **Er (der Bleistift) ist billig.** It is cheap.
> **Sie (die Klasse) ist hier.** It is here.
> **Es (das Buch) ist grau.** It is gray.

However, reference to neuter nouns indicating people, *e.g.*, **das Fräulein** 'the young lady,' **das Mädchen** 'the girl,' may be made in accordance with the sex of the person:

> **Es/sie (das Mädchen) ist hier.** She is here.

1.2 The Nominative Case Subjects of sentences are in the nominative case. All nouns and pronouns in the vocabularies are listed in that case.

1.3 The Present Tense In vocabularies, verbs are listed in the infinitive form. The infinitive of most German verbs ends in **-en**: **lern-en**, **sag-en**; however, a few verbs have only **-n**: **tu-n**. That part of the verb preceding the infinitive ending is called the *stem*.

1.3,1 The infinitive form of a verb is the same as that of the first and third persons plural in the present tense: **wir lern-en** 'we learn'; **sie lern-en** 'they learn.' The same form is used in the second person (corresponding to the English 'you' form, singular and plural): **Sie lern-en** 'you learn'.

1.3,2 The first person singular of the present tense is made by adding **-e** to the stem: **ich lern-e** 'I learn.'

1.3,3 The third person singular of the present tense is made by adding **-t** to the stem: **er, sie, es lern-t** 'he, she, it learns.'
    The **-e-** of the stem of most strong verbs is changed to **-i-** or **-ie-** in the third person singular: **er, sie, es sprich-t** 'he, she, it is speaking.' (This change will be discussed further in Lesson 6.1,5*.)

1.3,4 As in English, the most common verbs are apt to be irregular. The present tense of **sein** 'be' is completely irregular and must be learned separately; in the present tense of **haben** 'have,' only the third person singular is irregular:

> **ich bin**   I am
>
> **er, sie, es ist**   he, she, it is   **hat**   has
>
> **wir, sie, Sie sind**   we, they, you are

1.3,5 Literal translations of such forms as *I am studying, I do study* do not exist in German. All one can say is **ich studiere.** Yet **ich studiere** must often be translated with these phrases, especially in negative sentences: **Hier studiere ich nicht** 'I am not studying here' or 'I do not study here.'

1.3,6 The present tense often corresponds to the future tense in English: **Jetzt haben wir Klasse** 'Now we'll have class.'

1.3,7 Summary of the personal pronouns:[†]

> **ich**   I   **wir**   we
>
> **er, sie, es**   he, she, it   **sie**   they
>
> **Sie**   you   you

---

    * References to the grammar sections of lessons will be made as here, by citing the lesson number and the paragraph number in the grammar section.
    † In everyday German, two pronouns are used in a form of address which corresponds to the English "thou" and "ye": **du** and **ihr**. These

1.3,8 Summary of verbs in the present tense:

	sagen	say	lernen	learn
ich	sage		lerne	
er, sie, es	sagt		lernt	
wir, sie, Sie	sagen		lernen	

	sprechen	speak	haben	have
ich	spreche		habe	
er, sie, es	spricht		hat	
wir, sie, Sie	sprechen		haben	

1.4 Word Order of Simple Sentences The word order of German sentences is often exactly like that of English sentences: **Ich habe ein Buch.** 'I have a book.' **Was ist das?** 'What is that?'

1.4,1 The fundamental rule of German word order is that in simple sentences the verb must be the second element. Compare:

[1] **Ich** [2] **habe** [3] **ein Buch.** 'I have a book.'
[1] **Jetzt** [2] **haben** [3] **wir** [4] **Klasse.** 'Now we'll have class.'

The first element may consists of several words, as in the sentence on page 2, line 16: [1] **In meiner Klasse** [2] **sind. . .*** From the point of view of word order, the phrase **In meiner Klasse** is equivalent to the single word **jetzt.**

1.4,2 In questions introduced by interrogatives, *e.g.*, by **was**

---

pronouns are restricted in use to God in prayer, to members of the family, to close friends, and to animals. Since for the present we are limiting ourselves to forms used in formal German, we will not treat these pronouns until later. They are followed by special verb forms which also will be treated later. If you see these pronouns in texts or hear them in speech, you will be able to translate the verb forms too.

* References to German material in the texts will be made by page number and line number, as here.

'what,' the verb is in second place. When no interrogative is used, the sentence begins with the verb: **Habe ich das Papier?** 'Do I have the paper?' **Lernen Sie etwas?** 'Are you learning something?'

1.4,3 As in English, commands also begin with the verb. The general way of expressing commands and requests is to use the infinitive form of the verb plus **Sie: Kommen Sie in die Klasse!** 'Come to class.' The exclamation point is used to conclude such sentences in German, although it is commonly omitted in English.

1.5 The German Consonants   Most German sounds cause little difficulty in pronunciation. In spelling German, symbols are used which differ from those of English, but after a short time these will not be troublesome, for German spelling is relatively consistent. (The German alphabet is discussed in Appendix i.) By far the best way to learn German sounds is to listen to them in sentences pronounced by competent speakers and to reproduce them as accurately as possible. Special exercises and explanations on pronunciation and spelling will be given in each lesson; more extended discussions are included in Appendix i. Work through the pronunciation exercises, imitating as nearly as possible the pronunciation of a native speaker of German.

1.5,1 Consonants whose sounds in German differ from those of English are: **ch, l, r, pf, tz/z.***

1.5,2 The sound **ch,** the last sound of **ich,** is made by producing friction between the tongue and the roof of the mouth.

---

* In the discussions of pronunciation, spelling symbols are represented by *italics*; symbols referring to sounds are enclosed in brackets. Thus [i:] is the symbol for the vowel of **beat.**

To produce this sound, say *ee* [i:], then pronounce with great friction the initial consonant of *hue*; then bring the two sounds, [i:] and [h], together. Then leave off the vowel of *hue* and you have the German word **ich.**

mich	me	**billig**	cheap	**noch**	still
Licht	light	**König**	king	**Buch**	book

1.5,3 In German, only an [l] with an *ee*-like quality is used. In American English, the [l] of most speakers has on *oo*-like quality. When learning German, aim for an *ee*-like [l].

lieb	dear	**leben**	live	**billig**	cheap	**eilen**	hurry

1.5,4 The German **r** is pronounced variously by different German speakers. The greater percentage of Germans make a trill with the uvula, the appendage of the back part of the roof of the mouth. According to the standard German pronunciation, however, **r** is trilled with the tip of the tongue. When learning German **r**, the best procedure is to imitate the **r** of one's instructor, whether it is uvular or tongue-trilled.

fahren	travel	**Fritz**		**rot**	red
lehren	teach	**grau**	gray	**rufen**	call

After vowels, **r** is often merely a glide:

hier here		**war** was		**wieder** again		**Morgen** morning

1.5,5 In pronouncing the consonant combinations **pf** and **tz** (the latter is also spelled **z**), there must be no gap between the two elements of each combination:

Opfer	offering	**Pfeiffer**		**Pfeife**	pipe
Katzen	cats	**Zeit**	time	**zu**	to, too

EXERCISES

A. Form sentences, using the following nouns, after the pattern:

> Hier ist der Professor.

The nouns alone will be given.

1. Klasse
2. Lehrer
3. Mädchen
4. Frau
5. Papier
6. Fenster
7. Herr
8. Name
9. Lehrerin
10. Freund
11. Buch
12. Bleistift
13. Tür

B. Form sentences, using pronouns as subjects, after the pattern:

> Hier ist der Professor.　Er ist hier.

Use the nouns listed under A above.

C. Form sentences for the following verbs and complements, using the subjects listed.

1. Wir sagen.　　Sie ... , ich ... , er ...
2. Ich träume.　　wir ... , sie ... , er ... , Sie ...
3. Hören Sie Deutsch?　... wir Deutsch?　... ich Deutsch?　... er Deutsch?
4. Sie sprechen gut.　　er ... gut, sie ... gut
5. Ich habe ein Buch.　　Wir ... ein Buch, Sie ... ein Buch
6. Er ist hier.　　ich ... hier, wir ... hier, Sie ... hier
7. Wir studieren Physik.　　ich ... Physik, er ... Physik
... Sie Physik, bitte!

D. Memorize the following sentence patterns and form other sentences in the same way.

A. Wir haben heute Klasse.
B. Heute haben wir Klasse.
C. Haben wir heute Klasse?

1. A. Wir lernen jetzt Deutsch.   B.   C.
2. A. Ich habe hier ein Buch.   B.   C.
3. C. Ist sie noch jung?   A.   B.
4. C. Sprechen wir jetzt Deutsch?   A.   B.
5. B. In der Klasse sind vier oder fünf Mädchen.   A.   C.
6. B. Hier habe ich das Papier.   C.   A.

E. Read the following questions and answers and use them as models for additional sentences.

A. 1. Wo ist die Klasse?   Die Klasse ist hier.
2. Wer spricht Deutsch?   Die Lehrerin spricht Deutsch.
3. Wie sind die Mädchen in der Klasse?   Die Mädchen in der Klasse sind schön.
4. Wo ist die Tür?   Die Tür ist da.
5. Was hat Inge?   Inge hat ein Buch.
6. Wo ist das Fenster?   Das Fenster ist dort.
7. Wer ist Fritz?   Fritz ist mein Freund.
8. Wie heißt der Herr?   Der Herr heißt Moeller.

B. 1. Was haben Sie da?   Ich habe ein Buch.
2. Was hat er da?   Er hat ein Buch.
3. Was hat sie dort?   Sie hat das Papier.
4. Was haben wir alle?   Wir haben ein Buch.
5. Wie heißt das Mädchen?   Sie heißt Inge.
6. Was haben wir jetzt?   Jetzt haben wir Stunde.
7. Wie heißen Sie?   Ich heiße (Fritz Moeller).
8. Sind Sie Frau König?   Nein, ich heiße (Inge Pfeiffer).
9. Was lernen wir jetzt?   Jetzt lernen wir Deutsch.
10. Was tun wir jetzt?   Wir sprechen und hören.

C. 1. Lernen wir heute Deutsch?   Ja, heute lernen wir Deutsch.

2. Ist der Professor hier? Nein, der Professor ist nicht hier.
3. Sind die Mädchen schön? Ja, die Mädchen sind schön.
4. Ist die Lehrerin ein Fräulein? Nein, sie ist eine Frau.
5. Ist der Bleistift billig? Ja, er ist billig.
6. Ist das Buch billig? Nein, es ist teuer.
7. Lernen wir jetzt Englisch? Nein, jetzt lernen wir Deutsch.
8. Ist das Papier rot? Nein, das Papier ist weiß.
9. Hat der Professor ein Buch? Ja, er hat ein Buch.
10. Haben wir heute Klasse? Ja, heute haben wir Klasse.

F. Translate in writing:

1. Here is the teacher.
2. Where is the class?
3. Today they have class. (For word order, see **1.4,1.**)
4. Now we are learning German. (See **1.3,5.**)
5. We all have a book. It is gray.
6. The paper is white.
7. Here is the pencil. It (See **1.1,5**) is red.
8. Come to the physics class, Mr. König. (See **1.4,3.**)
9. Do you have the book?
10. Yes, I have it and I have the paper too. (Translate *too* with **auch** before **das Papier.**)
11. We are speaking German.
12. The woman teacher is called Mrs. König.
13. Four or five girls in the class are pretty.
14. Is the teacher already here?

G. Free conversation. Make up sentences which are appropriate to the following situation:

You are going to German class and you meet a friend. Say good morning to him. Tell him you are learning German. The teacher is in the classroom. He asks you to make simple sentences, such as giving your name, asking the name of some-one else, pointing out things (a book, the door, the window) and describing them (the book is cheap, the door is red), and so on. Then say good-bye.

BRIEF CONVERSATION

In der Klasse

WALTER KRENN: Guten Morgen, Herr Moeller! Wie geht's — und was tun
 Sie jetzt in der Klasse? Studieren Sie nun?
FRITZ MOELLER: Ich lerne jetzt Deutsch, aber sprech' es noch nicht.
 Ich höre und sag', was die Lehrerin spricht:
 (Lehrerin) ,,Hier ist das Fenster, und dort ist die Tür.
 Rot ist der Bleistift und weiß das Papier.''
WALTER: Da kommt Fräulein Inge! So jung und so schön!
INGE: Sehr angenehm! Danke!
FRITZ und INGE: Auf Wiedersehen!

LESSON 2

Walter kauft Bücher

[handwritten: z. B. = zum Beispiel]

THE ACCUSATIVE CASE

PREPOSITIONS REQUIRING THE ACCUSATIVE CASE

NOUN PLURALS

THE GERMAN VOWELS

TEXT

WALTER *is browsing in the University Bookstore. He has the following conversation with a sales clerk* (Verkäufer).

VERKÄUFER: Was wünschen Sie, bitte?
WALTER: Ich möchte ein paar Bücher kaufen.
VERKÄUFER: Für welchen Kurs soll es sein?
WALTER: O, ich brauche sie für keinen Kurs. Ich möchte
    etwas für mich lesen, Romane oder Detektiv-Geschichten. 5
    Haben Sie z.B. „Welt ohne Liebe?"
VERKÄUFER: Nein, das Buch kenne ich nicht. Aber ich kann
    es für Sie bestellen. Wie ist Ihr Name, bitte?

WALTER: Ich heiße Krenn. Walter Krenn. — Gut. Dann
10   möchte ich noch diese vier Bücher kaufen: „Der Weg ins
Dunkle," „In achtzig Tagen um die Welt," „Drei Männer
gegen ein Tier" und „Sechs Personen suchen ein Wort."
Und dann geben Sie mir, bitte, noch zwölf Bleistifte, zwei
Hefte fürs Examen und etwas Papier.
15 VERKÄUFER: Das Ganze macht siebzehn Dollar und fünfund-
zwanzig Cent.
WALTER: O, ich habe leider kein Geld bei mir.
VERKÄUFER: Und wer bezahlt diese Sachen?
WALTER: Schicken Sie die Rechnung an meinen Vater. Sie
20   kennen ihn sicher. Mein Vater ist Professor an der Univer-
sität. Er kommt jeden Tag in die Stadt.
VERKÄUFER: Da müssen Sie Herrn Webber fragen.
WALTER: Wen muß ich fragen?
VERKÄUFER: Herrn Webber. Er ist unser Direktor. Sehen
25   Sie den Herrn da drüben? Er kommt gerade durch die
Tür. Gehen Sie und fragen Sie ihn. Ohne seinen Namen
kann ich keine Rechnung schreiben. Und er kennt sicher
Ihren Vater.
WALTER: Ja, er kennt uns schon.

IDIOMS AND VOCABULARY

> **ein paar**   a couple, a few
> **z.B. (zum Beispiel)**   for example, e.g.
> **Wie ist Ihr Name?**   What is your name?

achtzig eighty
an on, to; up, to; at
bei at, with, near, by, among,
   at the house of
bestellen order
bezahlen pay
bitte please
der Brief, -e letter

brauchen need, require, use
dieser, diese, dieses this
   [**der**-*word*]
drüben over there
dunkel dark
das Dunkle dark
durch through
das Examen, – examination

fragen ask (for information)
fünfundzwanzig twenty-five
für for [*prep. only*]
ganz whole, entire
das Ganze whole
geben give
  er gibt he gives
gegen against
gehen go
das Geld, -er money
gerade just, now, straight-(way)
die Geschichte, -n story
das Heft, -e notebook
Ihr your [**ein**-*word*]
jeder, jede, jedes each, every [**der**-*word*]
ich, er kann I, he can; am, is able
kaufen buy
kennen be acquainted with, know
der Kurs, -e course
leider unfortunately
lesen read
  er liest he reads
die Liebe love
machen make, do
der Mann, ̈-er man, husband
mir (to) me
ich möchte I'd like
ich, er muß I, he must; have to, has to

müssen (we, you, they) must, have to
ohne without
die Person, -en person
die Rechnung, -en bill
der Roman, -e novel
die Sache, -n thing
schicken send
schreiben write
sechs six
sehen see
  er sieht he sees
sein his [**ein**-*word*]
sicher sure(ly), safe, secure
siebzehn seventeen
es soll it should, is to
die Stadt, ̈-e city
suchen look for, seek
der Tag, -e day
das Tier, -e animal
um around, about; at, for [*prep.*]
die Universität, -en university
der Vater, ̈- father
wann when
der Weg, -e way, road
welcher, welche, welches which, who [**der**-*word*]
die Welt, -en world
wer who
  wen whom [*acc.*]
das Wort, ̈-er word
wünschen wish
zwei two
zwölf twelve

GRAMMAR

2.1 The Accusative Case

2.1,1 The accusative is called the objective case in English grammar. In English, only pronouns have distinct objective forms. Compare:

Nominative	**ich** I	**er** he	**wir** we	**wer** who
Accusative	**mich** me	**ihn** him	**uns** us	**wen** whom

The accusative of the other German pronouns, **sie, es, Sie,** is **sie, es, Sie.**

2.1,2 For nouns in the accusative case, only masculines are marked by a special form of the **der**-words and **ein**-words. The masculine nouns themselves are, with few exceptions, alike in the nominative and accusative. For feminine and neuter nouns, the nominative and accusative forms are always alike. They are also alike in the plurals of nouns of all genders.

The following examples show the accusative of nouns with **der, die, das,** another **der**-word and an **ein**-word.

> **Er sieht den (diesen, Ihren) Brief.**
> He sees the (this, your) letter.
> **Er sieht die (diese, ihre) Rechnung.**
> He sees the (this, her) bill.
> **Er sieht das (dieses, ein) Tier.**
> He sees the (this, an) animal.
> **Er sieht die (diese, unsere) Bücher.**
> He sees the (these, our) books.

2.1,3 Most verbs take an accusative object, as in the preceding examples. The verb **sein,** however, is followed by the nominative. **Wie ist Ihr Name?** 'What is your name?'

If one gives one's profession, an article is not used before the noun: **Mein Vater ist Professor.** 'My father is a professor.'

2.1,4 The accusative is also used to indicate definite time: **Er kommt jeden Tag in die Stadt.** 'He comes to town every day.'

2.2 Prepositions Requiring the Accusative Case In English, all prepositions take the objective case. In German, various cases may follow prepositions.

2.2,1 The following prepositions always take the accusative:

durch 'through': **Er kommt gerade durch die Tür.** 'He is just coming through the door.'

für 'for': **Ich brauche sie für keinen Kurs.** 'I don't need them for any course.'

gegen 'against': **Drei Männer gegen ein Tier.** 'Three men against one animal.'

ohne 'without': **Welt ohne Liebe.** 'World without love.'

um 'around, about; for; at [*with time*]': **Kommt er nicht jeden Tag um diese Stunde?** 'Doesn't he come every day at this hour?'

2.2,2 The following nine prepositions take the accusative if the verb indicates motion toward a place:

an 'on (to), to': **Schreiben Sie an Ihren Vater.** 'Write to your father.'

auf 'on, upon': **Geht Walter auf die Straße?** 'Is Walter going out to (on) the street?'

hinter 'behind, after': **Fritz macht einen Punkt hinter den Namen.** 'Fritz is putting a period after the name.'

in 'into': **Der Weg ins Dunkle.** 'The way into the dark.'

neben 'beside, next to, near': **Stellen Sie es neben das Fenster!** 'Put it beside the window.'

über 'over, across, concerning': **Das Tier kommt gerade über den Weg.** 'The animal is just coming across the road.'

unter 'under, among': **Ich lege die Rechnung unter die Hefte.** 'I'll lay the bill under the notebooks.'

vor 'before, in front of': **Sie geht vor die Klasse und schreibt.** 'She goes before the class and writes.'

zwischen 'between': **Legen Sie das Papier zwischen die Bücher.** 'Lay the paper between the books.'

2.2,3 A few contractions of preposition and article are commonly used in speaking and occasionally in writing, *e.g.*, **ans = an das, aufs = auf das, ins = in das.**

2.3 Noun Plurals As in English, there are various ways of forming plurals of nouns. (1) There may be no additional ending: **der Lehrer, die Lehrer** (compare *sheep, sheep*). (2) The ending **-e** may be added: **der Brief, die Briefe.** (3) The ending **-er** may be added: **der Mann, die Männer.** (4) The ending **-en** or **-n** may be added: **die Person, die Personen** (compare *ox, oxen*). In addition, some plural forms may have a change in vowel: **Mann, Männer** (compare *man, men*). Such a change is indicated in vocabularies by putting umlaut marks, ¨, over the hyphen after the noun. The signs ¨ after **Vater** indicate that the plural is **Väter**; the signs ¨e after **Stadt** indicate that the plural is **Städte**; the signs ¨er after **Buch** indicate that the plural is **Bücher.**

2.3,1 In German, nouns are classified by the ways in which their plurals are formed; these must be learned for every noun. Plurals have been indicated in the vocabulary for Lesson 2; all the nouns of Lesson 1 are listed here in accordance with the ways in which their plurals are formed.

Group 1. Nouns adding no ending in the plural: **das Fenster, die Fenster; der Lehrer, die Lehrer; das Mädchen, die Mädchen.**

Group 2. Nouns adding **-e** in the plural: **der Bleistift, die Bleistifte; der Freund, die Freunde; das Papier, die Papiere.**

Group 3. Nouns adding **-er** in the plural: **das Buch, die Bücher.**

Group 4. Nouns adding **-en** or **-n** in the plural: **die Frau, die Frauen; die Klasse, die Klassen; die Lehrerin, die Lehrerinnen; die Minute, die Minuten; die Stunde, die Stunden; die Tür, die Türen; der Herr, den Herrn** *(accusative singular)*, **die Herren; der Name, den Namen** *(accusative singular)*, **die Namen; der Professor, die Professoren.**

2.3,2 The nominative and accusative plural of **der, die, das** is **die** for all genders. The ending **-e** is added to all **der**-words and **ein**-words in the nominative and accusative plural, *e.g.*, **diese** 'these,' **welche** 'which,' **keine** 'no.' (As is true also of the English indefinite article, *a, an*, there is no plural of **ein**; **ein Buch** 'a book,' **Bücher** 'books.')

2.4 The German Vowels There are seven vowels in German, all of which are either short or long. Do not confuse the terms 'short' and 'long' with these terms as they are used for English vowels: a short German vowel is really about half the length of a long German vowel. Contrast **Stadt** 'city' with **Staat** 'state'; contrast **in** with **ihn**. The best method of learning to pronounce the German vowels is to imitate carefully a competent speaker; be especially careful to clip the short vowels as he does.

in in	**ihn** him	**Rum** rum	**Ruhm** glory
denn for	**den** that one	**offen** open	**Ofen** stove
	Stadt city	**Staat** state	

2.4,1 Vowels with umlaut marks (··) over them are called *umlaut*, or *modified*, vowels. These are: **ü, ö,** and **ä.** The tongue positions for **i** and **e** are used in pronouncing **ü** and **ö,** but the lips are rounded. Compare:

ihn him   **grün** green   **Heer** army   **hör'** listen
dick fat   **Stück** piece   **kennen** know   **können** be able to

The umlaut vowel **ä** is equivalent to **e**: pronounce the first syllable of **Mädchen** as though it were spelled **Med.**

EXERCISES

A. Make additional sentences on the basis of those given here, substituting the words in parentheses for those in heavy type.

1. Ich habe **den Bleistift.** (the book, the letter, the money)
2. Er kennt **die Stadt.** (the woman teacher, the story)
3. Er sucht **das Tier.** (the girl, the teacher)
4. Fragen Sie **den Vater!** (the friend, the woman)
5. Ich höre **die Klasse.** (the door, the gentleman)
6. Kennen Sie **den Lehrer?** (the city, the word, the course)
7. Wir fragen **das Mädchen.** (the professor, the man)

B. Follow the directions for exercise A.

1. Wir suchen **ihn.** (her, them)
2. Er kennt **uns.** (me, them, you)
3. Er fragt **sie.** (you, me, us)
4. Wir schicken **sie.** (her, him)
5. Heute brauche ich **sie** hier. (them, him)
6. Wir fragen **sie.** (him, them, you)

C. Follow the directions for exercise A.

1. Ich habe **mein Buch** hier. (my pencil, his letter)

2. Wir suchen **einen Freund.** (his father) *examen*
3. Er schreibt jetzt **sein Buch.** (his name, his examination)
4. Wir haben **einen Lehrer.** (a pencil, a novel)
5. Er kennt **meine Lehrerin.** (your friend) *ihrenfreund*
6. Wir sehen **ihren Freund.** (his woman teacher) *seine lehrerin*
7. Wir haben **kein Buch.** (no paper)
8. Ich kenne **keine Frau** in der Klasse. (no girl)
9. Fragen Sie **Ihre Lehrerin!** (your professor)
10. Wir hören **ihren Vater** hier. (her teacher)

D. Put the nouns of exercises A and C (those printed in heavy type) and the substitutes given in parentheses into the plural.

E. Follow the directions for exercise A.

1. Wir gehen **durch die Klasse.** (around the city)
2. Schreiben Sie es **in das Buch!** (for your father)
3. Wir lesen es **für ihn.** (without her)
4. Er geht **um die Universität.** (into the city)
5. Finden Sie es **ohne ihn?** (for him)
6. Sie schreibt die Geschichte **in das Heft.** (in the book)
7. Die Lehrerin kommt **in die Tür.** (into class)
8. Die Herren gehen **um die Stadt.** (behind the university)

F. Read the following questions and answers and use them as models for additional sentences.

A. 1. Was tut Walter? Er kauft Bücher.
2. Was möchte Walter lesen? Er möchte Romane lesen.
3. Kennt der Verkäufer die Bücher? Nein, er kennt sie nicht.
4. Wer bezahlt die Sachen? Sein Vater bezahlt die Sachen.
5. Was ist Walters Vater? Walters Vater ist Professor.
6. Wann kommt er in die Stadt? Er kommt jeden Tag in die Stadt.

7. Was ist Herr Webber?   Herr Webber ist Direktor.
8. Kennt Herr Webber Walters Vater?   Ja, er kennt ihn.

B. 1. Für welchen Kurs braucht Walter die Bücher?   Er
       braucht sie für keinen Kurs.
    2. Kauft Walter „Welt ohne Liebe?"   Nein, er bestellt
       es nur.
    3. Wer sucht ein Wort?   Sechs Personen suchen ein Wort.
    4. An wen schickt der Verkäufer die Rechnung?   Er
       schickt die Rechnung an Walters Vater.
    5. Kommt Walters Vater heute in die Stadt?   Ja, er
       kommt jeden Tag in die Stadt.
    6. Wo ist der Direktor?   Er geht gerade durch die Tür.
    7. Ohne was kann Walter die Bücher nicht haben?   Er
       kann sie ohne den Namen des Direktors nicht haben.

G. Translate into German:

1. Walter is looking for (seeks) his friends.
2. Who is ordering the books?
3. Ask the man, please.
4. Do you have the book *King for* (**auf**) *One Day?*
5. The girl has no pencil.
6. I see my teacher now.
7. We are writing our story in the notebook.
8. Which letter do you wish?
9. He knows every way into the city.
10. He is sending his friend to (**auf**) the university.
11. Are they going without me?
12. What does she have against us?
13. We are reading about (**über**) the world.
14. I hear his father.

H. Free conversation.

You go to the bookstore to buy a few books.   You ask for
detective stories.   Then you buy pencils, paper, and notebooks

for an examination. The clerk tells you the total cost is five dollars. You find you have no money, and you tell the clerk to send the bill to your father. He writes out the bill. You say good-bye.

BRIEF CONVERSATION

Das Geld

FRITZ MOELLER *is waiting for the mailman* (Briefträger). MRS. VOGEL, *his landlady, comes up to him in the hallway.*

FRAU VOGEL: Guten Morgen, Herr Moeller. Was kann ich für Sie tun? Suchen Sie etwas?

FRITZ MOELLER: Ich warte nur auf [wait for] den Briefträger. Kommt er nicht jeden Tag um diese Stunde?

FRAU VOGEL: Ja, um zehn Uhr. Da ist er schon. Gerade kommt er durch die Tür.

FRITZ MOELLER: Hat er etwas für mich?

FRAU VOGEL: Ja, einen Brief für Sie. — Herr Moeller, heute [today] ist der sechste Oktober, und ich brauche mein Geld.

FRITZ MOELLER: Frau Vogel, Sie kennen meinen Vater nicht. Hier schickt er mir einen Brief, und hier ist das Geld für Sie.

FRAU VOGEL: Danke sehr. — Schreiben Sie an Ihren Vater und fragen Sie ihn, wann er in die Stadt kommt. Ich möchte ihn sehen.

Die mit den schwarzen Haaren

THE DATIVE CASE

PREPOSITIONS REQUIRING THE DATIVE CASE

WORD ORDER OF ELEMENTS IN THE PREDICATE

INTONATION

TEXT

KLAUS MOEHLENBROCK *meets his classmate,* HEINRICH
SEEMANN, *in the cafeteria at lunch.*

KLAUS: Guten Tag, Herr Seemann, wie geht es Ihnen? Darf
ich mich zu Ihnen setzen?
HEINRICH: Ja gewiß. Ich möchte auch gern mit Ihnen sprechen.
5 KLAUS: Das freut mich sehr. Was tun Sie heute nach der
Klasse? Sind Sie um drei Uhr frei?
HEINRICH: Nein. Ich bin leider nicht frei. Ich muß nach

26

der Klasse gleich nach Hause fahren. Das tue ich nicht gern, aber ich muß.

KLAUS: Warum?   10

HEINRICH: Meine Mutter ist krank, und mein Vater ist diese Woche nicht zu Hause. Da muß ich meiner Mutter helfen. Sie ist allein zu Hause.

KLAUS: Das tut mir aber leid. Sind Ihre Schwestern denn nicht zu Hause?   15

HEINRICH: O nein. Die sind schon seit einer Woche in Colorado.

KLAUS: In Denver?

HEINRICH: Nein, auf dem Lande, bei Boulder. Wir sind im Sommer nie in der Stadt. Wir sind immer auf dem Lande.   20

KLAUS: So, so! —Dann kann ich also nach der Deutschstunde nicht mit Ihnen ins Kino gehen.

HEINRICH: Das tut mir wirklich leid. Aber ich will Ihnen etwas sagen. Kommen Sie heute abend doch zu uns. Meine Kusine aus dem Osten ist heute abend bei uns, und die müs-   25 sen Sie kennenlernen.

KLAUS: Die mit den schwarzen Haaren? Ist die denn nicht in Neuyork?

HEINRICH: Ja, die mit den schwarzen Haaren. Heute morgen hat sie uns ein Telegramm geschickt [sent]: BIN AUF DER   30 REISE NACH LOS ANGELES. MUSS MORGEN WEITER. KEINEM MENSCHEN ETWAS VON MEINER REISE SAGEN!

KLAUS: Das brauchen Sie mir nicht zweimal zu sagen. Das gefällt mir sehr. Ich werde [shall] um acht Uhr bei Ihnen sein. Ich danke Ihnen. Auf Wiedersehen!   35

IDIOMS AND VOCABULARY

auf dem Lande   in the country
Das freut mich sehr.   I am very glad (about that).
Das gefällt mir sehr.   I like that very much; that pleases me a lot.
Das tut mir (aber) leid.   I am (really) sorry about that.

... doch ...   Why don't you ...
Guten Tag!   Hello.
heute abend   this evening
heute morgen   this morning
Ich möchte gern.   I'd like to.
kennen-lernen   get to know, meet
nach Hause   home(ward)
zu Hause   at home

acht   eight
allein   alone
also   therefore
danken [*dat.*]   thank
ich, er darf   I, he may; I
have, he has permission
denn [*adv.*]   anyway, and; tell
me
der, die, das [*demonst. pron.*]
this, that (one)
doch   nevertheless, please;
why don't you?
fahren   travel, go (by vehicle)
er fährt   he travels, goes
gern(e) [*See Idioms*]   gladly
gewiß   certain
gleich   immediately
das Haar, -e   hair
helfen [*dat.*]   help
er hilft   he helps
immer   always
das Kino, -s   movies
krank   sick
die Kusine, -n   cousin [*female*]
das Land, -er   country

der Mensch, -en   human
being
mit   with; [*adv.*] along
morgen   tomorrow
der Morgen, –   morning
die Mutter, –   mother
nach   after, to
nie, niemals   never
der Osten   the East
die Reise, -n   trip
schwarz   black
die Schwester, -n   sister
seit   since, for
setzen   set
der Sommer, –   summer
das Telegramm, -e   telegram
die Uhr, -en   clock, watch;
um... Uhr   at... o'clock
von   from, of, about
warum   why
weit   far, wide
weiter   further, on
wirklich   really
ich, er will   I want, he wants to
die Woche, -n   week
zweimal   twice, two times

GRAMMAR

3.1 The Dative Case

3.1,1 In English grammar there is no dative case. The German dative can be understood from patterns like: 'Tell me his name.' 'I'll give the teacher a book.' In these English illustrations, *me* and *the teacher* are indirect objects. In German they appear in the dative case. In English we can distinguish them from direct objects by their order: the indirect objects always precede the direct objects. However, if *to* is put in front of them, words used as indirect objects may be placed after direct objects, *e.g.*, 'I gave a book to the teacher.'

3.1,2 The dative is marked by special endings of **der**-words and **ein**-words:

Er gibt das dem (diesem, seinem) Lehrer. 'He is giving that to the (this, his) teacher.'

Er gibt das der (jeder, meiner) Lehrerin. 'He is giving that to the (each, my) teacher.'

Er gibt das dem (diesem, einem) Mädchen. 'He is giving that to the (this, a) girl.'

Er gibt das den (diesen, seinen) Lehrern. 'He is giving that to the (these, his) teachers.'

3.1,3 There is no special ending in the dative singular for most nouns, but monosyllabic masculine and neuter nouns occasionally add **-e,** as in the phrase **zu Hause** 'at home.' In the dative plural, **-n** is added to all nouns other than those already ending in **-n** or those which make plurals in **-s**: **den Freunden, den Lehrern, den Mädchen.**

3.1,4 Pronouns have special forms in the dative:

Er gibt mir die Uhr. 'He's giving me the watch.'

Ich gebe ihm die Uhr. 'I'm giving him the watch.'
Er gibt ihr die Uhr. 'He's giving her the watch.'
Er gibt uns die Uhr. 'He's giving us the watch.'
Er gibt ihnen die Uhr. 'He's giving them the watch.'
Er gibt Ihnen die Uhr. 'He's giving you the watch.'

3.1,5 The dative is used in German as the case of the indirect object:

Ich will Ihnen etwas sagen. 'I want to tell you something.'

3.1,6 The dative is also used for the only object after certain verbs. These verbs will be marked with [*dat.*] in vocabularies, as is **danken,** and must be memorized as verbs taking the dative. Up to the present you have had:

danken : Ich danke Ihnen. 'I thank you.'
gefallen : Das gefällt mir. 'I like that.'
helfen : Sie hilft ihrer Mutter. 'She is helping her mother.'

You have also had the verbal phrase **leid tun :**

   Das tut mir leid. 'I am sorry about that.'

3.2 Prepositions Requiring the Dative Case

3.2,1 The following prepositions always take the dative:

   aus 'out of, from': **Meine Kusine aus dem Osten ist bei
   mir.** 'My cousin from the East is at my place.'

   bei 'at (the place/home of)': *See example after* **aus.**

   mit 'with': **Ich möchte gern mit Ihnen sprechen.**
   'I'd like to speak with you.'

   nach 'after, towards, according to': **Was tun Sie heute
   nach der Klasse?** 'What are you doing today after
   class ?'

   seit 'since, for': **Die sind schon seit einer Woche in
   Colorado.** 'They have already been in Colorado a week.'

(Note particularly the meaning of seit *when it is used with noun phrases indicating time and the present tense of the verb. Such combinations are to be translated with the English present perfect.)*

von 'from, of, by': **Keinem Menschen etwas von meiner Reise sagen.** 'Don't tell anyone anything of (about) my trip.'

zu 'to, at': **Kommen Sie heute abend doch zu mir.** 'Why don't you come to my place this evening?'

3.2,2 The prepositions already given in Lesson 2.2,2 take the dative when no motion toward a place is involved:

an 'at': **Mein Vater ist Professor an der Universität.** 'My father is a professor at the university.'

auf 'on, upon': **Bin auf der Reise nach Los Angeles.** 'Am on the way to Los Angeles.'

hinter 'behind': **Die Uhr ist hinter der Tür.** 'The clock is behind the door.'

in 'in': **Wir sind im Sommer nie in der Stadt.** 'We're never in the city in summer.'

neben 'beside, next to, near': **Die Rechnung ist neben dem Buch.** 'The bill is beside the book.'

über 'over, concerning': **Sehen Sie es dort über dem Fenster?** 'Do you see it there over the window?'

unter 'under, among': **Das Mädchen sucht ihren Bleistift unter dem Tisch.** 'The girl is looking for her pencil under the table.'

vor 'before, in front of': **Wir sehen sie vor der Stunde.** 'We see her before class.'

zwischen 'between': **Seine Kusine steht zwischen meinem und ihrem Vater.** 'His cousin is standing between my father and hers.'

3.2,3 A few contractions of prepositions and **dem** are commonly used in speaking and occasionally in writing, *e.g.*, **am = an dem, beim = bei dem, im = in dem, vom = von dem, zum = zu dem.**

3.3 Word Order of Elements in the Predicate

3.3,1 If a German sentence begins with an element, usually adverbial, other than the subject, the *verb* stands in *second place* and is followed directly by the subject. (See page 27, line 12, **Da muß ich...**; page 27, line 30, **Heute morgen hat sie...**). Occasionally the first element is the object, as on page 27, line 33, **Das brauchen Sie. . . .**

3.3,2 In German, elements that complement or complete the finite verb stand at the end of the clause. The most common such elements are infinitives and participles:

> **Ich möchte auch gern mit Ihnen sprechen.** 'I'd also like to talk with you.'

With finite forms of **sein** the complement may be an adjective:

> **Sind Sie um drei Uhr frei?** 'Are you free at three o'clock?'

3.3,3 In general, the order of adverbial modifiers in German is fixed. Modifiers indicating time precede those indicating place:

> **Ich gehe jetzt in die Schule.** 'I am going to school now.'

3.3,4 Indirect objects in German precede direct objects when the direct object is a noun:

> **Ich gebe dem Lehrer (ihm) ein Buch.** 'I give the teacher (him) a book.'

But, as in English, the accusative object is first if it is a pronoun:

> **Ich gebe es dem Lehrer (ihm).** 'I give it to the teacher (him).'

3.4 Intonation One of the most important markers in speech is the sentence melody, or intonation. It informs the listener when sentences are concluded, what the feeling of the speaker is, which words in the sentence are important, and so on. Fortunately for us, the sentence melody of simple sentences in German is much like that of English. To acquire it, you must first of all produce German the way you do English: by phrases and by whole sentences rather than by syllables or by words. If you imitate your teacher or recorded materials in this respect, you will readily acquire the basic German intonations.

3.4,1 Practice these and similar sentences from the texts of Lessons 1 through 3. Note the drop at the end of each; this is the normal sentence intonation.

1. Das freut mich sehr.
2. Wir sind immer auf dem Lande.
3. Wie geht es Ihnen?

Note the rise in voice at the end of the following sentences; this is characteristic of questions that are not introduced by an interrogative and of statements of doubt.

1. Darf ich mich zu Ihnen setzen?
2. Sind Sie um drei Uhr frei?
3. In der Stadt?

EXERCISES

A. Make additional sentences on the basis of those given here, substituting the suggested words for those in heavy type.

1. Ich kann **meiner Lehrerin** helfen. (my professor, their mother)
2. Das gefällt **meinem Freund.** (the girl, his sister, their father)
3. Sagen Sie das **dem Lehrer!** (my cousin, our mother)

4. Ich fahre mit **meinem Professor.** (her sister, their father)
5. Sie sind in **dem Park.** (the class, the city)

B. Put the nouns of exercise A (those printed in heavy type) and the substitutes for them in the plural.

C. Follow the instructions for exercise A.

1. Sie gehen mit **uns.** (you, her, him)
2. Ich muß **ihr** helfen. (them, you, him)
3. Er will **mir** etwas sagen. (us, you, her)
4. Sie haben **ihm** ein Telegramm geschickt. (me, her, them)

D. Follow the instructions for exercise A.

1. Ich schicke **dem Vater** ein Telegramm. (his sister, her mother, him)
2. Die Kusine sagt **ihrem Freund** etwas von der Reise. (her professor, her teacher, the girls)
3. Sie gibt **ihm** das Papier. (his father, your sister, me)
4. Er macht **mir** etwas. (him, us, them)

E. Follow the instructions for exercise A.

1. Heute abend helfe ich **meiner Mutter.** (my father, his teacher, the professor)
2. Die Reise gefällt **ihm** nicht. (the girls, his friend)
3. Das tut **mir** leid. (him, us, her)
4. Warum helfen Sie **dem Professor** nicht? (your mother, me, my sister)

F. Follow the instructions for exercise A.

1. Er ist heute abend bei **uns.** ([at] her, his, their [place])
2. Nach der Stunde fahre ich mit **meiner Kusine.** (her sister, my father, my friends)

3. Seit **dem Winter** bin ich in dieser Stadt. (the summer, eight o'clock)
4. Er kommt heute abend zu **Ihnen.** (us, me)
5. Sie schreibt etwas von **ihrer Reise.** (the German class, her sister, the class)
6. Sie sprechen mit **meinem Vater.** (their mother, the teachers, his friends)
7. Das ist mein Freund aus **Chikago.** (the East, the city, the class)

G. Follow the directions for exercise A.

1. Sie ist seit einer Woche in **der Stadt.** (the class, the house)
2. Sie finden den Brief zwischen **mir** und **ihm.** (her and us, them and me)
3. Das brauchen wir vor **der Stunde.** (the German class, the trip)
4. Ich fahre neben **meiner Mutter.** (our friend, her, his cousin)
5. Das Mädchen hinter **meinem Bruder** sagt etwas. (me, his friend, my father)
6. Das Telegramm sehen Sie da auf **dem Heft.** (the book, the paper)
7. Sie ist Lehrerin an **der Schule.** (the university)
8. Was ist das da über **dem Haus?** (the clock, the university)

H. Follow the directions for exercise A.

1. **Heute abend** kann ich ins Kino gehen. (then, after German class)
2. **Im Sommer** sind wir auf dem Lande. (tomorrow, this evening)
3. **Da** muß ich mit ihm sprechen. (then, this morning)
4. **Für welchen Kurs** soll es sein? (for which bill, for which cousin)

I. Follow the directions for exercise A.

1. Ich möchte nach dem Examen **mit ihm sprechen.** (go to the movies, drive home)
2. Morgen kann ich **gehen.** (come, help)
3. Ich will das **finden.** (have, learn, buy)
4. Das brauchen Sie mir nicht zweimal zu **sagen.** (write, send)

J. Follow the directions for exercise A.

1. Er ist **seit einer Woche in der Stadt.** (in school since this morning)
2. Ich will **um fünf Uhr bei Ihnen** sein. (at my mother's after the class)
3. Er ist **heute morgen nicht zu Hause.** (not in class this evening)
4. Wir sind **im Sommer nie in der Stadt.** (never at home after the German class)

K. Read the following questions and answers and use them as models for additional sentences.

1. Wer möchte mit Klaus sprechen? Heinrich möchte mit Klaus sprechen.
2. Was tut Heinrich nach der Klasse? Er fährt nach Hause.
3. Warum muß er nach Hause? Seine Mutter ist krank.
4. Wo sind seine Schwestern? Sie sind in Colorado.
5. Wann sind die Moehlenbrocks immer auf dem Lande? Im Sommer sind sie auf dem Lande.
6. Wer kommt heute abend aus dem Osten? Heinrichs Kusine kommt aus dem Osten.
7. Was für (what kind of) Haare hat die Kusine? Sie hat schwarze Haare.
8. Nach welcher Stadt fährt sie? Sie fährt nach Los Angeles.
9. Wo will Klaus um acht Uhr sein? Er will bei Heinrich Seemann sein.

time before place

L. Translate into German:

1. I am sorry, but he is not at my house. (Use **bei**)
2. He must be in the country.
3. The exam is today.
4. Come to our place tonight at eight o'clock.
5. Hans and Fred go home immediately after class.
6. We've been in the city for a week.
7. We must help them with the things.
8. Are you free after class tomorrow?
9. Unfortunately they don't like that.
10. Do you see the money under the paper next to the window?
11. Do you know the girl with the black hair?
12. I want to thank him for the telegram.

M. Free conversation.

You see your friend Fritz after class. You ask him what he will do after the class, whether he will be free at five o'clock. He says he is, but that his cousin is at his house and wants to go to the movies. He can't go, however, for his mother is sick. You are free, and will go with her. After the movie you will be at Fritz' place. You thank him, and say good-bye.

BRIEF CONVERSATION

Geburtstagsgeschenke

KLAUS MOEHLENBROCK: Guten Abend, Herr Moeller. Was tun Sie in der Stadt? Sie sind nicht bei den Büchern?
FRITZ MOELLER: Nein, ich suche etwas für meine Freundin. Inge Pfeiffer hat morgen Geburtstag. Kennen Sie sie nicht? Ich studiere immer mit ihr.

KLAUS: Ja, ich kenne sie seit vier Wochen. — Warum geben
Sie ihr nicht eine Uhr oder ein Paar Ohrringe? Wie gefällt
Ihnen diese Uhr im Fenster, zwischen den Ringen?

FRITZ: Sehr schön. Aber sie möchte Bücher haben. — Gehen
Sie ins Kino?

KLAUS: Nein, ich komme aus dem Kino und gehe nach Hause.

FRITZ: Nun, ich sehe Sie morgen auf der Universität.

KLAUS: Ja, vor der Physikstunde. Auf Wiedersehen!

LESSON 4

Wie gefällt Ihnen diese Aussicht?

THE GENITIVE CASE

WORD ORDER OF DEPENDENT CLAUSES

PRONUNCIATION

TEXT

While other students are in class, KLAUS MOEHLENBROCK takes advantage of the warm spring afternoon to show the sights to ELEANOR SANDERS, his friend's attractive cousin from the East.

KLAUS: Es ist wirklich sehr nett, Fräulein Sanders, daß Sie heute noch hier sind.

ELEANOR: Ja, ich danke Ihnen, daß Sie so gut sind, mir Ihre Stadt zu zeigen.

KLAUS: O, in solcher Gesellschaft ist mir das ein Vergnügen. 5
Und für die Kusine meines Freundes habe ich immer Zeit.

ELEANOR: Es ist aber doch schade, daß Heinrich nicht mit uns fahren kann.

KLAUS: Nun ja, aber er hat jetzt Physikstunde. Während
10   dieser Stunde bin ich frei. Hier sind wir am Fluß. Wie gefällt Ihnen diese Aussicht?

ELEANOR: Wirklich wunderbar. Sagen Sie mir, Herr Moehlenbrock, wo wohnen Sie nun hier?

KLAUS: Jenseits des Flusses und weit außerhalb der Stadt.
15   Sehen Sie dort den Berg?

ELEANOR: Ja.

KLAUS: Sehen Sie auch das gelbe Haus gerade unterhalb des Berges?

ELEANOR: Ja, ich kann es sehen.

20 KLAUS: Nun, das ist unser Haus.

ELEANOR: Hat Ihr Vater vielleicht eine Bank?

KLAUS: O nein, er ist nur ein Aktionär [stockholder] der Bank. Aber er ist Direktor einer Baugesellschaft [construction company] und Präsident der Handelskammer [chamber of
25   commerce].

ELEANOR: Dann hat er wohl immer viel zu tun?

KLAUS: Ja, er ist an zwei Tagen während der Woche auf Reisen. Aber abends ist er wieder zu Hause.

ELEANOR: Wollen wir nicht weiter fahren? Es ist hier so
30   heiß in der Sonne.

KLAUS: Ist Ihnen die Sonne nicht angenehm, trotz der Hitze? Denken Sie, in Neuyork haben Sie jetzt oft Regen oder Schnee.

ELEANOR: Ja, das ist wahr. — Aber ich muß noch zur Bank und
35   etwas Geld holen. Ohne Geld kann ich nicht weiter fahren.

KLAUS: Das tut mir aber leid. Jetzt ist die Bank schon geschlossen [closed], wegen der Arbeit an den Büchern. — Aber ich habe gerade hundert Dollar bei mir und leihe Ihnen
40   gerne, was Sie brauchen. Schicken Sie mir dann das Geld aus Los Angeles.

ELEANOR: Sie meinen hundert und fünf Dollar?

KLAUS: Nein, natürlich nur hundert Dollar — und dann vielleicht ein Bildchen von Ihnen.

ELEANOR: Vielleicht. Statt des Geldes? — Aber es wird spät.   45
Ich habe nur noch zwanzig Minuten bis zur Abfahrt des Zuges.

KLAUS: Aber ich kann Sie ja in acht Minuten zur Bahn fahren.

IDIOMS AND VOCABULARY

Es ist schade. It is too bad.
Ich habe gerade ... I happen to have ...

abends in the evening(s)
die Abfahrt, -en departure
angenehm pleasant
(an)statt in place of
die Arbeit, -en work
außerhalb outside of
die Aussicht, -en view
die Bahn, -en train, railroad
die Bank, -en bank
der Berg, -e mountain, hill
das Bild, -er picture
das Bildchen,– little picture*
bis until; as far as
der Bruder, ⸚ brother
daß [*conj.*] that
denken think
das Ende, -s, -n end

der Fluß, -sses, ⸚e river
das Fräulein, – young lady; Miss
gelb yellow
die Gesellschaft, -en company, party
das Haus, ⸚er house
heiß hot
die Hitze heat
holen (go and) get, fetch
hundert hundred
jenseits on the other side of
leihen lend
meinen mean, have an opinion, think
natürlich naturally, of course
nett nice
nun now, well

* The suffixes -chen and -lein, which can be added to most nouns, form diminutives, like English book*let*, gos*ling;* often the diminutive connotes endearment, as in English lamb*kin*. All such nouns are neuter: **das Fräulein, das Mädchen, das Väterchen.** As in **Vater,** a o u vowels of the original noun take an umlaut when the noun becomes a diminutive.

oft often
der Regen, - rain
der Schnee snow
sehr very
sein [ein-*word***]** his, its
solcher [der-*word***]** such
die Sonne, -n sun
spät late
trotz in spite of
unterhalb below
das Vergnügen, – pleasure, fun
viel much, a lot
vielleicht perhaps
wahr true

während during
wegen on account of
werden become, get
  er wird he becomes, gets
wieder again
wohl probably, well, indeed
wohnen dwell, reside, live
wollen want to
  ich, er will I, he want(s) to
wunderbar wonderful
zeigen show
die Zeit, -en time
der Zug, ̈-e train
zwanzig twenty

GRAMMAR

4.1 The Genitive Case

4.1,1 The genitive corresponds to the English possessive. It is marked by special forms of **der**-words and **ein**-words. Most masculines and all neuter nouns have **-s** or **-es** endings; although **-s** is the common form of the ending, **-es** may be used for monosyllabic nouns, and it must be used for nouns that end in an [s] sound, such as **Flusses**. There is no genitive ending in the feminine or in the plural of nouns of all genders.

  Sie ist die Schwester des (dieses, meines) Lehrers.
    'She is the sister of the (this, my) teacher.'

  Sie ist die Schwester der (dieser, unsrer) Lehrerin.
    'She is the sister of the (this, our) teacher.'

  Ist dies das Bild des (dieses, seines) Mädchens? 'Is this the picture of the (this, his) girl?'

  Sehen Sie die Arbeit der (dieser, seiner) Männer?
    'Do you see the work of the (these, his) men?'

Instead of **unseres** and **unserer** one usually finds the shortened forms **unsres** and **unsrer.**

4.1,2 The genitive is used to indicate possession and to show relationship between two nouns. It usually follows the noun which it modifies, as in the following examples:

Sehen Sie das Buch meines Vaters? 'Do you see my father's book?'

Das ist die Schwester seines Freundes. 'That is his friend's sister.'

4.1,3 The genitive is also used after some prepositions:

(an)statt 'in place of, instead of': **Statt des Geldes?** 'Instead of the money?'

trotz 'in spite of': **...trotz der Hitze?** '... in spite of the heat?'

während 'during, in the course of': **Während dieser Stunde bin ich frei.** 'During this hour I'm free.'

wegen 'because of': **Er muß eine Reise machen, wegen seines Buches.** 'He has to take a trip because of his book.'

außerhalb 'outside of': **Jenseits des Flusses und weit außerhalb der Stadt.** 'On the other side of the river and far outside the city.'

unterhalb 'below': **Sehen Sie auch das Haus gerade unterhalb des Berges?** 'Do you also see the house just below the mountain?'

diesseits 'on this side of': **Ich kenne das Haus diesseits des Flusses.** 'I know the house on this side of the river.'

jenseits 'on the other side of': *See example after* **außerhalb.**

4.2 Word Order of Dependent Clauses

4.2,1 In dependent clauses beginning with conjunctions like **daß** 'that,' the finite verb stands at the end:

Es tut mir leid, daß er heute nicht kommt. 'I am sorry that he isn't coming today.'

4.2,2 As in English, infinitives may be used in separate clauses with objects or with other modifiers. In such constructions the infinitives must stand at the end:

Es freut mich sehr, Ihnen die Stadt zu zeigen. 'I am very happy to show you the city.'

4.3 Pronunciation When **b d g** are final in words or syllables, they are pronounced [p t k]:

ab	**Bild**	**Berg**
unterhalb	**Geld**	**Weg**
siebzehn	**Mädchen**	**Zug**

When **b d g** are followed in the same syllable by another consonant, usually **s** or **t**, they are also pronounced [p t k]:

gibt   abends   Tags

If, however, a vowel follows, they are pronounced [b d g]. Contrast:

geben : gibt   Bilder : Bild   Wege : Weg

Many native Germans, especially those from north Germany, pronounce final **g** like **ch**.

4.3,1 Final **-ig** is pronounced like. **ich**; the following words rhyme with **natürlich:**

billig   zwanzig   König 'king'

4.3,2 The combination **-ng** is pronounced [ŋ], as in German **jung** and English *young*. Before **k**, [ŋ] is spelled with **n** in the two languages, as in **denken** and *think*.

singen   Rechnung   dunkel   danke

EXERCISES

A. Make additional sentences on the basis of those given here, substituting the suggested words for those in heavy type.

1. Das ist der Bleistift **des Mädchens.** (of the woman teacher, of the mother)
2. Er ist Präsident **der Handelskammer.** (of the bank, of the company) *des Vaters des Fräuleins*
3. Das Bild **der Kusine** ist schön. (of the mother, of the young lady) *der Gesellschaft*
4. Da sehen Sie das Haus **der Lehrerin.** (of the company, of the friend) *des Freundes* *der Väter*
5. Ich finde den Brief **der Mutter** nicht. (of the father, of the girl) *des Mädchens*
6. Sie sehen dort **das Häuschen** der Gesellschaft. (the little picture) *das Bildchens*
7. Zeigen Sie mir **das Büchlein** der Frau! (the little sister) *das ... schwesterlein*

B. Put the nouns in heavy type in exercise A and the substitutes for them in the plural.

C. Follow the directions for exercise A.

1. Das ist die Schwester **seines Freundes.** (of my mother, of their friends)
2. Das Haus **seines Vaters** ist schön. (of her professor, of my teacher)
3. Wir besuchen die Schwester **meines Vaters.** (of his friend, of our mother)
4. Sein Vater ist Präsident **der Handelskammer.** (of a company, of our bank)
5. Wir wohnen im Haus **seines Vaters.** (of my cousin, of his brother)

6. Ich danke Ihnen für das Buch **Ihres Vaters.** (of your friend, of her mother)
7. Das Haus **meines Vaters** ist am Fluß. (of the company, of the woman)

D. Follow the directions for exercise A.

1. Trotz **der Hitze** gehe ich heute in die Stadt. (the rain, the snow)
2. Das rote Haus unterhalb **des Bergs** ist unser Haus. (the university, the railroad)
3. Wir wohnen diesseits **des Flusses.** (the mountains, the railroad)
4. Er wohnt da wegen **der Gesellschaft.** (the view, the river)
5. Außerhalb **der Stadt** ist es nicht so heiß. (the bank, the houses)
6. Da kommt ihre Kusine statt **meiner Schwester.** (my friend, her mother)
7. Während **der Stunde** sehe ich Fräulein Schmidt. (the German class, the trip)

E. Follow the directions for exercise A.

1. Es tut mir leid, daß er nicht **kommt.** (writes, goes)
2. Abends ist es angenehm, durch den Park zu **kommen.** (go)
3. Er sagt, daß er während der Woche oft **liest.** (writes, goes)
4. Meinen Sie, daß er kommen **kann?** (has to, wants to)
5. Es gefällt mir nicht, morgen zu **schreiben.** (look, go)

F. Read the following questions and answers, using them as models for further sentences.

1. Für wen hat Klaus immer Zeit? Für die Kusine seines Freundes hat Klaus immer Zeit.
2. Warum kann Heinrich nicht mit ihnen fahren? Heinrich hat jetzt Physikstunde.

3. Wo wohnt Klaus? Er wohnt außerhalb der Stadt.
4. Was für ein Haus sieht Eleanor? Sie sieht ein gelbes Haus.
5. Was tut der Vater während der Woche? Während der Woche ist er oft auf Reisen.
6. Warum muß Eleanor zur Bank? Sie muß Geld holen.
7. Wer leiht ihr das Geld? Klaus leiht ihr das Geld.
8. Von wem (whom) möchte Klaus ein Bildchen haben? Er möchte ein Bildchen von Eleanor haben.
9. Wie viele Minuten hat Eleanor bis zur Abfahrt des Zuges? Eleanor hat nur zwanzig Minuten.
10. Wer fährt sie zur Bahn? Klaus fährt sie zur Bahn.

G. Translate in writing:

1. We are living in the house of his teacher during this summer.
2. We have no work today because of the party.
3. He thinks that it is already too hot.
4. He is showing her the city in spite of the snow.
5. After the rain it really gets hot.
6. They live on the other side of the mountains.
7. I consider (**finden**) my sister's watch very pretty.
8. They are showing him the pictures of their teachers.
9. On account of the heat we are going to the movies.
10. During the day I write a lot.

H. Free conversation.

Show a visitor your town from a near-by hilltop. Point out your home, your school, the river, the railroad, the bank, the house of a friend, and so on. He asks for more details. Indicate the position of these points of interest with regard to one another. Then drive him back to town, continuing your description.

BRIEF CONVERSATION

Mit wem spreche ich?

The telephone rings in Professor Niebuhr's house; Mrs.
Niebuhr *answers.*

Hallo! Hier Frau Niebuhr. —
Nein, mein Mann ist jetzt nicht zu Hause. —
O, Sie sprechen von dem Bruder meines Mannes. Ja, der
wohnt gerade bei uns. Ja, er ist Professor der Biologie und
der Autor eines Buches. —
Eine Autorität in der Welt der Tiere? O, ja, das ist er. —
Nein, es tut mir leid, daß Sie nicht mit ihm sprechen können.
Er ist beim Präsidenten der Universität. —
Ja. Er ist während der Woche noch hier. Aber am Ende
der Woche muß er eine Reise nach Neuyork machen, wegen
seines Buches. —
Mit wem spreche ich? — Herr Fritz Moeller? —
Ich will es ihm sagen. Telefonieren Sie ihm morgen um zehn
Uhr. Er freut sich sehr, mit Ihnen zu sprechen.

LESSON 5

Leider ist sie nicht mehr hier

THE PAST TENSE AND THE PAST PARTICIPLE OF WEAK VERBS

COMPOUND TENSES: THE PRESENT PERFECT AND THE
PAST PERFECT

TRANSLATING GERMAN INTO ENGLISH

PRONUNCIATION

TEXT

Um halb fünf Uhr war Klaus Moehlenbrock im „Co-op."
Er brauchte eine neue Füllfeder. Er hatte seine eigene Füll-
feder seit zwei Stunden gesucht und nicht gefunden. Ein
Mann im Laden fragte ihn: „Was wünschen Sie, bitte?"
Klaus hörte ihn nicht. Er träumte und sagte nichts. Der   5
Mann wiederholte seine Frage: „Was wünschen Sie, bitte?
Womit kann ich dienen?" „Verzeihen Sie, bitte," sagte
Klaus, „ich habe Sie nicht gehört. Ich möchte eine Füllfeder
kaufen. Ohne meine Feder kann ich nicht studieren."

10 Der Mann legte drei Federn vor Klaus auf den Tisch.
„Diese kostet drei Dollar fünfzig, diese kostet sieben Dollar
fünfundsiebzig, und diese hier kostet elf Dollar". Klaus
wartete und rechnete. Dann antwortete er: „Gut. Ich nehme
die für drei Dollar fünfundsiebzig. Die ist gut genug für
15 mich." „Sie meinen wohl drei Dollar fünfzig!"
Dann telefonierte er noch Heinrich Seemann und dankte
ihm für den schönen Abend.
Auf der Straße war starker Verkehr. Viele Leute drängten
sich [crowded] vor dem Laden und warteten auf das grüne
20 Licht. Unter den Leuten begegnete Klaus einem Herrn.
Es war Professor Niebuhr. Klaus grüßte ihn und wollte schnell
vorbei. Doch Herr Niebuhr drehte sich um [turned around]
und sagte: „Guten Abend, Herr Moehlenbrock. Ich habe
gehört, daß Sie heute nicht in der Physikstunde waren. Ich hatte
25 geglaubt, Sie wären [might be] krank."
„Nein," sagte Klaus, „ich war nicht krank." „Dann sind
Sie zu Hause gewesen und haben gearbeitet?" „Nein, ich
habe auch nicht gearbeitet. Ich habe Fräulein Sanders die
Stadt gezeigt." „Fräulein Sanders? Ist das nicht die Kusine
30 von Herrn Seemann? Ist sie noch hier?" „Nein. Sie ist
heute nachmittag nach Los Angeles gereist. Leider."
Das rote Licht wurde grün, und die Menschen eilten über
die Straße. Nur Klaus Moehlenbrock wartete noch. Er
träumte.

IDIOMS AND VOCABULARY

auch nicht   not … either
Guten Abend.   Good evening.
nicht mehr   no longer
(um) halb fünf (Uhr)   (at) four-thirty (o'clock)
Verzeihen Sie!   Pardon me.

der Abend, -e evening   **arbeiten** work
antworten [*dat.*] answer   **auf** up, upon, on

bald   soon
begegnen [*dat.*]   meet
dienen   [*dat.*] serve
eigen [*adj.*]   own
eilen   hurry
elf   eleven
die Feder, -n (**Füllfeder**)
  pen (fountain pen)
finden   find
  gefunden [*pptc.*]   found
die Frage, -n   question
fünfundsiebzig   seventy-
  five
fünfzig   fifty
genug   enough
gesucht [*pptc. of* **suchen**]
  looked for
gewesen [*pptc. of* **sein**]   been
glauben   believe, think
grün   green
grüßen   greet
halb   half
interessant   interesting
kosten   cost
der Laden, ⸚   store
legen   lay, put, place
die Leute [*pl. only*]   people

das Licht, -er   light
der Mittag, -e   noon
  heute mittag   this noon
nehmen   take
neu   new
nichts   nothing
rechnen   figure
reisen   travel
schnell   fast, quick
sich [*reflexive*]   himself, herself, itself; themselves; each
  other
sieben   seven
stark   strong
die Straße, -n   street
telefonieren   telephone
der Tisch, -e   table
über   across, over, concerning
unter   under, among
der Verkehr   traffic
vor   in front of; ago
vorbei   past, by, over
war [*past of* **sein**]   was
warten auf [*acc.*]   wait for
wiederholen   repeat; review
womit   with what, how

GRAMMAR

5.1 The Past Tense and the Past Participle of Weak Verbs

In German as in English, there are two classes of verbs, *regular* (*e.g.*, **danken, dankte** 'thank, thanked'), and *irregular* (*e.g.*, **geben, gab** 'give, gave'). In German grammar, the regular verbs are referred to as *weak*, the irregular as *strong*.

5.1,1 The past tense of weak verbs is formed by adding **-te** or **-ten** to the stem:

> **Ich (er) kaufte eine Feder.** 'I (he) bought a pen.'
> **Wir (sie, Sie) kauften eine Feder.** 'We (they, you) bought a pen.'

5.1,2 Verbs with stems ending in **t** or **d** and those ending in a consonant (other than **r** or **l**) plus **m** or **n** add **-e-** before any ending beginning with **t**: **kostet** 'costs,' **kostete** 'cost,' **gekostet** 'cost'; **rechnet** 'figures,' **rechnete** 'figured,' **gerechnet** 'figured.'

5.1,3 The past participle [*pptc.*] of weak verbs is formed by adding **-t** to the stem and by prefixing **ge-: ge-kauf-t** 'bought.' A verb with an unaccented first syllable, however, does not take the **ge-: studiert** 'studied,' **wiederholt** 'repeated.'

5.1,4 The past tense of **haben** is irregular in having two **t**'s:

> **ich (er) hatte**   **wir (sie, Sie) hatten**

The past participle, however, is regular: **gehabt.**

5.2 Compound Tenses: The Present Perfect and the Past Perfect

5.2,1 As in English, the present perfect and the past perfect are formed by using an auxiliary with the past participle. For most verbs the auxiliary is **haben.**

The present perfect is made with present forms of **haben** plus the past participle:

> **ich habe gekauft**   'I have bought'
> **er (sie, es) hat gekauft**   'he (she, [it]) has bought'
> **wir (sie, Sie) haben gekauft**   'we (they, you) have bought'

The past perfect is made with past forms of **haben** plus the past participle:

ich (er, sie, es) hatte gekauft   'I (he, she, it) had bought'
wir (sie, Sie) hatten gekauft   'we (they, you) had bought'

5.2,2 The past perfect is used as in English:

Klaus hatte ihn nicht gehört.   'Klaus hadn't heard him.'

5.2,3 The present perfect is used much more widely in German than in English. In conversation it is virtually the only form used to indicate past time; see page 49, line 8, **Ich habe Sie nicht gehört.** 'I didn't hear you.'

In narrative, on the other hand, the past is used; see page 49, line 5, **Klaus hörte ihn nicht.** 'Klaus didn't hear him.'

Accordingly, while the present perfect of German will be used in sentences where the English present perfect would be used, it will also be used to correspond to some uses of the English past tense.

5.3 Translating German into English   The first principle of translation is conversion of an idiomatic text into the idiom of another language.   If the language from which we are translating, such as German, uses the present perfect where the past is used in English, our finished translation must use only past tense forms in those contexts.   And the proper form of the past—whether the simple, *e.g.*, "I went," the emphatic, *e.g.*, "I did go," or the progressive, *e.g.*, "I was going," must be selected.   **Ich habe ihn nicht gesehen** must be translated 'I didn't see him', not 'I saw him not.'; in a suitable context, however, it may be translated 'I have not seen him.'   Your own idiom will determine the style of your translation, although you must, of course, include the entire content of the German text in your translation.

A correct idiomatic translation will enable someone with no knowledge of German to understand fully the meaning of the original, and it will give the translator a better understanding of English and German and of language in general.   So-called

"literal translations" are of little value because one can understand them only by checking back on the original and because
anyone can produce them without mastering the content of the
material he is supposedly translating.

5.4 Pronunciation   The German [š] is spelled **sch** before
vowels and before **l, m, n, r,** and **w**:

> schon   schlafen   schmieren 'smear'
> schnell   schreiben   schwarz

Before **p** and **t** it is spelled simply with **s**:

> spät   spielen   sprechen
> Stadt   stark   Bleistift

The pronunciation [š] is used before **p** and **t** only at the beginnings of words and syllables; it is not used in such words as
ist and **Fenster**.

5.4,1   The accent generally falls on the first syllable of German
words.   There are two large groups of exceptions: (1) Verbs
with prefixes containing an **e**-vowel, such as **begégnen, be-
súchen** (compare English *befriend*); (2) Foreign words, such as
studíeren.   Many words of foreign origin that have been
taken into German are accented on the last syllable, *e.g.*, **Physík,
Universität.**
A few verbs with longer prefixes are accented on the stem
syllable, *e.g.*, **wiederhólen**.   All verbs with unaccented first
syllable omit **ge-** in the past participle.

EXERCISES

A. Make additional sentences on the basis of those given
here, substituting the suggested words for those in heavy type.

1. Die Kusine **fragte** seinen Vater.   (heard, greeted)
2. Das **glaubte** der Herr nicht.   (wished, learned)

vor + time = ago

Lesson 5   55

3. Die Mädchen **telefonierten** weiter. (waited, figured)
4. Der Herr setzte sich und **träumte**. (studied, worked)
5. Ihr Vater **kaufte** das Buch. (needed, sent) *brauchte schickte*
6. Die Menschen **wollten** über die Straße. (hurried)
7. Der Professor wartete eine Minute, und dann **wiederholte**
   er: (asked, said)

B. Follow the directions for exercise A.

1. Mein Freund **antwortete** der Lehrerin. (thanked, met)
2. Das Fräulein **kaufte** eine Füllfeder. (had, needed)
3. Wir **wohnten** dann in der Stadt. (studied, searched)
4. Vor fünf Wochen **arbeitete** er noch. (waited, traveled)
5. Der Mann **zeigte** ein Buch. (had, bought)
6. Während der Deutschstunde **studierte** er. (worked, *gearbeit* reviewed) *wiederholt*
7. Was **wünschte** er? (believed, answered)

C. Follow the directions for exercise A.   *gefragt, geglaubt*

1. Was haben Sie **gehört**? (asked, believed)
2. Sie hat ein Buch **gehabt**. (used, showed)
3. Wo haben Sie das **gekauft**? (learned, searched)
4. Nach der Stunde haben wir **gearbeitet**. (studied)
5. Wo hat er denn **gewohnt**? (waited, searched)
6. Haben Sie das dort **gehört**? (fetched, bought) *gekauft*
   geholt

D. Review the sentences of exercise C and put them into
the past perfect, using also the verbs suggested in parentheses.
Then review the sentences of B and put only the original sentences in the present perfect and the past perfect.

E. Substitute pronouns for the subjects in heavy type in the
following sentences, making appropriate changes in the verb
where necessary.

1. **Der Herr** wartete eine Stunde. (we, they)
2. **Der Professor** hat das Buch auf den Tisch gelegt. (I, we)

3. Hatte **er** das vor der Klasse gesagt? (they, I)
4. Um sieben Uhr reiste **das Mädchen** nach Kalifornien. (we, they)
5. **Unser Freund** besuchte uns oft in Los Angeles. (they, she)
6. Hatten **Sie** das nicht gehört? (he, she)
7. **Der Doktor** grüßte und sagte: Guten Tag! (they, we)
8. **Er** hat das auch geglaubt.· (I, we, they)

F. Read the following questions and answers and use them as models for further sentences.

1. Was wünschte Klaus zu kaufen? Er wünschte eine Füllfeder zu kaufen.
2. Hörte Klaus den Mann? Nein, er träumte und hörte ihn nicht.
3. Was legte der Mann auf den Tisch? Er legte drei Federn auf den Tisch.
4. Wem begegnete Klaus auf der Straße? Er begegnete Professor Niebuhr.
5. Was hatte der Professor gehört? Er hatte gehört, daß Klaus nicht in der Klasse war.
6. Hatte Klaus zu Hause gearbeitet? Nein, Klaus hatte Fräulein Sanders die Stadt gezeigt.
7. Ist Fräulein Sanders noch in der Stadt? Nein, sie ist nach Los Angeles gereist.
8. Wer träumte, statt über die Straße zu gehen? Klaus Moehlenbrock träumte.

G. Translate in writing:

1. It was half-past four and he was hurrying home(ward).
2. His sister was working in the store.
3. We (went and) got the table for him.
4. Did he buy the pen?
5. This notebook costs two dollars.
6. The professor had just repeated the question.

7. She was waiting for her friend and daydreaming.
8. We met him this noon at the university.
9. Who answered his mother?
10. I haven't found that story in these books.

H. Free conversation.

Describe a scene you saw in a bookstore. A young lady was buying a fountain pen and had a hard time making up her mind. One of her friends came along. She greeted him. They started to talk. After a while she looked at the clerk again and her friend showed her a red pen. She liked the price but not the color. She then looked at a green pen. After she had heard its price she bought a pencil.

BRIEF CONVERSATION

Das war meine Kusine

HEINRICH SEEMANN *and* WALTER KRENN *are leaving the classroom together.*

HEINRICH: Die Physikstunde war heute ja sehr interessant.

WALTER: Ja, wir haben heute viel gelernt. Ich glaube, daß wir bald ein Examen haben. Wir haben noch nie [never before] so viel in einer Stunde gearbeitet. —

HEINRICH: Es ist schade, daß Klaus nicht da war.

WALTER: O? Vielleicht hatte er viel Vergnügen.

HEINRICH: Wie meinen Sie das?

WALTER: O, heute mittag begegnete ich ihm auf dem Weg zum Fluß. Er ging neben einer jungen Dame [lady] mit schwarzen Haaren. Ich grüßte ihn und drehte mich nach ihm um. Aber er hörte nicht, was ich sagte.

HEINRICH: Ja, das war meine Kusine. Klaus wollte ihr die Stadt zeigen.

LESSON 6

Menschen spielen im Park

THE PAST TENSE AND THE PAST PARTICIPLE OF

STRONG VERBS

VERBS WITH *SEIN* AS AUXILIARY

PRONUNCIATION

TEXT

Am Nachmittag war es sehr heiß. Viele Studenten waren an den Fluß gegangen, der im Süden der Stadt durch einen kleinen Park fließt. Es ist dort gewöhnlich kühl und angenehm, und die Stunden fliegen schnell vorbei. Viele Leute
5 waren im Wasser und schwammen. Einige lagen in der Sonne, um braun zu werden, und andere lagen im Schatten [shade], um weiß zu bleiben. Vier junge Leute spielten mit einem großen Ball. Sie warfen den Ball über das Wasser, hin und her, hin und her. Einmal stolperte [stumbled] der junge Mann,

der den Ball gefangen hatte, und er fiel ins Wasser, gerade   10
zwischen ein paar Mädchen. Die Mädchen erschraken und
schrieen, aber es schien ihnen nicht unangenehm zu sein.

Unter einem Baume saßen Inge Pfeiffer und Fritz Moeller
und lernten Deutsch zusammen. Sie hatten seit sechs Wochen
fleißig gearbeitet, und jetzt lasen, schrieben und sprachen sie   15
nur noch Deutsch. „Wir werden nächstes Jahr in Heidelberg
studieren," sagten sie.

Ein paar Kinder sprangen am Fluß entlang und warfen Steine
ins Wasser. Aber Herr Hansen, der Badewart [lifeguard],
saß auf einer Bank und sah sie nicht. Er las die Zeitung.   20
„Ich möchte wissen," sagte Fritz Moeller, „was er in der
Zeitung findet. Es gibt doch selten etwas Neues." „O doch,"
sagte Inge, „es geschieht immer etwas. Gestern habe ich
gelesen: ‚Meteor fällt in Arizona.' ‚Polizei* fängt Bankräuber
[... robber].' Heute wird in der Zeitung stehen: ‚Auto fährt   25
gegen einen Baum. Fahrer [driver] stirbt auf dem Wege zum
Krankenhaus [hospital].' Und dann sagen Sie, daß es selten
etwas Neues gibt." „Ja, und Frau Schmidt bekommt Zwil-
linge [twins]!" rief Fritz. „Das meine ich ja gar nicht! Glauben Sie, wir werden in dieser Zeitung lesen, daß man die   30
Ursache des Krebses [cause of cancer] gefunden hat? Oder
daß ein Mensch eine wunderbare Symphonie komponiert
hat?" „Wir müssen die Dinge nehmen, wie sie kommen,"
antwortete Fräulein Pfeiffer. „Doch es wird spät. Es hat
gerade fünf Uhr geschlagen. Um sechs Uhr werden wir   35
essen. Dann muß ich zu Hause sein."

Als sie zum Wagen gingen, lachte Fritz Moeller: „Da sehen
Sie, wie Herrn Hansen die Zeitung gefällt." Herr Hansen saß
noch in der Sonne und schlief. Die Zeitung war ihm aus der
Hand gefallen.   40

---

* In the future try to guess the meanings of new words. Up to now
we have given in brackets those new words which are not in the lesson
vocabulary. Only the harder ones will be given in brackets from now
on; all, however, will be listed in the German-English vocabulary in the
back of the book.

IDIOMS AND VOCABULARY

[am Fluß] entlang   along [the river]
am Nachmittag   in the afternoon
es gibt; es gab   there is (are); there was (were)
Es steht in der Zeitung   It says in the paper
Es steht im Buch   It says in the book
gar nicht   not at all

als   when, than, as
ander   other
das Auto, -s   car
der Ball, ⁻e   ball
die Bank, ⁻e   bench
der Baum, ⁻e   tree
bekommen, a, o   get, receive
bleiben, ie, (ist) ie   stay, remain
braun   brown
der, die, das [*relative pron.*] which, who, that
das Ding, -e   thing
einige   some, a few
einmal, zweimal (etc.) once, twice (etc.)
erschrecken, a, (ist) o, i become frightened
essen, aß, gegessen, ißt   eat
fallen, ie, (ist) a, ä   fall, drop
fangen, i, a, ä   catch
fleißig   industrious, diligent
fliegen, o, (ist) o   fly
fließen, o, (ist) o   flow
geben, a, e, i   give
gefallen, ie, a, ä [*dat.*]   please

geschehen, a, (ist) e, ie happen
gestern   yesterday
gewöhnlich   usual(ly)
groß   large, big, tall
die Hand, ⁻e   hand
hin und her   back and forth
das Jahr, -e   year
das Kind, -er   child
klein   little
kühl   cool
lachen   laugh
lesen, a, e, ie   read
liegen, a, e   lie (rest)
man   one, 'they'
der Nachmittag, -e   afternoon
nächst [*adj. only*]   next
ein paar   a couple, a few
der Park, -s   park
rufen, ie, u   shout, call
scheinen, ie, ie   seem, appear, shine
schlafen, ie, a, ä   sleep
schlagen, u, a, ä   beat, hit, strike

schreien, ie, ie scream, yell
schwimmen, a, (ist) o swim,
  float
sein, war, ist gewesen, ist
  be
selten seldom, rare
sitzen, saß, gesessen sit
spielen play
springen, a, (ist) u jump
stehen, stand, gestanden
  stand
der Stein, -e stone
sterben, a, (ist) o, i die
der Student, -en, -en student

der Süden south
treffen, a, o, i meet, hit
um . . . zu in order to
un- [*negative prefix*] un-, in-,
  im-, dis-
verstehen, verstand, ver-
  standen understand
der Wagen, – car
das Wasser, – *or* (–) water
werfen, a, o, i throw
wissen, wußte, gewußt,
  weiß know (a fact)
die Zeitung, -en newspaper
zusammen together
zwischen among, between

GRAMMAR

6.1 The Past Tense and the Past Participle of Strong Verbs Strong verbs undergo a vowel change in the past tense (*e.g.*, **geben, gab** 'give, gave'), and add **-en** rather than -t in the past participle (*e.g.*, **gegeben** 'given').

6.1,1 One can make all the forms of any verb if he knows its infinitive, its past singular, its past participle, and its third person singular present. These are called the *principal parts.* The principal parts of all strong verbs used in Lessons 1 through 5 will be given in this lesson and must be memorized.

Strong verbs will be listed in lesson vocabularies from here on according to the pattern **sehen, a, e, ie;** the principal parts of **sehen** are accordingly **sehen, sah, gesehen, sieht.**

6.1,2 The past tense forms of strong verbs are:

for **ich, er, sie, es :** the second principal part, *e.g.*, **ich sah**
  'I saw.'

for **wir, sie, Sie :** this form plus **-en,** *e.g.,* **wir sahen** 'we saw.'

6.1,3 The past participle of strong verbs is made by adding **-en** to the stem and, except for the verbs covered by the rule in Lesson 5.1,3, by prefixing **ge-** ; *e.g.,* **ge-seh-en.**

6.1,4 Because the irregularity of strong verbs consists in the internal change of vowels, the principal parts of each verb must be learned separately. There are three groups of strong verbs:

Group 1. Those that have the same vowel in the past and past participle, *e.g.,* **schreiben, schrieb, geschrieben, schreibt.**

Group 2. Those that have different vowels in the first three principal parts, *e.g.,* **helfen, half, geholfen, hilft.**

Group 3. Those that have the same vowel in the present and past participle, *e.g.,* **geben, gab, gegeben, gibt.**

For the most part, those verbs which are irregular in English will be strong in German. Some vowel changes are also the same in the two languages, *e.g.,* **springen, sprang, gesprungen** 'spring, sprang, sprung'; **sehen, sah, gesehen** 'see, saw, seen.' Use such verbs as patterns when you are learning the principal parts of German verbs.

6.1,5 Most strong verbs with **-e-** in the stem change it to **-i-** or **-ie-** in the third singular present; most strong verbs with **-a-** change it to **-ä-**. All such verbs will be indicated by the addition of a fourth principal part; when there is no such change in the present, only three principal parts will be listed.

6.1,6

Group 1

bleiben	blieb	ist geblieben	*stay*
leihen	lieh	geliehen	*lend*

Lesson 6

	scheinen	schien	geschienen	*seem, shine*
	schreiben	schrieb	geschrieben	*write*
	schreien	schrie	geschrieen	*scream*
B.	fliegen	flog	ist geflogen	*fly*
	fließen	floß	ist geflossen	*flow*
IRREGULAR	stehen	stand	gestanden	*stand*
	verstehen	verstand	verstanden	*understand*
				learn

Group 2

A.	finden	fand	gefunden		*find*
	schwimmen	schwamm	ist geschwommen		*swim*
	springen	sprang	ist gesprungen		*jump*
B.	erschrecken	erschrak	ist erschrocken	erschrickt	*become frighten*
	helfen	half	geholfen	hilft	*help*
	nehmen	nahm	genommen	nimmt	*take*
	sprechen	sprach	gesprochen	spricht	*speak*
	sterben	starb	ist gestorben	stirbt	*die*
	werfen	warf	geworfen	wirft	*throw*
IRREGULAR	gehen	ging	ist gegangen		*go*
	liegen	lag	gelegen		*lie*
	sitzen	saß	gesessen		*sit*
	werden	wurde	ist geworden	wird	*become*

Group 3

A.	essen	aß	gegessen	ißt	*eat*
	geben	gab	gegeben	gibt	*give*
	geschehen	geschah	ist geschehen	geschieht	*happen*
	lesen	las	gelesen	liest	*read*
	sehen	sah	gesehen	sieht	*see*
IRREGULAR	kommen	kam	ist gekommen		*come*
	bekommen	bekam	bekommen		*receive*

B.

| fahren | fuhr | ist gefahren | fährt | *go, drive* |
| schlagen | schlug | geschlagen | schlägt | *strike* |

C.

fallen	fiel	ist gefallen	fällt	*cut down*
gefallen	gefiel	gefallen	gefällt	*please*
fangen	fing	gefangen	fängt	*catch*
schlafen	schlief	geschlafen	schläft	*sleep*

D.

| heißen | hieß | geheißen | | *to be called* |

6.1,7 Verbs with a prefix undergo the same vowel changes as the simple verbs; *e.g.*, **verstehen** is like **stehen**, **gefallen** like **fallen**.

6.1,8 The principal parts of most weak verbs can readily be made from the stem or the infinitive in accordance with the rules given in Lesson 5.1 and 5.2 *e.g.*, **spielen, spielte, gespielt.** A few verbs, however, have the endings of weak verbs, but also undergo vowel or consonant changes in the stem. You have had:

denken	dachte	gedacht	
kennen	kannte	gekannt	
haben	hatte	gehabt	hat
wissen	wußte	gewußt	ich, er weiß

Review also the principal parts of **sein, war, ist gewesen, ist.**

6.2 Verbs with *SEIN* as Auxiliary Some German verbs use forms of **sein** rather than **haben** as auxiliary. You are familiar with this practice in archaic English, *e.g.*, Matthew ii.11: "And when they *were* come into the house..." [not "when they *had*"]. These verbs are intransitive; they indicate either change of position, *e.g.*, **ist gefahren, ist gereist, ist begegnet,** or change of condition, *e.g.*, **ist erschrocken.** Two others are **ist geblieben, ist gewesen.**

We indicate such verbs by placing **ist** before them, as in the list above and in vocabularies.

Compare the present perfect and the past perfect of **fahren** and **helfen**:

ich bin gefahren	ich habe geholfen
er (sie, es) ist gefahren	er (sie, es) hat geholfen
wir (sie, Sie) sind gefahren	wir (sie, Sie) haben geholfen
ich (er, sie, es) war gefahren	ich (er, sie, es) hatte geholfen
wir (sie, Sie) waren gefahren	wir (sie, Sie) hatten geholfen

6.3 Pronunciation   The sounds [f s v z] are pronounced as in English, but are in part spelled differently:

[f] may be spelled with **f** or **v**:

fangen   oft   vier   von

[v] is generally spelled with **w**, but in a few foreign words it is spelled with **v**:

was   wie   wer   Universität

[s] does not occur at the beginning of words. Within a word or at the end, it may be spelled with **ss**, **s**, or **ß**; **ss** is generally used after short vowels, **ß** after long vowels and diphthongs:

aus	ist	uns	liest
essen	müssen	wissen	Wasser
heißen	aß	wußte	grüßen

[z] is spelled with single **s**, and occurs at the beginnings of words before vowels and within words between vowels:

sein	so	sehr
lesen	reisen	dieser

66 *Lesson 6*

When the **s** of words like **lesen** and **reisen** comes to stand finally or between consonants, it is pronounced [s]. Contrast:

lesen: las   reisen: reiste   dieser: dies

EXERCISES

A. Make additional sentences on the basis of those given here, substituting the suggested words for those in heavy type.

1. Am Nachmittag **sprachen** wir nur Deutsch. (read, wrote)
2. Er **blieb** bis neun Uhr. (stood, sat)
3. Der Herr **fand** das Kind nicht. (saw, took)
4. Die Kinder gingen, aber sie **fingen** nichts. (received, understood)
5. Er stand am Fluß und **schrie.** (read, laughed)
6. Das junge Mädchen **fiel** ins Wasser. (jumped, went)
7. Trotz der Hitze **schlief** er. (drove, helped)
8. Es **floß** weiter. (flew, went)
9. Wie **hieß** er? (died, slept)
10. Es **geschah** ihm nichts. (pleased)
11. Die Mädchen **lagen** auf der Bank. (ate, sat)
12. Der junge Student **wurde** braun. (was, stayed)

B. Review the sentences of exercise A, putting them (*a*) into the present perfect, (*b*) into the past perfect.

C. Follow the directions for exercise A.

1. Der Student **trifft** seinen Freund an der Bahn. (sees, finds)
2. Der Stein **liegt** im Wasser. (is, stays)
3. Das **bleibt** immer so. (flows, happens, comes, seems, becomes)
4. Wer **spricht** denn da so lange? (eats, reads, writes)
5. Es gibt nichts, was Fritz nicht **versteht.** (does, sees, knows)

6. Natürlich weiß kein Mensch, daß das Mädchen gut **fliegt.** (swims, jumps)
7. Der König **hilft.** (dies, falls)
8. Das Kind **wirft** den Ball. (catches, strikes [schlagen], hits [treffen], takes)
9. Der Professor **trifft** den Studenten zweimal. (calls, sees)
10. Das Bild **gibt** er gern. (gets, takes)
11. Ein so gutes Kind **schreit** selten. (speaks, strikes)

D. Review the sentences of exercise C, putting them (*a*) into the present perfect, (*b*) into the past perfect.

E. Fill in the blanks with appropriate verb forms, (*a*) in the present tense, (*b*) in the past tense.

1. Auf der Bank im Park _____ ein Mann.
2. Er _____ die Zeitung.
3. Der junge Mann _____ einen Ball über das Wasser.
4. Sein Freund auf der anderen Seite _____ den Ball nicht.
5. Der Ball _____ ins Wasser.
6. Drei Mädchen _____ in der Sonne, um braun zu werden.
7. Ein Fluß _____ im Süden der Stadt durch einen Park.
8. Ich _____ jede Woche einen Brief nach Hause.
9. _____ Sie jeden Abend durch den Park?
10. Der junge Mann _____ jeden Morgen bis acht Uhr.
11. In dieser Stadt _____ nie etwas Neues.
12. Um acht Uhr _____ es kühl.

F. Give the German for the English sentences below. The word order will be exactly the same as that of the pattern sentences.

1. Viele Leute waren im Wasser.
   A. Many children were playing in (**auf**) the street.
   B. Many students were sitting under the trees.
   C. Some money was lying by the door.

2. Aber Herr Hansen sah sie nicht.
   A. But the student didn't understand him.
   B. But the thing didn't hit it.
   C. But my friend didn't say that.

3. Es hat gerade fünf Uhr geschlagen.
   A. She just threw the ball.
   B. He has usually sent the bill.
   C. They have always given the money.

4. Viele Studenten waren an den Fluß gegangen.
   A. The children had been swimming in the river.
   B. The girls had been reading in the house.
   C. The people had remained in the country.

5. Sie hatten seit sechs Wochen fleißig gearbeitet.
   A. He had studied diligently for two years.
   B. She had worked alone for three days.
   C. I had been asking diligently for five weeks.

G. Questions and answers.

1. Wo waren Fritz und Inge an dem heißen Nachmittag? Sie waren im Park.
2. Was taten vier junge Leute? Sie warfen einen Ball über das Wasser.
3. Warum schrieen die Mädchen? Der Ball war ins Wasser gefallen.
4. Warum lagen die Leute in der Sonne? Sie lagen in der Sonne, um braun zu werden.
5. Warum lagen einige nicht in der Sonne? Um weiß zu bleiben.
6. Was tat Herr Hansen? Erst las er die Zeitung, später schlief er.
7. Was stand in der Zeitung? Nicht viel stand in der Zeitung.
8. Woher wissen wir, daß Herr Hansen nichts in der Zeitung fand? Er schlief.

H. Translate in writing:

1. The students were sitting under a tree and were reading the newspaper.
2. Some children were swimming in the river.
3. That happened at six o'clock this morning.
4. Inge and her sister were still sleeping.
5. The girl from the South was called Miss Herrero; now her name is Mrs. Schmidt.
6. His friend had worked there for two weeks.
7. The teacher was sitting near the window and didn't see him.
8. He read the telegram twice.
9. The ball fell between his car and the tree.
10. The children were going along the river and looking for their ball.

I. Free conversation.

Describe a day at a picnic — how you drove to a park by a river, how you met your friends there. You played ball together and went swimming. Later you ate. After coming home you read the newspaper, studied until seven, and then slept well.

BRIEF CONVERSATION

Klaus ist wohl sehr nervös!

WALTER KRENN *sees* HEINRICH SEEMANN *sitting in the Student Union lobby.*

WALTER: Was tun Sie hier? Warten Sie auf Klaus Moehlenbrock?

HEINRICH: Ja, ich wollte Tennis mit ihm spielen.

WALTER: Sie brauchen nicht zu warten. Er kommt doch nicht mehr.

HEINRICH: Wieso [how so]? Haben Sie ihn getroffen?

WALTER: Ja, er saß ganz allein in der Bibliothek [library].

HEINRICH: Was, bei der Arbeit? Was las er denn?

WALTER: Ich kann nicht sagen, daß er studierte. Vor ihm lagen ein paar Bücher; aber er arbeitete nicht mit den Büchern. Ich glaube, er träumte.

HEINRICH: Haben Sie mit ihm gesprochen?

WALTER: Ja, ich setzte mich [sat down] zu ihm und fragte, was er geschrieben hatte. Einen Brief, sagte er. Aber dann sprang er auf, warf den Brief in den Papierkorb [wastebasket], nahm seine Bücher und fuhr nach Hause.

HEINRICH: Er ist wohl sehr nervös gewesen.

LESSON 7

Der dreizehnte Mai

REVIEW OF NOUN PLURALS

NUMERALS

THE FUTURE TENSE

PRONUNCIATION

TEXT

Herr Schneider, der Geschäftsführer [manager] des neuen
Lebensmittelgeschäfts [grocery store], war vor zwei Wochen
in die Stadt gekommen. Aber während dieser Zeit hatte er
noch kein Haus für seine Familie gefunden. Er brauchte ein
großes Haus mit fünf Schlafzimmern, denn er hatte eine große 5
Familie — zwei Söhne und vier Töchter. Und manchmal
kamen auch seine Verwandten, ihn zu besuchen, seine Brüder,
Schwestern, Onkel, Vettern, Kusinen und Tanten, und die
kamen gewöhnlich mit ihren Familien.
Herr Schneider suchte also eine Wohnung. In den Zeitungen 10

der Stadt las er, daß viele Wohnungen zu haben waren, aber die
waren entweder zu klein oder zu teuer oder beides. Er ging
zu einem Agenten. Er hatte ihn mit geschlossenen Augen unter
den Namen vieler Agenten im Telefonbuch gefunden. Der
15 Mann zeigte ihm zwölf Häuser, vier Tage lang, aber Herr
Schneider fand nicht gerade, was er wünschte. Am nächsten
Tag fuhren sie durch viele Straßen bis an das Ende der Stadt.

Die Bäume blühten [were blooming] in den Gärten, die Vögel
sangen in den Zweigen, die Blumen lachten in der Sonne — und
20 Herr Schneider hatte frohe Gefühle im Herzen. In einem
Garten lag ein Haus, alt, dunkel und verlassen. Es hatte viele
Fenster, Türen, Türmchen [little towers] und Giebel [gables]
und schien hundert Jahre alt zu sein.

„Das nehme ich,“ sagte Herr Schneider. „Hier habe ich
25 Platz für alle meine Bücher und Bilder. In dieses Zimmer
können wir drei Betten stellen. Hier neben die Küche wird
meine Frau alle ihre Teller, Gläser, Töpfe [pots] und Pfannen
stellen. Und hier haben wir Platz für unsere Tische und
Stühle — und Musikinstrumente.“ „Musikinstrumente?“
30 fragte der Agent. „Ja, unsere Familie ist sehr musikalisch.
Meine Söhne spielen Saxophon und Trompete, und meine
Töchter spielen Klavier, Cello, Flöte und Ziehharmonika
[accordion]. Meine Frau singt immer in der Küche, und
manchmal singe ich auch.“

35   „Dann sollten Sie hier keine Schwierigkeiten haben.“ „Wie
meinen Sie das?“ „Ja, sehen Sie, die früheren Besitzer haben
hier nie lange gewohnt. Einer ist nach vierzehn Tagen gestorben. Der zweite hat in drei Monaten Bankerott gemacht [went
broke]. Der dritte ist nach vier Wochen die Treppe hinunter
40 gefallen, und hat sich beide Beine gebrochen. Wissen Sie, es
soll hier Geister geben. Man hört sie nachts durchs Haus
gehen: Der erste Besitzer und seine beiden Frauen —.“
„Das ist das beste Haus für uns — wenn meine Tanten zu
Besuch kommen. Hier ist Ihr Scheck. Und in drei Tagen
45 werden wir einziehen [move in]. Welches Datum haben wir
heute?“ „Freitag, den dreizehnten Mai.“

*future
aux + ing
(werden)*

IDIOMS AND VOCABULARY

vier **Tage lang**   for four days
vierzehn **Tage**   two weeks
zu **Besuch**   for a visit

das Auge, -s, -n   eye
beide   both
das Bein, -e   leg
der Besitzer, –   owner
best (gut, besser)   best (good, better)
besuchen   visit
das Bett, -s, -en   bed
die Blume, -n   flower
brechen, a, o, i   break
denn [*conj.*]   for
dreizehn   thirteen
dreizehnt-   thirteenth
der dritte   third
das Ende, -s, -n   end
entweder ... oder   either ... or
der erste   first
die Familie, -n   family
der Freitag, -e   Friday
froh   glad, happy
früher   earlier
der Garten, ¨   garden
das Gefühl, ‒e   feeling
der Geist, -er   ghost, spirit
das Glas, ¨er   glass
das Herz, -ens, -en   heart
hinunter   down(ward)
die Küche, -n   kitchen

lange   a long time
manchmal   occasionally
der Monat, -e   month
die Nacht, ¨e   night
nachts   at night
neben   beside, next to
der Onkel, –   uncle
der Platz, ¨e   place, space, room
schließen, o, o   shut, close
die Schwierigkeit, -en   difficulty
singen, a, u   sing
der Sohn, ¨e   son
sollen   ought to, be said to
stellen   set, put, place
der Stuhl, ¨e   chair
die Tante, -n   aunt
der Teller, –   plate
die Tochter, ¨   daughter
die Treppe, -n   stairs
verlassen, ie, a, ä   leave
der Verwandte, -n, -n   relative
der Vetter, -n [*male*] cousin
vierzehn   fourteen
der Vogel, ¨   bird
voll   full
wenn   if, when(ever)

wieviel how much	das **Zimmer,** – room
wie viele how many	das **Schlafzimmer,**– bed-
die **Wohnung, -en** apartment	room
ziehen, zog, gezogen pull,	der **Zweig, -e** twig, branch
draw	der **zweite** second

NOTE. Many German proper names have a meaning, just as do English proper names. Compare the following:

(der) König	King
(der) Pfeiffer	Piper
(der) Schneider	Taylor
(der) Seemann	Saylor/sailor

Moehlenbrock is an archaic word meaning "millrace," whereas Niebuhr means "neighbor." You might try to find out the meaning of other German names in your class or neighborhood. The spelling of many German names has been changed in order to preserve their original sound: Eisenhower, Hoover, Stine, etc.

GRAMMAR

7.1 Review of Noun Plurals   In Lesson 2.3 we noted four ways of making noun plurals. Here we will deal with the types of nouns that belong to each group. (For a full inflection of selected nouns belonging to each group, see Appendix 2.)

7.1,1 Nouns of Group 1 add no ending in the plural. They generally have two syllables and end in **-el, -en,** or **-er.** Most are masculine; some are neuter, including all words ending in **-chen** and **-lein**; and there are two feminines: die **Mutter,** die **Tochter.** Other examples of nouns in Group 1 are

der Vogel, der Garten, der Bruder, and **das Fenster.**

7.1,2 Nouns of Group 2 add **-e** in the plural. They are generally monosyllables in the singular and may be masculine, feminine, or neuter; most monosyllabic masculines belong to this group. Examples are **der Baum, die Hand, das Jahr.**

7.1,3 Nouns of Group 3 add **-er** in the plural. They are almost all neuter and most are monosyllables in the singular. Examples are **das Buch, der Mann.**

7.1,4 Nouns of Group 4 add **-en** or **-n** in the plural. They are almost all feminine, but a few are masculine: the masculines add **-en** in all forms but the nominative singular. Most feminine nouns belong to this group. Examples are **die Arbeit, die Bank, die Lehrerin, der Mensch, der Student.**

7.1,5 Nouns which differ in some form from group 4 are:

der Herr, den, dem, des Herrn; die, den, der Herren
der Name, den, dem Namen, des Namens; die, den, der Namen
der, den, dem Vetter, des Vetters; die, den, der Vettern
das Herz, dem Herzen, des Herzens; die, den, der Herzen
das Auge, dem Auge, des Auges; die, den, der Augen

Inflected like **das Auge** are **das Bett** and **das Ende.**

The plurals of some nouns taken into German from other languages in recent times are formed with **-s**; examples are **der Park, die Parks; das Kino, die Kinos.** All plural case forms of such nouns end in **s**.

7.2 Numerals

7.2,1 The cardinal numerals are:

1 **eins**	11 **elf**	20 **zwanzig**
2 **zwei**	12 **zwölf**	30 **dreißig**
3 **drei**	13 **dreizehn**	40 **vierzig**
4 **vier**	14 **vierzehn**	50 **fünfzig**
5 **fünf**	15 **fünfzehn**	60 **sechzig**
6 **sechs**	16 **sechzehn**	70 **siebzig**
7 **sieben**	17 **siebzehn**	80 **achtzig**
8 **acht**	18 **achtzehn**	90 **neunzig**
9 **neun**	19 **neunzehn**	100 **hundert**
10 **zehn**		

Numerals above 20 are made on the pattern which is used in the nursery rhyme 'four-and-twenty blackbirds'; they are written as one word, *e.g.*, **vierundzwanzig.**

7.2,2 The ordinal numerals from "first" to "tenth" are:

first	**der erste**	sixth	**der sechste**
second	**der zweite**	seventh	**der sieb(en)te**
third	**der dritte**	eight	**der achte**
fourth	**der vierte**	ninth	**der neunte**
fifth	**der fünfte**	tenth	**der zehnte**

7.2,3 The pattern for giving the hour is: **Es ist (ein) Uhr.** 'It is (one) o'clock.'

For giving minutes after the hour, **nach** is used; for minutes before the hour, **vor** is used.

Es ist zwanzig Minuten nach zwei. 'It is twenty minutes after two.'

Es ist fünf Minuten vor neun. 'It is five minutes to nine.'

To indicate quarter hours, **Viertel** 'quarter' is used, *e.g.*, **Viertel nach zwölf** 'quarter after twelve'; **Drei Viertel drei** (or **dreiviertel drei**) 'a quarter to three.'

To indicate the half-hour, one uses **halb** 'half' preceding the numeral for the next hour, *e.g.*, **Es ist halb vier.** 'It is three-thirty.'

7.2,4 The pattern for giving the day of the month is:

Heute ist der dritte April. 'Today is the third of April.'

For the names of months and days of the week, see Appendix 5.

7.3 The Future Tense. The future tense is made with forms of **werden** plus the infinitive, *e.g.*, **Wir werden nächstes Jahr in Heidelberg studieren.** 'We shall study in Heidelberg next year.'

The future of **studieren** is:

> ich werde studieren
> er (sie, es) wird studieren
> wir (sie, Sie) werden studieren

The present tense is used to indicate future time in German when future meaning is clear from the context, as on page 72, line 24, **Das nehme ich.** 'I'll take that.'

7.4 Pronunciation In unstressed syllables **e** indicates a vowel [ə] that is like the second vowel of *sofa, animal,* and *cinema.* In German, unlike English, this sound is always spelled with **e.** Contrast the sounds of the stressed **e** and the unstressed **e** in **Treppe.**

> **frage Gefühl Kusine Vergnügen**

7.4,1 The contrast between short and long vowels was discussed in Lesson 2.4. Various devices are used to indicate that vowels are long:

The vowel symbol may be followed by **h**:

> **ihn früh nehmen Söhne Bahn wohnen Uhr**

The vowel symbol may be repeated:

> **Schnee Haar Boot**

The spelling **ie** indicates a long [i:]; contrast **bin**: **Biene** 'bee':

> **sie viel wieder ziehen**

Short vowels may be indicated by doubling the following consonant; contrast **können : König; denn : den; Vetter : Väter.**

Most syllables ending in two consonants have short vowels:

Kind   Berg   Hand   Sommer   Mutter

EXERCISES

A. Make additional sentences on the basis of those given below, substituting the suggested words for those in heavy type.

1. Vor zwei Wochen bin ich in diese **Läden** gegangen. (rooms, gardens)
2. Die **Besitzer** schienen sehr alt zu sein. (uncles, windows)
3. Haben Sie das den **Mädchen** gesagt? (mothers, fathers)
4. Die Namen der **Vögel** habe ich nicht verstanden. (brothers, daughters, young ladies)
5. Die **Zimmer** waren sehr schön. (birds, cars)
6. Dieses Jahr brauchen wir die **Wagen.** (plates, small doors)

B. Follow the directions for exercise A.

1. In dieses Zimmer will er die **Instrumente** stellen. (things, chairs)
2. Ich möchte zwei **Bleistifte** kaufen. (balls, tables)
3. Da waren die **Bäume** sehr klein. (mountains, rivers)
4. Sie hat nicht mit den **Königen** gesprochen. (sons, people)
5. Die **Jahre** gehen schnell vorbei. (days, months)
6. Bei Tisch konnte ich seine **Söhne** nicht sehen. (hands, legs)
7. Heute werden die **Wege** heiß sein. (trains, cities)
8. Der Herr kennt Ihre **Gefühle.** (wishes)
9. Ihre Mutter hat die **Telegramme** geschickt. (papers, tables)
10. Am Abend lag Schnee auf den **Zweigen.** (trees, cities)

C. Follow the directions for exercise A.

1. Er hat uns die vier **Bilder** gegeben. (books) *Bücher*
2. Wie heißen die **Kinder** dort? (men) *Männer*
3. Sie sagt, sie hat gestern **Geister** gesehen. (lights) *Lichter*
4. Er hat uns die **Gelder** noch nicht gegeben. (glasses) *Gläser*
5. Jetzt sind die **Bücher** teuer. (houses) *Häuser*

D. Follow the directions for exercise A.

1. Heute abend besuche ich die **Schwestern.** (cousins, *Kusinen* woman teachers) *Lehrerinnen*
2. Diese **Frauen** kenne ich schon lange. (professors, *Professoren* apartments, views) *Wohnungen*
3. Solche **Arbeiten** finde ich zu lang. (questions, hours) *Fragen Stunde*
4. Er hat an drei **Gesellschaften** geschrieben. (families, *Familien* banks) *Banken*
5. Morgen schickt er uns natürlich die **Uhren.** (newspapers, flowers) *Zeitungen*, *Blumen*
6. Sechs **Wochen** lang hat es schon hier gestanden. (minutes, hours) *Minuten*, *Stunden*
7. Die Wagen meiner **Vettern** kenne ich schon. (aunts, students) *Tanten*, *Studenten*
8. Wer hat die **Treppen** gesucht? (pens) *Federn*
9. Mein Freund kennt die **Banken** der Stadt. (railroads, *Bahnen* streets) *Strassen*
10. Die **Blumen** waren sehr teuer. (apartments, doors) *Wohnungen Türen*
11. Die **Lehrerinnen** singen oft. (gentlemen, students) *Herren Studenten*
12. Ich habe die **Betten** nicht gesehen. (names, human beings) *Namen menschen*
13. Viele **Uhren** brauche ich wirklich nicht. (eyes, difficulties) *Augen*, *Schwierigkeiten*

E. Follow the directions for exercise A.

1. Zweimal sind seine **Vettern** krank gewesen. (sons, *Söhne* daughters) *Töchter*

2. Er hat uns für die **Zeitungen** gedankt.   (books, *Bücher*
pencils) *Bleistifte*

3. Die **Stühle** hat meine Mutter dort gefunden.   (beds,
pictures) *Betten* , *Bilder*

4. Er will die **Teller** leider nicht nehmen.   (tables, lights) *Tische Lichter*

5. Das hat den **Männern** gewiß geholfen.   (fathers, professors) *Professoren* *Väter*

6. Auf der Reise waren die **Frauen** wirklich sehr krank.
(gentlemen, uncles) *Herren* , *Onkel*

7. Ihre **Bücher** sind sehr schön.   (hands, eyes) *Hände Augen*

8. Haben Sie in vielen **Wohnungen** gewohnt?   (cities,
houses) *Städten* , *Häuser*

9. Während der zwei **Stunden** hat er viele Telegramme
geschickt.   (days, weeks) *Tagen* , *Wochen*

10. Eines Tages werde ich die **Instrumente** holen.   (cars,
children) *Kinder* *Autos*

F. Fill in the blanks with appropriate noun forms:

1. Mein Freund Waldemar ist erst vor zwei *Wochen* in diese
Stadt gekommen.

2. Wir wohnen schon seit ____ hier. *Jahren*

3. In unserer Familie haben wir *Kinder* (children), *Söhne* ____ (sons)
und *Töchter* ____ (daughters).

4. In der Küche sind *Teller* , *Tische* und *Stühle* .

5. In meinem Zimmer habe ich *Tisch* und *Stuhl* .

6. Der erste Besitzer hatte zwei *Söhne*

7. Ich nehme immer *Bücher* mit in die Klasse.

8. In den Zweigen singen die ____.

9. Ich wohne nur vier ____ (streets [blocks]) von hier.

10. In dieser Stadt gibt es zwei ____ (newspapers).

G. Give German equivalents for the English sentences below
The word order will be exactly the same as in the pattern sentences.

1. In drei Tagen werden wir einziehen.
   A. He will go in four weeks.
   B. After two months it will happen.
   C. They will come in six days.
2. Hier wird meine Frau ihre Gläser finden.
   A. Here my mother will buy the flowers.
   B. There his friend will find his books.
   C. Here her uncle will see his daughters.
3. Freitag, den dreizehnten Mai.
   A. Friday, the twelfth of April.
   B. Friday, the seventh of August.
   C. Friday, the fourth of September.
4. Der Mann zeigte ihm zwölf Häuser, vier Tage lang.
   A. The man showed him ten houses for three days.
   B. My father showed her eight apartments for two days.
   C. The teacher showed him twenty notebooks for three hours.
5. Es ist jetzt vierzehn Minuten vor drei.
   A. It is now twenty to four.
   B. It was then two minutes to five.
   C. It is only ten to six.

H. Questions and answers.

1. Wann war Herr Schneider in die Stadt gekommen? Er war vor zwei Wochen in die Stadt gekommen.
2. Warum brauchte er ein großes Haus? Er hatte viele Kinder.
3. Wie viele Kinder hat Herr Schneider? Er hat sechs Kinder, zwei Söhne und vier Töchter.
4. Wer besuchte die Familie Schneider manchmal? Die Verwandten besuchten die Familie Schneider, die Brüder und Schwestern, Onkel und Tanten, Vettern und Kusinen.
5. Wo fand Schneider endlich ein Haus? Er fand ein Haus in einem Garten am Ende der Stadt.

6. Was hat die Familie Schneider alles? Schneiders haben Betten, Tische, Stühle, Gläser, Teller und Musikinstrumente.
7. Wer singt in der Küche? Herr Schneiders Frau singt in der Küche.
8. Wer besuchte das alte Haus noch? Geister besuchten das alte Haus.

I. Translate in writing:

1. His uncle had come to the city two weeks previously.
2. She had not yet found a room near the university.
3. Her relatives often went to visit them.
4. The cars were either too fast or too small.
5. On the next day they left their apartment.
6. In the kitchen there were many plates, glasses, doors, and chairs.
7. His daughters write stories and his wife sings.
8. The owner died after three weeks.
9. Today is the twentieth.
10. We'll eat at six o'clock.

J. Free conversation:

Describe how friends of yours move to the city and set out to find a house. They look at various apartments, but these are too small. Most of the houses are very old. They want one with three bedrooms, for they have a large family. The agent tells them that one large house has noisy neighbors. At another, many children are running through the garden. Finally they find a beautiful house outside of town, but it is very expensive.

BRIEF CONVERSATION

Der erste heisse Tag

HANS FISCHER *passes by as* FRITZ MOELLER *is waiting for his class.*

HANS: Was machen Sie denn jetzt? Ich habe Sie schon ein paar Wochen nicht gesehen.

FRITZ: Ich war gestern nachmittag im Park.

HANS: So? Waren viele Menschen da?

FRITZ: Viele Menschen? Die ganze Stadt war draußen [out there], Studenten, Lehrer, alles — Männer, Frauen und Kinder. Es war der erste heiße Tag in diesem Jahr.

HANS: Also darum [therefore] war's in den Läden so still. Im Co-op gab es mehr [more] Verkäufer als Leute, die etwas kaufen wollten.

FRITZ: Warum sind Sie nicht auch gekommen? Inge und ein paar andere Mädchen waren auch draußen.

HANS: O, ich hatte meine Arbeiten zu machen. Ich habe vier Briefe geschrieben, in mehreren [several] Büchern gelesen und dann noch zwei Stunden geschlafen.

FRITZ: Als wir nach Hause fuhren, waren Autos auf allen Straßen. Die Polizei hatte alle Hände voll. Um sieben Uhr gab's zwei Unfälle [accidents].

HANS: Ja, ich habe es in der Zeitung gelesen. — Werden Sie heute nachmittag wieder in den Park fahren?

LESSON 8

Eine schreckliche Nacht

INFLECTION OF ADJECTIVES

COMPARATIVES AND SUPERLATIVES

COMPOUNDS WITH *DA-*

PRONUNCIATION

TEXT

Herr Schneider wohnte schon vier Wochen in dem großen, alten, verlassenen Haus. Als die Tage länger und heißer wurden, schickte er seine Familie in die Ferien. Sein ältester Sohn und seine älteste Tochter waren nach Kalifornien gefahren.
5 Seine Frau war mit drei jüngeren Kindern nach Colorado gereist. Die jüngste Tochter war bei Verwandten auf dem Lande zu Besuch. Herr Schneider war so froh wie ein Kind, daß er einmal allein war.

Als er bei einbrechender [approaching] Dunkelheit nach Hause

fuhr, wunderte er sich über den starken Verkehr auf der Straße. 10
Er wollte schneller fahren, aber ein Polizist warnte ihn: „Bitte,
fahren Sie etwas langsamer — und auf der rechten Seite der
Straße. Die linke muß für die Feuerwehr [fire department]
frei bleiben. Es brennt hier nämlich."

Herr Schneider hatte eine dunkle Ahnung im Herzen. Als 15
er endlich zum äußersten Ende der Stadt kam, sah er, daß es
sein Haus war, das brannte. Schneller als gewöhnlich eilte er in
seinen Garten. Viele Leute standen um das brennende Haus,
neugierig und schweigend.

„Da ist nicht mehr viel zu machen [to be done]," sagte ein 20
Feuerwehrmann. „Die meisten Stücke haben wir gerettet."
Herr Schneider sah alle die alten Tische und Stühle und Betten
unter den Bäumen. Da stand auch der neue Fernseh-Apparat
[television set] (er war nur halb versichert). Und daneben lagen
die wertvollen Musikinstrumente. „Das Klavier war leider zu 25
schwer," sagte ein Feuerwehrmann.

„Aber wo sind denn meine vielen Bücher — alle meine
amerikanischen und deutschen Detektiv-Romane?" „Das tut
mir leid. Sie können ja sehen: auch die unteren Räume stehen
schon in hellen Flammen. Bei dem geringen Wasserdruck 30
[water pressure] ist nichts zu machen." Es war eine schreckliche Nacht für Herrn Schneider.

Nach einigen Tagen bekam er im Geschäft einen Brief.
Der war vom Präsidenten seiner Firma:

den 15. Juni 35

Sehr geehrter Herr Schneider!
Ich habe gehört, daß vorgestern Ihr altes Haus abgebrannt ist.
Das tut mir sehr leid, aber kein Angestellter [salaried employee]
unserer Firma sollte in solch einem alten Kasten wohnen.
Hiermit leihen wir Ihnen zehntausend Dollar. Bauen Sie sich 40
ein etwas moderneres Haus.
Mit besten Wünschen,

Ihr ergebener
GEORGE A. JEFFERSON

IDIOMS AND VOCABULARY

auf Ferien on vacation
in die Ferien on vacation
Ihr ergebener yours (*literally:* your devoted)
Sehr geehrter dear (*literally:* very honored)

die Ahnung, -en foreboding, idea
als [*after comparative*] than
alt, älter, ältest old, older, oldest
amerikanisch American
äußerst extreme
bauen build
brennen, brannte, gebrannt burn
es brennt there's a fire
daneben beside it
die Dunkelheit, -en darkness
endlich finally, at last
die Ferien [*pl. only*] vacation
das Feuer, – fire
die Flamme, -n flame
gering insignificant, small
das Geschäft, -e business
heiß, heißer, heißest hot, hotter, hottest
hell bright, light
jung, jünger, jüngst young, younger, youngest
der Kasten, ¨ chest, box, crate
lang, länger, längst long, longer, longest
langsam slow
link- left
machen make, do
mehr [*cf.* **viel**] (any) more, (any) longer
nämlich namely, you know, you see
neugierig curious, inquisitive
der Raum, ¨e room, space
recht right, correct, quite, all right
retten rescue, save
der Schnupfen cold
schrecklich terrible
schwer heavy
die Seite, -n side, page
das Stück, -e piece
der Verkehr traffic
versichern insure
vorgestern day before yesterday
warnen warn
wertvoll valuable
sich wundern über [*acc.*] be surprised at
der Wunsch, ¨e wish

GRAMMAR

8.1 Inflection of Adjectives Adjectives are inflected for case and gender. They may be preceded by **der**-words (**dieser** 'this,' **jener** 'that,' **jeder** 'each,' **mancher** 'many a,' **solcher** 'such a,' **welcher** 'which'), or by **ein**-words (**kein** 'no,' **mein** 'my,' **unser** 'our,' **sein** 'his, its,' **ihr** 'her, their,' **Ihr** 'your'), or they may stand alone before nouns.

8.1,1 Adjectives following any of the **der**-words take **-en** endings in all but five forms; in these the ending is **-e**.

N	dieser starke Mann		
		diese schöne Frau	dieses junge Kind
A	diesen starken Mann		
		diese schöne Frau	dieses junge Kind
D	diesem starken Mann		
		dieser schönen Frau	diesem jungen Kind
G	dieses starken Manns		
		dieser schönen Frau	dieses jungen Kinds

N |	diese starken Männer		
A \)		diese schönen Frauen	diese jungen Kinder
D	diesen starken Männern		
		diesen schönen Frauen	diesen jungen Kindern
G	dieser starken Männer		
		dieser schönen Frauen	dieser jungen Kinder

8.1,2 For adjectives following any of the **ein**-words, the endings are the same as those of adjectives following **der**-words except in three of the five forms with **-e**: the nominative singular masculine has **-er**; the nominative/accusative singular neuter has **-es**.

ein starker Mann   **ein junges Kind**

8.1,3 If no **der**-word or **ein**-word stands before an adjective, the adjective's endings are the same as those of **dieser** except in the genitive singular masculine and neuter, which have **-en**, *e.g.,* **trotz schrecklichen Verkehrs** 'in spite of terrible traffic,' and **bei einbrechender Dunkelheit** 'in the approaching darkness.'

8.1,4 If an adjective stands after the noun it modifies or if it is used adverbially, it takes no ending:

> **Herr Schneider war so froh wie ein Kind.** 'Mr. Schneider was as happy as a child.'
> **In einem Garten lag ein Haus, alt und dunkel.** 'In a garden a house was situated, old and dark.'
> **Die Stunden fliegen schnell vorbei.** 'The hours fly past quickly.'

As is seen in this last example, adverbs are made from adjectives without adding endings. One common adverb is exceptional; it is **lange**, an old adverb for **lang**.

8.1,5 The present participle is made by adding **-d** to the infinitive, *e.g.,* **schlafend** 'sleeping,' from **schlafen** 'sleep.' The most common use of the present participle is as an adjective, *e.g.,* **das brennende Haus** 'the burning house.'

The past participle, too, is used adjectivally, *e.g.,* **die geretteten Stühle** 'the rescued chairs.'

8.1,6 Adjectives may be used as nouns. When so used, they are capitalized but keep their adjectival inflection, *e.g.,* **der Verwandte** 'the [*male*] relative,' **ein Verwandter** 'a [*male*] relative,' **keine Verwandte** 'no [*female*] relative.' In translating such adjectives *one* must often be supplied, *e.g.,* **Der Neue gefällt mir besser.** 'The new one pleases me more.'

8.2 Comparatives and Superlatives As in English, the comparative form of adjectives is made by adding **-er**, the superlative by adding **-st** or **-est.** The resulting forms are inflected like simple adjectives, *e.g.*, **schnell, schneller, der schnellste** 'fast, faster, fastest': **ein schnellerer Wagen** 'a faster car,' **der schnellste Wagen** 'the fastest car.'

The stem vowel **a, o,** or **u** of some common monosyllabic adjectives is changed to **ä, ö,** or **ü** in the comparative and superlative forms:

alt	**älter**	**der älteste**
lang	**länger**	**der längste**
groß	**größer**	**der größte**
jung	**jünger**	**der jüngste**

If the final consonant of an adjective is **-s** or **-t**, **-est** is used in the superlative form, as in **älteste.** A few common adjectives have further irregularities (see also the superlative of **groß**):

gut	**besser**	**der beste**
viel	**mehr**	**das meiste**
nah	**näher**	**der nächste**

Phrases like "more interesting" or "most interesting" are never used in German. The German comparative and superlative forms are always indicated by suffixes, not by preceding adverbs, *e.g.*, **interessanter, der interessanteste.**

8.3 Compound with da- Compounds of **da-** or **dar-** plus preposition correspond to English phrases of preposition plus *it, e.g.*, **darin** 'in it,' 'in them'; compare the archaic 'therein.' If the preposition begins with a consonant, **da-** is used, *e.g.*, **dadurch** 'through it,' **daneben** 'beside it'; if the preposition begins with a vowel, **dar-** is used, *e.g.*, **darauf** 'on it,' **darüber** 'over it.'

8.4 Pronunciation The consonant **k** is pronounced before **n** in German. Contrast:

        Knie: knee   **Knoten:** knot

The consonants **qu** are pronounced [kv]:

    Quelle source   **Quadrat** square   **bequem** comfortable

The letter **j** pronounced [y] as in *yes*:

ja yes   **Jahr** year   **jener** yon   **jung** young

Words like **Universität** 'university' do not have an initial [y]; compare also the pronunciation of **Urán** 'uranium' with its English equivalent.

EXERCISES

A. Make additional sentences on the basis of those given below, substituting the suggested words for those in heavy type.

1. Er hat zwei Wochen in der **alten** Stadt gewohnt.   (small, terrible)
2. Die **meisten** Bücher haben mir nicht gefallen.   (largest, heaviest)
3. Das **kleinere** Kind fand sein Geld nicht.   (younger, more industrious)
4. Die **alte** Frau hat uns ein wunderbares Bild gezeigt.   (nice, smaller)
5. Am nächsten Tag fanden sie das **weiße** Haus.   (red, cheap)
6. Liest sie die **neueste** Zeitung?   (American, old)
7. Die **gelben** Blumen gefallen mir nicht.   (red, bigger)

B. Follow the directions for exercise A.

1. Sie hat ihm etwas **Schwarzes** gegeben.   (green, beautiful)
2. **Neues** gibt es in der Zeitung nicht.   (true/truth, unpleasant [things])
3. Drei **lange** Wochen hat er hier gelegen.   (expensive, wonderful)
4. Einige **junge** Leute standen da.   (glad, strong)

C. Follow the directions for exercise A.

1. Sein **roter** Wagen ist wunderbar.   (newest, green)
2. Ein **neues** Haus war zu haben.   (better, other)

3. Ich habe keinen Platz für meine **alten** Bücher. (many, own, valuable)
4. Der Fluß fließt durch einen **schönen** Park. (certain, pleasant)
5. Die Kinder spielten mit ihrem **roten** Ball. (new, yellow)
6. Der Student hat ein **langes** Buch gelesen. (American, German)

D. Follow the directions for exercise A.

1. Die **Angestellten** sind sehr spät gekommen. (relatives, youngest ones)
2. Der neue Professor ist immer sehr **schnell** gefahren. (well [good], early)
3. Während der Ferien wurden unsere Tage **länger**. (hotter, more pleasant)
4. Der **junge** Student schien sehr fleißig zu sein. ([who was] writing, new)
5. In der Stadt hat er nichts **Angenehmes** gefunden. (new, cheap)
6. Die **Fleißigsten** sind nicht immer die Besten. (quickest, earliest)
7. Das **neue** Mädchen spielte Klavier. (next, largest)
8. Die Lehrer haben **später** gearbeitet. (longer, more industriously)
9. Als sie im Park saßen, wurde es sehr **unangenehm**. (cool, late)
10. Das kleine Mädchen war die **jüngste**. (freest, fastest, most natural)

E. Give German equivalents for the English sentences below. The word order will be exactly the same as in the pattern sentences.

1. Die jüngste Tochter war bei Verwandten.
   A. His oldest cousin was at home.

B. Her largest son was on vacation.

C. The most interesting child was with (**bei**) relatives.

2. Bitte, fahren Sie etwas langsamer!
   A. Read somewhat faster, please.
   B. Come a bit earlier, please.
   C. Write somewhat more beautifully, please.

3. Die Tage wurden länger und heißer.
   A. The nights grew longer and cooler.
   B. The flowers grew bigger and more beautiful.
   C. His children seemed younger and more inquisitive.

4. Schneller als gewöhnlich eilte er in seinen Garten.
   A. He was going to his class later than usual.
   B. He was driving into the city more slowly than usual.
   C. She hurried to her train more quickly than usual.

5. Herr Schneider war so froh wie ein Kind.
   A. The box was as big as a car.
   B. His cousin was as old as his brother.
   C. The professor was as happy as his students.

F. Questions. In succeeding lessons we will not give German answers to the questions. To help you recall the story, however, we will give phrases or short sentences in English after each question. Remember to answer each question with a complete sentence.

1. Wie lange wohnte Herr Schneider in seinem Haus? [four weeks]
2. Wo war seine Familie? [on vacation]
3. Welches Kind war bei Verwandten? [his youngest daughter]
4. Wie gefiel es Herrn Schneider, allein zu sein? [he was as happy as a child]
5. Warum mußte er eines Abends langsamer fahren? [there was a fire]

6. Wer fuhr auf der linken Seite der Straße? [the fire department]
7. Was sah er in seinem Garten? [a lot of people]
8. Welches Instrument wurde nicht gerettet? [the piano]
9. Von wem bekam er einen Brief? [the president of his firm]
10. Was sollte er mit dem Geld machen? [build a more modern house]

G. Translate in writing:

1. Some students were reading the newest German novels.
2. Is today the twelfth or the thirteenth of April?
3. It is really an unpleasant Friday for me.
4. On this cool day we will work hard.
5. Their relatives came on a visit day before yesterday.
6. Yesterday the younger students were on vacation.
7. The novel wasn't as long as her letter.
8. (The) most students write better than he.
9. He put the most valuable instruments in his apartment.
10. This white house has the largest garden on the street.

H. Free Conversation.

Tell about a friend's last vacation. His older brother was in Colorado, and he and his younger sister were going to meet him. School lasted longer than he had thought it would. He drove faster than usual, and a policeman warned him. John said he was sorry and drove on, more slowly. — His brother lived in a large old house. He had many books and musical instruments. The younger brother and sister stayed there three weeks on their vacation.

BRIEF CONVERSATION

Romantische Abende

INGE PFEIFFER *and her friend* BETTY *discuss plans for next summer's vacation.*

BETTY: Wohin werden Sie im kommenden Sommer fahren?

INGE: Am liebsten nach dem Osten. Ich habe die großen Städte noch nie gesehen. Meine älteste Schwester hat sich einen neuen Wagen gekauft, und wenn ich mit ihr gehe, will sie die ganze Reise für mich bezahlen. Ist das nicht wunderbar? — Was werden Sie tun?

BETTY: Es gibt nichts Schöneres, als bei hellem Tage in der Sonne zu liegen und zu träumen. Ein Verwandter von mir hat ein altes Haus in Michigan an einem kleinen See [lake]. Da bin ich schon seit langer Zeit nicht mehr gewesen.

INGE: Das klingt [sounds] sehr romantisch.

BETTY: Am besten gefallen mir die Abende. Da sitzt man am Wasser bei einbrechender Dunkelheit und singt alte Lieder [songs].

INGE: ... und bekommt einen Schnupfen. Sie müssen vorsichtig [careful] sein!

LESSON 9

Wie man Schnupfen bekommt

RELATIVE PRONOUNS

SUBORDINATING CONJUNCTIONS

INTERROGATIVES

PRONUNCIATION

TEXT

Heinrich Seemann, den wir schon in einer früheren Aufgabe
getroffen haben, war ein guter Student. Jeden Nachmittag
stand er im Laboratorium und arbeitete mit seinen Gläsern
und Retorten, wie es ein guter Student tut. Und jeden Abend
saß er hinter seinen Büchern. Er studierte Chemie und wollte   5
Ingenieur bei der Ölindustrie werden.
Der Professor, unter dem er arbeitete, war ein berühmter
Mann. Er hatte vor mehreren Jahren den Nobelpreis bekommen, weil er eine große Entdeckung gemacht hatte. Er hatte

95

10 nämlich eine Substanz gefunden, mit der man den Schnupfen
heilen konnte.
   Auch Heinrich wollte ein berühmter Mann werden. Während
die anderen Menschen schliefen, stand er im Laboratorium und
rechnete und experimentierte. Er goß ein dunkles Öl von
15 einem Glas ins andere. Nachdem er es in der einen Retorte
gemischt hatte, analysierte er es in einer anderen. Er ließ es
heiß werden und kühlte es ab. Er beobachtete und rechnete.
Aber er merkte nicht, wie es im Raum immer kälter wurde.
Und ehe die Nacht vorbei war, hatte er einen schrecklichen
20 Schnupfen.
   Als Heinrich am nächsten Morgen im Krankenhaus erwachte,
saß sein Professor neben seinem Bett. „Womit haben Sie
gestern abend experimentiert?" „Mit der gleichen Substanz,
die ich Ihnen vor ein paar Tagen gezeigt habe." „Und was war
25 das Resultat Ihrer Beobachtungen?" „Nichts, was mir nicht
schon früher bekannt war."
   „Aber warum haben Sie nicht auf das Thermometer gesehen?
Wer ein guter Ingenieur werden will, muß auch seine Umwelt
[environment] beobachten. Nun, es tut mir leid, daß Sie dabei
30 einen solchen Schnupfen bekommen haben. Sie sind wirklich
ein Opfer der Wissenschaft geworden. Hier, nehmen Sie
diese drei Pillen und in drei Tagen werden Sie wieder gesund
sein. Auf Wiedersehen!" Sobald Heinrich die Medizin
geschluckt [swallowed] hatte, ging es ihm besser.

IDIOMS AND VOCABULARY

Es geht mir gut.   I am (feeling) all right.
immer (kält)er   (cold)er and (cold)er
vor ein paar Tagen   a few days ago

**abkühlen, kühlte ab, abge-
   kühlt**   cool off
die Aufgabe, -n   lesson
bekannt   (well) known

beobachten   observe
die Beobachtung, -en   observation
berühmt   famous

dabei in the process
ehe = bevor before
die Entdeckung, -en discovery
erwachen (ist) awake
gesund healthy
gießen, o, o pour
gleich same, equal
heilen heal
hinter behind
lassen, ließ, gelassen, läßt
have (something done), let,
leave, permit
mehrere several
merken notice

mischen mix
nachdem [*conj.*] after
nah, näher, nächst near,
nearer, next
das Öl, -e oil
das Opfer, – victim, sacrifice
pfeifen, pfiff, gepfiffen
whistle
sobald as soon as
während [*conj.*] while
weil because
wer he who, whoever
die Wissenschaft, -en
science

NOTE: English *when* corresponds to three German words:
wenn — in the present and future: page 72, line 43: Wenn
meine Tanten zu Besuch kommen. 'When my aunts come
to visit.'
wann — in questions: Wann kommen Sie? 'When are you
coming?'
als — usually in the past: Als sie zu Besuch kamen, ...
'When they came for a visit, ...'

GRAMMAR

9.1 Relative Pronouns

9.1,1 The usual relative pronoun is **der, die, das.** It has the
same forms as the definite article, except that **-en** is added in the
three genitive singular forms **(dessen, deren, dessen),** in the
dative plural **(denen),** and in the genitive plural **(deren).** (The
ss in the masculine and neuter singular indicates that the
preceding vowel is short.)

The case taken by the relative pronoun is determined by its function in its own clause, *e.g.* **Einmal stolperte der junge Mann, der den Ball gefangen hatte.** 'Once the young man stumbled who had caught the ball.' Here **der** is the subject of the relative clause, and therefore it is in the nominative case. The gender and number of the relative pronoun are determined by the noun to which it refers. Since **der junge Mann** is masculine and singular, so is the relative pronoun.

Note this further example: **Es war sein Haus, das brannte.** 'It was his house that was burning.' Because **das** is the subject of **brannte,** it is in the nominative case. **Haus** is singular and neuter, and hence the relative is singular and neuter.

9.1,2 Relative pronouns corresponding to "whoever" and "whatever" are **wer** and **was.** **Wer ein guter Ingenieur werden will, muß seine Umwelt studieren.** 'Whoever wants to become a good engineer must study his environment.' Here **wer** is the subject of the verb in the main clause as well as of the verb in the dependent clause, as is *whoever* in the English equivalent.

After **nichts, etwas,** and **alles, was** is used as a relative pronoun. **Er fand nichts, was ihm gefiel.** 'He didn't find anything that pleased him.' It is also used as a relative pronoun after neuter superlative adjectives and in references to an entire preceding clause:

Das Beste, was er bekommen hat…. 'The best thing that he received…'

Fritz versicherte den Wagen, was er bis jetzt vergessen hatte. 'Fred insured the car, [*a thing*] which he had forgotten to do until now.'

9.1,3 In relative clauses the finite verb stands at the end. One must observe its position in order to distinguish relative pronouns from definite articles or demonstratives, *e.g.*, **der** 'he, that one.'

9.2 Subordinating Conjunctions Clauses introduced by most conjunctions have the finite verb at the end. Such conjunctions are:

als 'when; as': **Es war spät, als er ging.** 'It was late when he went.'

bevor 'before': **Bevor er erwachte, hatte er einen Schnupfen.** 'Before he awoke, he had a cold.'

daß 'that': **Es ist nett, daß Sie heute noch hier sind.** 'It is nice that you are still here today.'

ehe 'before': **Er ging, ehe ich 'Auf Wiedersehen' sagte.** 'He left before I said good-bye.'

nachdem 'after': **Er kam, nachdem die Schule aus war.** 'He came after school was out.'

ob 'if, whether': **Er fragt, ob wir das verstehen.** 'He asks whether we understand that.'

obgleich 'although': **Obgleich er nichts sagte, wußte er es.** 'Although he didn't say anything, he knew it.'

sobald 'as soon as': **Sobald er es getan hat, kann er gehen.** 'As soon as he has done it, he may go.'

während 'while': **Er schlief, während der Professor sprach.** 'He was sleeping while the professor was talking.'

weil 'because': **Er tat es, weil er mußte.** 'He did it because he had to.'

wenn 'if; when': **Wenn seine Freundin abfährt, geht er mit.** 'When his girl friend drives off, he goes along.'

wie 'as, how': **Wir müssen die Dinge nehmen, wie sie kommen.** 'We have to take things as they come.'

9.2,1 If the subordinate clause precedes the main clause, it is followed immediately by the verb of the main clause. Contrast the following sentence with the sentence after **während** above:

Während die anderen Menschen sprachen, schlief er. 'While the other people were speaking, he was sleeping.'

9.2,2 The conjunctions **aber** 'but,' **denn** 'for,' **oder** 'or,' **sondern** 'but [*rather*],' and **und** 'and' have no effect on the word order: **Und was war das Resultat Ihrer Beobachtungen?** 'And what was the result of your observations?'

9.3 Interrogatives Interrogatives are used as in English to introduce questions. The interrogative pronoun referring to persons is: nominative **wer,** accusative **wen,** dative **wem,** genitive **wessen**; referring to things, it is: nominative and accusative **was.**

> **Wessen Buch ist das?** 'Whose book is that?'
> **Was war seine Entdeckung?** 'What was his discovery?'

If a preposition plus an interrogative refers to a thing, a compound may be used which consists of **wo-** or **wor-** plus the prepositions: **Womit haben Sie experimentiert?** 'With what did you experiment?' (Compare the archaic or legal English 'wherewith.') Before consonants, **wo-** is used: **wodurch** 'through what.' Before vowels, **wor-** is used: **worin** 'in what.' Note the similarity of **wo-**compounds to **da-**compounds, which were treated in Lesson 8.3.

The interrogative adjective is **welcher, welche, welches: Welchen Bleistift möchten Sie haben?** 'Which pencil would you like to have?'

Interrogative particles are **wann** 'when,' **warum** 'why,' **wie** 'how,' and **wo** 'where.' **Wie gefällt ihm die Zeitung?** 'How does he like the paper?' Like other interrogatives, these may be used to introduce indirect questions; the finite verb must then stand at the end of the clause: **Da sehen Sie, wie Herrn Hansen die Zeitung gefällt.** 'There you see how Mr. Hansen likes the paper.'

9.4 Pronunciation In pronouncing German, syllables and words must be kept sharply distinct. Practice sentences such as the following, avoiding slurring the unstressed syllables of such words as **ehe, antwortete,** and **beobachtete.**

Es ist fünf Uhr.

Das war unangenehm.

Weil er mußte, hat er es getan.

Wir warteten, bis sie antwortete.

Ehe ich ging, sprachen wir lange.

Er beobachtete und beobachtete und hat nichts gesehen.

EXERCISES

A. Make additional sentences on the basis of those given below, substituting the suggested words for those in heavy type and making any necessary changes in the rest of the sentence.

1. **Der Herr,** der dort wohnte, schien sehr alt zu sein. (the woman, the people)
2. **Das Kind,** das unter dem Baum gestanden hatte, lief ins Wasser. (the student, her sister)
3. **Die Kusine,** mit der er spielte, sprach gut Deutsch. (the male cousin, a girl)
4. **Die Wohnung,** die wir dort gesehen haben, war neu. (the house, the train)
5. **Der Sohn,** der sehr bekannt war, spielte Klavier. (a young lady, the brothers)
6. In **der Zeitung,** die er bekommen hatte, gab es nichts Neues. (the book, the novel)
7. **Die Detektiv-Romane,** die er abends las, waren nicht berühmt. (the newspapers, the book)
8. **Wer** nicht stehen kann, wird fallen. (whatever)

B. Follow the directions for exercise A.

1. **Was** haben Sie dort gesehen? (whom)
2. **Welche Aufgabe** hat er gelesen? (which book, which letters)
3. **Warum** ist er so spät gekommen? (how, when)

4. **Mit einem Bleistift** hat er die Aufgabe geschrieben? (with what)
5. **Wer** steht dort vor dem Haus? (what)
6. **Welches Mädchen** war bei Verwandten? (son, aunt)
7. **Wo** hat der Professor gesprochen? (why, how)

C. Connect the following pairs of clauses with the conjunctions in parentheses:

1. Sie waren an den Fluß gegangen. Es war sehr heiß. (weil, während, denn)
2. Das Mädchen schrie. Es hatte den Ball gefangen. (ehe, aber, als)
3. Sie saßen unter einem Baum. Sie lernten Deutsch. (und während, als)
4. Ich las in der Zeitung. Er hatte ein Buch geschrieben. (daß, wie)
5. Sie saß in der Sonne. Sie schlief nicht. (but, although)
6. Es war ein schrecklicher Tag. Sein Haus brannte ab. (for, because)

D. Give German equivalents for the English sentences. The word order will be exactly the same as in the pattern sentences.

1. Heinrich, den wir schon getroffen haben, war ein guter Student.
   A. The man whom we saw earlier was his older brother.
   B. The woman, whom you noticed already, was her former teacher.
   C. The girl whom you met yesterday is his younger sister.

2. Der Professor, unter dem er arbeitete, war ein berühmter Mann.
   A. The gentleman with whom he drove was a new student.
   B. The man to whom he was talking was his old professor.
   C. The woman near whom he stood was a young teacher.

3. Er hatte eine Substanz gefunden, mit der man den Schnupfen heilen konnte.
   A. He had bought a newspaper in which he could read the letter.
   B. He had seen a family in which the children had valuable instruments.
   C. She had written a book from which one could learn physics.

4. Während die anderen Menschen schliefen, stand er im Laboratorium.
   A. As soon as the other students came, he went to the movies.
   B. Before his young brother talked, he came to his house.
   C. While her older sisters were reading, she was helping in the kitchen.

5. Aber er merkte nicht, wie es immer kälter wurde.
   A. But he didn't notice that she drove faster and faster.
   B. Or we didn't know why he wanted more and more.
   C. For he didn't say that the books were getting more and more expensive.

6. Womit haben Sie gestern abend experimentiert?
   A. What did you write with last night?
   B. On what did he fall this morning?
   C. With what did he work yesterday?

7. Nichts, was früher bekannt war.
   A. Nothing that was valuable earlier.
   B. Everything that was known yesterday.
   C. Something that was good day before yesterday.

8. Wer (ein) Ingenieur werden will, muß seine Umwelt beobachten.
   A. Whoever wants to become a professor must buy many books.
   B. Whoever wants to make discoveries must study science.
   C. Whoever wants to see that man must ask his brother.

9. Es tut mir leid, daß Sie einen Schnupfen bekommen haben.
   A. I am sorry that you made that discovery.
   B. He is sorry that you read that letter.
   C. We are sorry that he took the car.

10. Sobald er die Medizin geschluckt hatte, ging es ihm besser.
    A. After he had drunk the medicine, he liked it better.
    B. When he had eaten a piece, he was feeling fine.
    C. Before he had read the newspaper, it seemed true to him.

E. Questions.

1. Wer war ein guter Student? (Heinrich Seemann)
2. Wo arbeitete er jeden Nachmittag? (in the laboratory)
3. Was tat er jeden Abend? (he sat behind his books)
4. Was wollte er werden? (an engineer)
5. Unter wem arbeitete er? (under a famous professor)
6. Warum war sein Professor berühmt? (he had made a great discovery)
7. Wann experimentierte Heinrich? (while other people slept)
8. Was merkte er eines Abends nicht? (that it got colder and colder in the room)
9. Wo erwachte er am nächsten Morgen? (in the hospital)
10. Wie wurde Heinrich wieder gesund? (the professor gave him three pills)

F. Translate in writing:

1. Several years earlier the professor had made a great discovery.
2. After his discovery he became famous.
3. The room in which Henry was working grew colder and colder.
4. He was feeling fine when he was studying.
5. While he stood in the room, he was figuring.

6. The oil which he poured into another glass was dark.
7. When the night was past, he was ill.
8. He observed something that he had not known before.
9. The professor was sorry that his student wasn't feeling well.
10. Before he awoke, he was healthy (well) again.

G. Free conversation.

Describe work in a laboratory. Discuss the work of the professor and the experiments of a student. Both are trying to find a cold remedy. They are working with a substance which they must observe carefully for its temperature changes. Up to the present their results have not made them famous.

BRIEF CONVERSATION

Sehr spät im Park

Walter Krenn *meets* Klaus Moehlenbrock *at lunch.*

Walter: Warum sind Sie gestern abend nicht zum Geologie-Klub gekommen?

Klaus: Weil ich das Feuer sehen wollte.

Walter: Welches Feuer? Wo hat es denn gebrannt?

Klaus: Nun, bei den Schneiders, in dem alten Haus, das hinter dem Park liegt, ganz am andern Ende der Stadt.

Walter: Das Haus, in dem es so viel Musik gibt?

Klaus: Ja, der alte Kasten, der so lange leer gestanden hat, daß kein Mensch ihn kaufen wollte.

Walter: War's denn ein großes Feuer?

Klaus: Ja, als ich hin kam, stand alles in hellen Flammen. — Warum fragen Sie?

Walter: O, ich frage mich nur, was Sie so spät im Park zu tun hatten — und so ganz allein.

Liebe unter dem Licht

REFLEXIVE VERBS

VERBS WITH SEPARABLE PREFIXES

VERBS WITH INSEPARABLE PREFIXES

PRONUNCIATION OF VOWELS

TEXT

Klaus Moehlenbrock, den wir in der fünften Aufgabe verlassen haben, konnte Eleanor Sanders nicht mehr vergessen. Sie war schon vor mehr als vier Wochen in Los Angeles angekommen. Sie hatte ihm auch schon längst [long ago] das Geld
5 zurückgeschickt, das er ihr geliehen hatte. Aber sie hatte ihm kein Bildchen beigelegt, zum Zeichen [as a sign], daß sie sich des Tages im Frühling erinnerte. Klaus wußte nicht, was er tun sollte, um Eleanor noch einmal zu begegnen.

Ein Tag nach dem anderen ging vorbei und das gleiche Spiel

wiederholte sich. Jeden Abend schlief er ein und dachte an 10
Eleanor, und jeden Morgen wachte er auf und hatte von ihr
geträumt. Eines Tages begegnete er Heinrich Seemann, der
sich inzwischen von seiner Krankheit erholt hatte. Aber
Heinrich hatte nichts von seiner Kusine gehört und erzählte nur
von seinen wissenschaftlichen Beobachtungen und Experimen- 15
ten. Dann drehte er sich um und ging ins Laboratorium.
Nein, Heinrich verstand ihn nicht. Klaus hatte die Entdeckung
gemacht, daß er sich in Eleanor verliebt hatte.
Klaus verlebte [spent] schreckliche Tage. Was sollte er tun?
Sollte er hinfliegen, sie besuchen und zu ihr von seiner Liebe 20
sprechen? Aber dann würde [would] sie ihn auslachen und er
würde mit traurigen Gefühlen im Herzen zurückkommen und
seine Liebe würde abgekühlt sein. — Eines Abends kehrte er
langsam in seine Wohnung zurück. Zu Hause brannte noch
Licht, und unter dem Licht fand sich [there was] ein Brief. 25
Der Brief war von Eleanor. Klaus setzte sich auf einen Stuhl
und las:

Lieber Klaus!

Ich weiß nicht, ob Sie sich an mich noch erinnern. Vor vielen
Wochen waren Sie so gut, mir Ihre Stadt zu zeigen. Heute kann 30
ich Ihnen mitteilen, daß ich in zwei Monaten wieder nach
Austin kommen werde. Mein Vater hat nämlich sein Haus
im Osten verkauft und eine Stellung [position] als Bankdirektor in
Houston angenommen. Sie werden sich wundern, warum ich
so lange nicht geschrieben habe. Aber ich wollte wissen, wie 35
sich die Dinge im Osten entwickeln würden. Ich habe mir
immer gewünscht, im Südwesten zu leben. Ich hoffe, daß es
Ihnen gut geht und bin mit den besten Wünschen

Ihre
E.

In dieser Nacht war Klaus Moehlenbrock der glücklichste
Mensch auf der ganzen Welt.

IDIOMS AND VOCABULARY

eines Abends (Tages) one evening (day)
[*gen. for indefinite time*]
denken an [*acc.*] think of
sich verlieben in [*acc.*] fall in love with
vier Wochen a month

an-fangen, fing an, ange-fangen, fängt an begin
an-kommen, kam an, ist angekommen arrive
an-nehmen, nahm an, an-genommen, nimmt an accept; assume
auf-wachen (ist) wake up
aus-lachen [*acc.*] laugh at
bei-legen enclose, add
drehen turn
sich um-drehen turn around
ein-schlafen, ie, (ist) a, ä fall asleep
entwickeln develop
sich erholen recover
sich erinnern [*with gen. or an plus acc.*] remember
erzählen tell
sich freuen enjoy, be happy
der Frühling spring
fünft- fifth
glücklich lucky; happy
hin-fliegen, o, (ist) o fly (to a place)

hoffen hope
inzwischen meanwhile
die Krankheit, -en sickness
leben live
lieb dear
mit-teilen inform, notify
ob whether, if
sich setzen sit down
das Spiel, -e game, play
die Stellung, -en position, job
traurig sad
vergessen, a, e, i forget
verkaufen sell
vorbei-gehen, ging vorbei, ist vorbeigegangen pass, go by
wissenschaftlich scientific
das Zeichen, – sign, token
zurück back, behind
zurück-kehren (ist) return, come back
zurück-kommen, a, (ist) o return, come back
zurück-schicken send back

GRAMMAR

10.1 Reflexive Verbs   Simple reflexive constructions are used in German as well as in English: **Er sah sich im Wasser.** 'He saw himself in the water.'   The term *reflexive verb* does not apply to the verbs in these constructions but rather to combinations of verb and reflexive pronoun which have a specific meaning that is different from the meaning of the simple verb, *e.g.*, **sich erinnern** 'remember' versus **erinnern** 'remind.'

10.1,1 Some reflexive verbs in German correspond in translation to English verbs plus adverbs: **sich setzen** 'sit down.' Others correspond to English intransitive verbs: **sich erholen** 'recover, get well again.'   Others correspond to English simple verbs: **sich erinnern** 'remember.'   In all reflexive constructions the reflexive pronoun is the object of the verb; if, as with 'remember,' a further object is used, this must be put into a prepositional phrase or into a construction which will be noted in vocabularies for individual verbs, *e.g.*, **ob Sie sich an mich noch erinnern** 'whether you still remember me'; **daß er sich in Eleanor verliebt hatte** 'that he had fallen in love with Eleanor.'

Only the third person and **Sie** 'you' have a special reflexive pronoun, **sich.** For other persons, forms of the personal pronoun are used.   Most verbs are accompanied by the accusative of the pronouns.   A few take the dative, *e.g.*, **sich wünschen.**   Only in the first person singular is there a difference in form from that of reflexive pronouns in the accusative: **ich habe mir immer gewünscht** 'I have always wished.'

10.1,2 The following forms illustrate the reflexive pronouns and various tenses of the verb:

ich setze mich	I sit down
er setzte sich	he sat down

sie hat sich gesetzt	she has sat down
wir hatten uns gesetzt	we had sat down
sie werden sich setzen	they will sit down
setzen Sie sich bitte	sit down, please

10.1,3 **sich** also means 'each other, one another': **Sie sahen sich an.** 'They looked at one another.'

10.2 Verbs with Separable Prefixes Many verbs in English are consistently used with certain adverbs, and when so used have a meaning different from that of the simple verb, *e.g.*, 'come back' versus 'come,' 'cool off' versus 'cool.' In German such verb phrases are written as single words in the infinitive: 'come back' as **zurückkehren,** 'cool off' as **abkühlen.** Because the "adverb" portion of such verb phrases comes before the verb in the German infinitive it is called a *prefix*, and because the prefix does not stand before the verb in all constructions, it is called *separable*. As infinitive forms of verbs are the ones memorized and listed in vocabularies, one learns, for example, the form **auf-wachen** 'wake up.' In vocabularies, a hyphen is generally put after the separable element in order to identify such verbs.

10.2,1 Many of the separable prefixes are also prepositions, *e.g.*, **an, auf, aus, bei, mit, um;** others are also adverbs, *e.g.*, **ab, hin, zurück.**

Verbs with separable prefixes have the accent on the prefix, *e.g.*, **án-kommen, éin-schlafen, zurück-kommen.**

10.2,2 When separable verbs are used in the present and past tenses and in the imperative, they are like English verbs in that the prefix stands at the end of the clause: **er kehrte zurück** 'he came back.'

In the compound tenses, however, the word order differs from that of English, for in German, infinitives and past participles must stand at the end of the clause: **Er wird früh aufwachen.**

'He will wake up early.' **Sie ist spät aufgewacht.** 'She woke up late.'

In the word order within subordinate clauses the two languages also differ, for in German the verb stands at the end; accordingly, the verb is preceded by the separable prefix, which is there joined to it: **als er aufwachte...** 'when we woke up...'.

10.2,3 In forming the past participle, the **ge-** is placed between the prefix and the verb, *e.g.*, **angekommen.**

If **zu** is used with the infinitive, it stands between the prefix and the verb, *e.g.*, **Sie brauchen das nicht anzunehmen.** 'You don't need to accept that.'

10.3 Verbs with Inseparable Prefixes Certain compound verbs always retain their prefixes. Their prefixes are accordingly called *inseparable.*

The most common inseparable prefixes are never found as individual words. They have an **e** vowel, which is always unstressed, as in English *betake*: **be- emp- ent- er- ge- ver- zer-.** Examples of verbs with inseparable prefixes are: **befinden, empfinden, entwickeln, erzählen, geschehen, verstehen, zerreißen.**

A few inseparable prefixes have more than one syllable, however, and some are also found as individual words. Prefixes of this type can be recognized from the position of the stress, as in **wiederhólen.** The position of the stress must be carefully noted because the same prefixes may also be accented and accordingly separable; for example, in **wiéder-sehen** the prefix is separable, as is indicated by the position of the stress on **wieder.**

10.3,1 Verbs with inseparable prefixes do not take the **ge-** in the past participle, *e.g.*, **besucht, erzählt, verkauft.** Nor do verbs in **-ieren,** *e.g.*, **studiert.**

10.4 Pronunciation of Vowels One of the essential differ-

ences in pronounciation between English and German is in
the manner of producing vowels. German vowels are pure;
English vowels are diphthongal. That is, the German vowels
are maintained steadily throughout, whereas the English vowels
end in a consonant. The vowels of English words like *see*
and *say* end in a *y*-like consonant; the vowels of words like
sue and *sow* in a *w*-like consonant. One must carefully avoid
carrying over into German this consonantal pronunciation.
Contrast:

knee: **nie**	Vee: **wie**	fear: **vier**
mare: **mehr**	lake: **leg'**	hair: **her**
tune: **tun**	noon: **nun**	roof: **ruf'**
four: **vor**	zone: **Sohn**	shone: **schon**

EXERCISES

A. Make additional sentences on the basis of those given
here, substituting the suggested words for those in heavy type
and making any necessary changes in the rest of the sentence.

1. **Der Herr** hat sich schnell umgedreht. (I, they, we)
2. **Wir** haben uns gefragt, warum er nicht gekommen ist.
   (my mother, they, I)
3. Soll **er** sich auf die Bank setzen? (we, they, I)
4. **Die Lehrerin** wiederholte sich oft. (I, the students)
5. **Ich** werde mich bald an seinen Namen erinnern. (we,
   my brother, the professor)
6. **Das junge Mädchen** hat sich schon längst erholt. (I,
   the students)
7. **Wir** erholten uns in einem großen Park. (my brother,
   the children)
8. **Eine Klasse** entwickelt sich oft schnell. (difficulties, a
   sickness)
9. Was wünschen **Sie** sich heute? (I, he)

B. Change the tenses of the verbs printed in heavy type as indicated.

1. Das Öl **kühlte** sich schnell ab. (pres., pres. perfect, future)
2. Jeden Abend **ist** der Ingenieur **zurückgekommen.** (past. perfect, past, present)
3. Als der berühmte Professor sprach, **schlief** die kleine Studentin **ein.** (pres. perfect, past perfect)
4. Er **nahm an,** daß ich das nicht weiß. (pres. perfect, past perfect, future)
5. Die Studenten **haben** das Thermometer **zurückgeschickt.** (past, present, future)
6. Er **fliegt hin,** um den Nobelpreis anzunehmen. (future, past, pres. perfect)
7. Sie **teilte** uns **mit,** daß sie die Aufgabe nicht versteht. (pres. perfect, past perfect, present)
8. Am nächsten Morgen **kam** er bei uns **an.** (pres. perfect, past perfect, future)
9. Ich war krank, als ich **aufwachte.** (pres. perfect, past perfect)
10. **Haben** Sie ihn wirklich **ausgelacht?** (past perfect)
11. Nach zehn Minuten **drehte** er sich **um** und **kehrte zurück.** (pres. perfect)
12. Das Öl **lege** ich Ihnen in diesem Glas **bei.** (past, future, pres. perfect)

C. Change as indicated the tenses of the verbs printed in heavy type.

1. Ich **habe** das Klavier **verkauft.** (past, past perfect)
2. Bei einbrechender Dunkelheit **kühlt** sie sich am äußersten Ende des Parks **ab.** (pres. perfect, past perfect)
3. Sein Experiment **hat** sich langsam **entwickelt.** (present, past, future)
4. Es war schon spät, als der Präsident seiner Firma ihn **besuchte.** (pres. perfect, past perfect)

5. Die jüngste Tochter **erzählte** von ihren Ferien. (present, future, pres. perfect)

6. **Haben** Sie den Fernseh-Apparat **vergessen?** (past, past perfect)

7. Ich **erhole** mich sehr schnell. (pres. perfect, past, future)

8. Wo **haben** Sie die Kinder **verlassen?** (past, past perfect)

9. Er **begegnete** uns auf der linken Seite der Straße. (pres. perfect, past perfect)

10. Der Besitzer des Hauses **verlebte** eine schreckliche Nacht. (past perfect, pres. perfect, future)

D. Replace the words printed in heavy type with the German equivalents of the words in parentheses.

1. **Er erinnert sich** gerne an den Abend im Konzert. (we remembered, they have remembered, will they remember?)

2. **Sie setzte sich** auf den Stuhl. (I will sit down, he had sat down, she is sitting down)

3. Das kleine Mädchen **hatte sich** in Klaus **verliebt.** (fell in love, has fallen in love, is falling in love)

4. **Ich frage mich,** ob **er** noch **kommen wird.** (we asked ourselves — he remembers her; he's asking himself — she'll laugh at him; she had asked herself — he had forgotten her)

5. **Er wunderte sich** über die vielen Menschen auf der Straße. (I am surprised, were you surprised? haven't you been surprised? they had been surprised)

E. Give German equivalents for the English sentences. The word order will be exactly the same as in the pattern sentences.

1. Der Direktor hatte seinen Wagen verkauft.
   A. The student had insured his watch.
   B. The gentleman had sent back his pictures.
   C. The professor had observed his difficulty.

2. Warum haben Sie die Rechnung angenommen?
   A. Why did he sell his house?
   B. When did the student recover?
   C. Why had you laughed at him?

3. Der Polizist hatte sich umgedreht und war zurückgekommen.
   A. Spring had begun and passed.
   B. Klaus had recovered and waked up.
   C. His friend had turned around and fallen asleep.

4. Sie war in Los Angeles angekommen.
   A. He had fallen asleep in a chair.
   B. They had gone by with their friend.
   C. She had returned on the train.

5. Klaus setzte sich auf einen Stuhl.
   A. He fell in love with his cousin.
   B. Henry is sitting down on (**auf**) the bed.
   C. She is recovering in the South.

6. Sollte er sie besuchen?
   A. Should she tell that?
   B. Should we sell it?
   C. Should I forget him?

F. Questions.

1. Wann war Eleanor in Los Angeles angekommen? (a month earlier)
2. Was hatte sie an Klaus zurückgeschickt? (the money she had borrowed)
3. Wen traf Klaus eines Tages? (Heinrich Seemann)
4. Was erzählte ihm sein Freund? (his scientific observations and experiments)
5. Welche Entdeckung hatte Klaus gemacht? (that he had fallen in love)
6. Warum wollte er nicht nach Los Angeles fliegen? (Eleanor would laugh at him)

7. Wo fand er eines Abends einen Brief? (under the light)
8. Wann wollte Eleanor nach Austin zurückkommen? (in two months)
9. Warum hatte sie so lange nicht geschrieben? (she wanted to wait for developments)
10. Was hatte sie sich immer gewünscht? (to live in the Southwest)

G. Translate in writing:

1. The disease developed as his wife had told him.
2. We arrive Friday at eleven o'clock and will return immediately after the game.
3. It is nice that he has not forgotten it.
4. A month ago his father sold their old house.
5. Eleanor told Klaus she hoped to see him again.
6. He fell asleep at once and woke up eight hours later.
7. The teacher wondered why the class found everything so difficult.
8. The two men understood each other extremely well.
9. Before he sat down he remembered the end of her letter.
10. His friend recalled the days when he was at (auf) the university.

H. Free conversation.

Discuss some types of students. One is always working in the laboratory, carrying out scientific experiments. Another has studied thoroughly the park at the other end of town. Another talks a great deal of her trips and of the places she has visited on vacation. Another spends much of his time in front of his television set.

BRIEF CONVERSATION

Ein neuer Bauplatz

MR. SCHNEIDER *calls on* MR. JOHNSON, *the agent who had sold him the old house.*

JOHNSON: Guten Morgen, Herr Schneider. Es freut mich sehr, Sie wiederzusehen. Was kann ich für Sie tun? Bitte, setzen Sie sich!

SCHNEIDER: Danke. — Sie wissen doch, was bei mir vor ein paar Tagen geschehen ist?

JOHNSON: Ja. Das hat mir leid getan. Ich bin sehr erschrokken, als ich in der Zeitung davon [about it] las. Ich hoffe, daß Sie sich von dem Schrecken [fright] erholt haben.

SCHNEIDER: O ja. Das Haus war ja versichert. Außerdem [besides] habe ich zehntausend Dollar bekommen. Nun will ich mir ein neues Haus bauen. Haben Sie einen Bauplatz, den ich mir ansehen kann?

JOHNSON: Ja gewiß. Kommen Sie mit! Ich bin noch heute morgen an einem Platz vorbeigegangen. Sie werden sich freuen [be happy], daß Sie mich besucht haben!

Musik auf dem Lande

THE PASSIVE VOICE

MODAL AUXILIARIES

PRONUNCIATION OF VOWELS

TEXT

Der ältere Herr Moehlenbrock hatte gehört, daß in der
Nachbarschaft gebaut wurde. Er sagte zu seiner Frau: „Ich
muß mir doch einmal ansehen, was da gebaut wird. Ich hoffe,
daß uns die Aussicht auf den Fluß nicht verdorben wird. Man
5 kann nie wissen." Aber Herr Moehlenbrock brauchte keine
Sorge zu haben. Das neue Haus wurde hinter ihnen gebaut,
auf der anderen Seite des Berges, wo das Land billiger war.
Im Garten des Nachbars wurde fleißig gearbeitet. Schon zehn
Bäume waren von den Arbeitern gefällt worden.

An der Straße hatte man Steine und Bretter abgeladen. Auf 10
dem ganzen Platz herrschte starker Betrieb [hustle and bustle].
Unter den Leuten traf Herr Moehlenbrock auch den neuen
Besitzer. „Guten Morgen," sagte er. „Ich wollte nur meinen
neuen Nachbar begrüßen. Darf ich mich vorstellen? Mein
Name ist Moehlenbrock." „Sehr angenehm," sagte der neue 15
Nachbar. „Mein Name ist Schneider. Es freut mich sehr,
mit Ihnen bekannt zu werden. — Dies ist wirklich eine schöne
Gegend." „Ja," sagte Herr Moehlenbrock. „Es gefällt uns
hier auch. Es wird ja manchmal ein bißchen einsam hier
draußen. Aber das läßt sich ertragen. — Denken Sie, es ist 20
schon zweimal bei uns eingebrochen worden. Aber die Polizei
hat die Diebe jedesmal gefaßt. — Übrigens haben Sie schon
Wasser? Wasser ist hier nicht immer leicht zu bekommen."
„O ja. Unsere Wasserleitung [water pipes] ist schon gelegt.
Ich hoffe, daß wir morgen angeschlossen werden." 25
   Es wurde eine Pause in der Arbeit gemacht. Herr Moehlenbrock sah, wie die Leute ihre Flasche Coca-Cola tranken. Dann
fuhr er fort: „Ich nehme an, es ist Ihnen nicht unangenehm, Ihre
Vorräte so weit aus der Stadt zu holen." „Kleinigkeit," sagte
Herr Schneider. „Unsere Vorräte werden uns immer ins Haus 30
gebracht. Ich bin nämlich Geschäftsführer des neuen Lebens-
mittelgeschäfts." — „So? Das ist ja sehr interessant. Sagen
Sie, haben Sie Familie?" — „Ja, sechs Kinder." — „Sechs
Kinder? Dann ist es wohl manchmal recht lebhaft [lively]
bei Ihnen?" — „Das mag sein. Wir sind eben alle etwas 35
musikalisch. Wie viele Kinder haben Sie?" „Nur einen
Sohn. Aber der geht schon auf die Universität." — „Das
ist ja großartig. Der sollte meinen Ältesten kennenlernen.
Der ist gerade aus Kalifornien zurückgekehrt und hat die
neueste Musik mitgebracht. Er spielt nämlich Saxophon. 40
Und das macht ihn beliebt. Es vergeht kaum eine Woche, in
der er nicht eingeladen wird." — „Ja, wir müssen ihn kennen-
lernen. — Nun, es hat mich sehr gefreut, mit Ihnen zu sprechen.
Viel Glück zum neuen Haus. Auf Wiedersehen!"

IDIOMS AND VOCABULARY

Kleinigkeit!   Nothing to it!

ab-laden, u, a, ä   unload
an-schließen, o, o   connect
an-sehen, a, e, ie   look at
der Arbeiter, –   worker
begrüßen   greet
beliebt   popular
ein bißchen   a bit, a little
das Brett, -er   board
bringen, brachte, gebracht
   bring
der Dieb, -e   thief
draußen   outside, out there
dürfen, durfte, gedurft,
   ich/er darf   be permitted,
   may
eben   just
ein-brechen, a, o, i   break
   in, burglarize
ein-laden, u, a, ä   invite
einsam   lonesome, lonely
ertragen, u, a, ä   put up
   with, bear
fällen   fell, cut down
fassen   seize, grasp, catch
fort-fahren, u, (ist) a, ä
   continue, drive on
sich freuen   be happy
die Gegend, -en   region,
   neighborhood

das Glück   luck, happiness
großartig   magnificent
herrschen   rule, prevail
kaum   hardly
kennen-lernen   get to know,
   meet
die Kleinigkeit, -en   trifle,
   little thing
leicht   easy
mögen, mochte, gemocht,
   ich/er mag   like; may
der Nachbar, -s, -n   neighbor
der Name, -ns, -n   name
die Pause, -n   pause, intermission
die Sorge, -n   care, sorrow
übrigens   by the way
verderben, a, (ist) o, i   spoil,
   perish
vergehen, verging, ist vergangen   pass (time), go
   away, go by
der Vorrat, ̈-e   supply, provision
vor-stellen   present, introduce
sich vor-stellen   introduce
   oneself; imagine

GRAMMAR

11.1 The Passive Voice When in either English or German we wish to report an action without specifying who is performing it, we use the passive voice, *e.g.*, **Unsere Vorräte werden immer ins Haus gebracht.** 'Our supplies are always brought into the house.' We could say as well: 'The delivery boy always brings our supplies into the house,' but such a statement employing the active voice would introduce a superfluous actor when we are merely interested in the action.

11.1,1 The passive voice is formed in German, as in English, by the use of the past participle plus an auxiliary. The auxiliaries, however, differ. In English, forms of *be* are used; in German, forms of **werden.** You already know the forms of **werden** (see Lesson 6.1,6), and accordingly no memorization of new forms is required. Because the present perfect and the past perfect of **werden** are made with the auxiliary **sein,** forms of **sein** are also used in the present perfect and past perfect forms in the passive. However, **ge-** is not used in the participle of **werden,** for generally the preceding participle has a **ge-**.
The following forms are given as a brief survey:

Present

ich werde gefragt   I am asked
er (sie, es) wird gefragt   he (she, it) is asked
wir (sie, Sie) werden gefragt we (they, you) are asked

Past

ich (er, sie, es) wurde gefragt I (he, she, it) was asked
wir (sie, Sie) wurden gefragt   we (they, you) were asked

Present Perfect

ich bin gefragt worden	I have been asked
er (sie, es) ist gefragt worden	he (she, it) has been asked
wir (sie, Sie) sind gefragt worden	we (they, you) have been asked

Past Perfect

ich (er, sie, es) war gefragt worden	I (he, she, it) had been asked
wir (sie, Sie) waren gefragt worden	we (they, you) had been asked

Future

ich werde gefragt werden	I shall be asked
er (sie, es) wird gefragt werden	he (she, it) will be asked
wir (sie, Sie) werden gefragt werden	we (they, you) will be asked

11.1,2 If the agency of the action is expressed in a passive construction, the agency is preceded by **von: Schon zehn Bäume waren von den Arbeitern gefällt worden.** 'Ten trees had already been felled by the workers.'

11.1,3 German sentences in the active as well as the passive may be introduced by **es.** The subject then must follow the verb. This construction resembles that of English sentences introduced by *there*: **Es vergeht kaum eine Woche, in der er nicht eingeladen wird.** 'There is hardly a week [*going by*] in which he is not invited.' **Es** is used similarly with the passive on page 119, line 26: **Es wurde eine Pause in der Arbeit gemacht.** 'There was a pause [*made*] in the work.'

In similar constructions **es** may be the sole subject: **Es ist** schon zweimal bei uns eingebrochen worden. 'There have already been two burglaries at our house.' If such constructions are introduced by a phrase or an adverb, **es** is omitted: **Im Garten des Nachbars wurde fleißig gearbeitet.** 'There was work going on diligently in the neighbor's garden.'

11.1,4 Personal pronouns may be used as indirect objects in passive constructions, *e.g.*, page 119, line 30: **... werden uns immer ins Haus gebracht.** ... 'are always brought into the house for us.' Pronouns may be used similarly in sentences in the active voice, and often they need not be included in the translation, *e.g.*, page 118, line 3: **Ich muß mir das doch einmal ansehen...** 'I'll really have to take a look at that [*for myself*].'

11.1,5 Some German writers attempt to avoid the passive. One type of substitute for the passive is the reflexive verb, *e.g.* (page 107, line 25), **Unter dem Licht fand sich ein Brief.** 'A letter was to be found under the light.' Another is the use of **man** one,' *e.g.*, **mit der man den Schnupfen heilen konnte** 'with which the common cold could be cured.'

11.1,6 The meaning of **werden** in any passage must be determined from the words following it. Accordingly, one must never interpret or translate a sentence with **werden** before one analyzes it completely. There are three common uses of **werden**:

(1) as a full verb, meaning 'become, grow, get':

    Es wird kalt. 'It is getting cold.'

(2) as auxiliary for the future:

    Er wird ihn fragen. 'He'll ask him.'

(3) as auxiliary for the passive:

    Er wird gefragt. 'He is being asked.'

11.2 Modal Auxiliaries German, like English, has a number of verbs which do little but tell the manner or mode of the subject's activity; the activity itself is usually indicated in an accompanying infinitive, *e.g.*, **Man kann nie wissen.** 'One can never know.' Because of their function, these verbs are called *auxiliaries*.

The meanings of modal auxiliaries are difficult to express by English equivalents, for they are used in a great number of idiomatic expressions. It is best, therefore, to learn entire passages in which they are used and to review lessons and vocabularies in which they have occurred.

11.2,1 In both German and English the modal auxiliaries are irregular in form. The chief irregularities are found in the present tense. The first and third person forms are alike in the singular, *e.g.*, **ich (er, sie, es) kann** 'I (he, she, it) can.' The plural forms in the present are the same as the infinitive.

dürfen be permitted, may   **können** be able, can
mögen may; like to   **müssen** must, have to
sollen ought to; be said to   **wollen** want to

ich (er, sie, es) darf	kann	mag
wir (sie, Sie) dürfen	können	mögen
ich (er, sie, es) muß	soll	will
wir (sie, Sie) müssen	sollen	wollen

The past tense is like that of weak verbs (with loss of umlaut): **ich (er, sie, es) durfte konnte mochte mußte sollte wollte**

11.2,2 When modal auxiliaries are used with an infinitive, the infinitive is not preceded by zu, *e.g.*, **Darf ich mich vorstellen?** 'May I introduce myself?' With most other verbs **zu** is used before infinitives as *to* is in English, *e.g.*, **Herr Moehlenbrock brauchte keine Sorge zu haben.** 'Mr. Moehlenbrock didn't need to have any worries.'

11.2,3 The verb **lassen** may also be used in constructions similar to those including modal auxiliaries, *e.g.*, **Das läßt sich ertragen.** 'That can be borne.' **Sie ließ ihn kommen.** 'She had him come.'

11.2,4 When modal auxiliaries are used in perfect tenses with another infinitive, the past participle of the modal is like the modal infinitive, *e.g.*, **Wir hatten uns um zwölf Uhr treffen wollen.** 'We had wanted to meet at twelve o'clock.' Contrast with this **Wir hatten kein Examen gewollt.** 'We had wanted no exam.' Because two successive infinitives are used, this pattern is often called the *double infinitive* construction.

Double infinitives must always stand at the end of their clauses. In dependent clauses the auxiliary directly precedes them.

11.3 Pronunciation of Vowels Although English does not have long vowels in contrast to short vowels, all English vowel sounds are prolonged before certain sounds. English vowels are relatively short before [p t k f s]:

sought   safe   cease

they are longer before such sounds as [b d g v z]:

sawed   save   seize

they are longer still before [m n l r] and when final:

saw   say   see

German vowels do not vary in this way. They must be pronounced as of equal length regardless of the following sounds. Since one tends to carry over one's native speech habits into a new language, one must attempt to pronounce German vowels with equal length, regardless of context. Practice:

lief	seht	gab	rot	Zug
viel	sehr	Jahr	Rohr	zur
Vieh	See	ja	roh	zu

EXERCISES

A. Change the passive forms in the following sentences successively to the present, the past, the present perfect, the past perfect, and the future.

1. Große Entdeckungen wurden von ihm gemacht.
2. Das Öl ist lange gemischt worden.
3. Der Professor war von seinen Nachbarn beobachtet worden.
4. Wird auf der anderen Seite des Berges gebaut?
5. Das schöne Mädchen ist von seiner Kusine vorgestellt worden.
6. Die Bücher wurden von der Lehrerin ins Zimmer gebracht.
7. Wie lange wurde hier gearbeitet?
8. Leider waren die Instrumente von den Studenten nicht mitgebracht worden.
9. Ich weiß nicht, was da abgeladen wird.
10. Sie wissen, daß hier Deutsch gesprochen wird.

B. Replace the words in heavy type with the words in parentheses:

1. **Die Vorräte werden** ins Haus **gebracht.** (the books ... had been sent, the letter ... was sent, the telegrams ... have been brought)

2. In der Nachbarschaft **wurde ein Haus gebaut.** (a discovery ... has been made, stones and boards ... had been unloaded, a thief ... was caught)

3. Mein Sohn **ist** von den Nachbarn **eingeladen worden.** (is being invited, was invited, had not been invited)

4. **Das Klavier war** nicht **gerettet worden.** (the window

... is being closed, the house door ... has been opened, the telephone [line] ... was laid)

5. Wissen Sie, wann **die Vorräte gebracht werden?** (the house ... has been sold, the university ... was built, the work ... has been begun)

C. Give the German for the English sentences. The word order will be exactly the same as that of the pattern sentences.

1. Ich hoffe, daß uns die Aussicht nicht verdorben wird.
   A. I believe that the letter won't be brought to us.
   B. I know that his friend hasn't been introduced to her.
   C. We hear that the picture hadn't been sent to you.

2. Ist Ihre Wasserleitung schon angeschlossen worden?
   A. Was their telephone connected yesterday?
   B. Had the trees already been cut down?
   C. Was his house broken into last night?

3. In der Nachbarschaft wurde gebaut.
   A. There is work going on in the garden.
   B. They had played the entire night. [There had been playing the entire night.]
   C. There has been talking in the next room.

4. Man hat die Diebe heute morgen gefaßt.
   A. A break was made in the work then.
   B. My cousin has been invited tonight.
   C. The supplies had already been fetched.

5. Herr Schneider wurde von seinem neuen Nachbar begrüßt.
   A. He had been visited by the owner.
   B. We have been invited by Mr. and Mrs. Schneider.
   C. I was asked by one of the workers.

D. Read and translate the following sentences. Then combine each element before a vertical line with each of the elements after it. For example, the second time you would read: Wir wollen Ihnen die Gegend zeigen. (This exercise is designed to illustrate how closely typical sentences with modal auxiliaries resemble each other syntactically.)

1. Wir wollen | eine Flasche Coca-Cola trinken.
2. Mein Bruder kann | Ihnen die Gegend zeigen.
3. Der Student sollte | von seinen Experimenten erzählen.
4. Auch der Vater muß | spät zurückkommen.
5. Sein Onkel durfte | das Land verlassen.
6. Er mag wohl | dort hinfliegen.

E. Replace the words in heavy type with the words in parentheses.

1. Herr Schneider **wollte** seinen Nachbar kennenlernen. (liked to, must, had wanted to, intends to)
2. **Sollen wir** eine Flasche Coca-Cola trinken? (would you like to, have they wanted to, had she been permitted to, hadn't they wanted to)
3. Mein Bruder **kann** Ihnen die Gegend zeigen. (wanted to, had wanted to, had been supposed to, has been obliged to)
4. Ich **kann** nicht jeden Abend in die Stadt kommen. (had wanted to, was permitted to, have liked to, had been compelled to)
5. Die Aussicht **darf nicht** verdorben werden. (wasn't supposed to, could not, had not been able to)

F. Change the tense of each of the following sentences to the present or the past, as appropriate. Then put sentences 1, 3, 4, and 8 into the present perfect and the past perfect.

1. Das Haus wurde während unsrer Ferien gebaut.
2. Kann ein Mädchen so einen Kasten machen?
3. Am Ende des Romans wird die schöne Frau gerettet.
4. Ich mag das Stück nicht.
5. Sollen wir den Studenten warnen?
6. Sie muß noch ihren Wagen versichern.
7. Heute abend sollen sie einziehen.

8. Nachts wird das Klassenzimmer geschlossen.
9. Wie lange darf er hier bleiben?

G. Questions.

1. Was hatte Herr Moehlenbrock gehört? (that a new house was being built)
2. Wo wurde das neue Haus gebaut? (behind them)
3. Warum baute man auf der anderen Seite des Berges? (the land was cheaper)
4. Wie viele Bäume waren gefällt worden? (ten)
5. Wie heißt der neue Nachbar? (Schneider)
6. Wie gefällt Herrn Schneider die Gegend? (fine)
7. Wann bekommt er Wasser? (the next day)
8. Muß Herr Schneider seine Vorräte selbst aus der Stadt holen? (no)
9. Wen wollen die Schneiders kennenlernen? (young Moehlenbrock)
10. Warum soll der Sohn so beliebt sein? (he plays the latest music)

H. Translate in writing:

1. First the boards were unloaded, and then a pause was made by the workmen.
2. "Nothing to it!" he said. "The box with the supplies has been brought into the kitchen."
3. In this region one can live outdoors.
4. Whoever wants to buy land can do it easily and cheaply.
5. You can hardly imagine how many trees have already been felled.
6. We must get to know our new neighbor.
7. Up to now the thieves have always been caught.
8. You'll be able to buy the supplies this afternoon if you want to.
9. I hope I've been understood by all.
10. During the intermission he is supposed to go and get the car.

I. Free conversation:

A new house is being built in front of the Pfeiffers' house. Two large trees have already been felled. Mrs. Pfeiffer hopes that their view of the city won't be spoiled. Then she gets to know the neighbors when they come to look at the place. The new neighbor's wife is worried about thieves. Mrs. Pfeiffer reassures her and discusses the advantages of the area. Supplies are brought out from the grocery store. The place is very quiet and one can sleep well. None of the neighbors have musical children. The two women become very good friends.

BRIEF CONVERSATION

Verändert und glücklich

FRITZ: Haben Sie Klaus Moehlenbrock schon zu sehen bekommen?

WALTER: Nein, warum?

FRITZ: O, Sie müssen mit ihm sprechen. Er ist ganz verändert [changed]. Ich kann nicht verstehen, was ihm geschehen ist.

WALTER: Nun, was mag ihm geschehen sein? Ich will ihn später fragen. Wir hatten uns um zwölf Uhr treffen wollen.

FRITZ: Ja, gestern abend ist er noch gesehen worden, wie er langsam und traurig nach Hause ging.

WALTER: Und heute?

FRITZ: Es ist nicht zu glauben, wie froh er ist. Heute morgen kommt er zur Universität, singend und pfeifend, und wird von allen freundlich begrüßt. Und die Fenster, die nicht geöffnet [opened] werden dürfen — wegen der Klima-Anlage [air conditioning] —, die macht er weit auf [open up].

WALTER: Man sagt, er soll einen Brief von seiner Freundin bekommen haben.

FRITZ: Vielleicht. Es läßt sich nicht beschreiben [describe], wie glücklich er ist.

LESSON 12

Verdorbener Appetit

SUBJUNCTIVE I

USES OF THE SUBJUNCTIVE I

PRONUNCIATION

TEXT

in the middle of

Es war mitten im Sommer. Die „Sommerschule" hatte
längst angefangen. Das Thermometer stand schon seit vierzehn Tagen auf hundert. Aber trotz der Hitze wurde fleißig
gearbeitet. Keine Wolke stand am Himmel, und kein Mensch
fragte, ob es abends vielleicht regnen werde.   5
Professor Niebuhr saß heute abend in der „Union." Er
hoffte, daß es hier etwas kühler sein werde, als in seiner
Wohnung. Denn er hatte noch keine Klima-Anlage [air
conditioning]. Während er aß, dachte er nach, worüber er

10 morgen in der Klasse sprechen wolle. Drüben am Fenster
saßen Fritz Möller und Inge Pfeiffer. Sie lasen zusammen das
Werk eines deutschen Dichters. Sie lasen, daß der Mensch
seine Gedanken auf die Wirklichkeit richten solle. Dann
werde er seine Aufgabe in der Welt schon [surely] erfüllen.

15 Klaus und Heinrich gingen durch den Raum. Sie grüßten
Professor Niebuhr und setzten sich an den nächsten Tisch.
Klaus lachte und wollte wissen, ob er das Examen bestanden
habe. Professor Niebuhr antwortete: „Ja, Sie haben einmal
recht tüchtig gearbeitet. Wenn Sie so fortfahren, bekommen

20 Sie noch ein B." Klaus und Heinrich sprachen leise mit
einander. Heinrich hatte heute nämlich einen Brief von seiner
Kusine erhalten, und er wollte seinem Freunde davon erzählen.
„Schön," sagte Klaus. „Ich habe mich immer schon gefragt,
warum Fräulein Sanders so lange stumm geblieben ist." Und

25 dann berichtete Heinrich, wie Eleanor viel länger in Los
Angeles geblieben sei, als sie zuerst geplant habe. Es gefalle
ihr dort sehr, und sie habe eine Stellung als Sekretärin gefunden.
Ihr Vater habe sein Haus im Osten verkauft und sei Bankdirektor in Houston geworden.

30 „Das weiß ich schon," unterbrach ihn Klaus. Aber Heinrich
fuhr fort: „Sie wissen aber nicht, was noch kommt." Und
dann erzählte er, daß Eleanor einen jungen Mann getroffen
habe, der ein großer Künstler zu werden verspreche. Sie
habe sich sehr in ihn verliebt und werde ihn gewiß noch heiraten.

35 Das war zuviel für Klaus. Er blickte finster vor sich hin, denn
sein Appetit war ihm verdorben.

Professor Niebuhr stand jetzt bei Fritz Möller und sagte:
„Was lesen Sie denn, wenn ich fragen darf?" Inge zeigte
auf eine Seite im Buch und Niebuhr las:

40   Er stehe fest [firm] und sehe hier sich um:
Dem Tüchtigen ist diese Welt nicht stumm!
„Ah, *Faust!*" sagte Professor Niebuhr. „Sie haben wirklich
nette Fortschritte [progress] gemacht!"

IDIOMS AND VOCABULARY

vor sich hin blicken stare

an-fangen, i, a, ä start, begin

berichten report

bestehen, bestand, bestanden pass; consist, exist

blicken look

davon about it

der Dichter, – poet

einander each other, one another

erfüllen fulfill, complete

erhalten, ie, a, ä = bekommen get, receive

finster = dunkel gloomy, dark

der Gedanke, -ns, -n thought, idea

heiraten marry

der Himmel, – heaven(s)

hin to that place

der Künstler, – artist

längst long ago

leise soft, quiet; in a low voice

nach-denken, dachte nach, nachgedacht think over, consider

regnen rain

richten (an, auf) direct

die Schule, -n school

stumm = schweigend silent, mute

tüchtig capable, able, excellent

unterbrechen, a, o, i interrupt

versprechen, a, o, i promise

das Werk, -e work [*esp. of art or literature*]

die Wirklichkeit reality

die Wolke, -n cloud

zuerst at first

zuviel, zu viel too much

GRAMMAR

12.1 Subjunctive I

12.1,1 When we report a statement indirectly we modify the verb in some way and, in writing, we do not use quotation marks. We could, of course, repeat the statement directly, *e.g.*, "I told him, 'Go tomorrow'." But we find it more natural to employ indirect quotation, *e.g.*, "I told him that he should go tomorrow." In English, many of these indirect quotations were formerly expressed without a verb like *should*: and indeed we still say, for example, "I suggested that he go tomorrow." Here the verb in the third person singular is just like that for the first person singular—not *goes* but *go*. The equivalent form in German is called the *subjunctive*.

12.1,2 If subjunctive forms are built on the present indicative, they are referred to as *subjunctive I* forms, *e.g.*, page 132, line 14, **werde**; line 10, **wolle**; line 13, **solle**. The subjunctive I differs from the indicative only in the third person singular; here, as for **ich, -e** is added to the stem; after **wir, sie, Sie** the ending is **-en.** The stem vowel of strong verbs, *e.g.*, **sprechen, sehen, fahren,** never is modified.

Present Subjunctive I

ich, er, sie, es habe	werde	spreche
wir, sie, Sie haben	werden	sprechen
ich, er, sie, es sehe	wolle	sei
wir, sie, Sie sehen	wollen	seien

The only irregular form in the present subjunctive I is the singular of **sein.**

12.1,3 The past subjunctive I corresponds to the present perfect indicative. The auxiliary is put in the subjunctive.

Past Subjunctive I

| ich, er, sie, es habe gesehen | sei geblieben |
| wir, sie, Sie   haben gesehen | seien geblieben |

12.1,4 The future subjunctive I corresponds to the future indicative, with the auxiliary in the subjunctive.

Future Subjunctive I

ich, er, sie, es werde sehen
wir, sie, Sie   werden sehen

12.1,5 In translating subjunctive I forms into English we generally use modal auxiliaries past or past perfect forms, for patterns like "I suggested that he *go* tomorrow" are infrequent. More frequent are patterns like those used in the following translations:

> **Klaus lachte und wollte wissen, ob er das Examen bestanden habe.** 'Klaus laughed and wanted to know whether he *had* passed the exam.'

> **Kein Mensch fragte, ob es abends vielleicht regnen werde.** 'No one asked whether it *would* perhaps rain in the evening.'

12.2 Uses of the Subjunctive I

12.2,1 The subjunctive I is generally used to signal the presence (or continuation) of an indirect quotation. On page 132, line 26, the forms **sei** and **habe** are to be expected after **berichtete** 'reported.' But in the following sentences the subjunctive I forms indicate that the quotation is continuing: **gefalle** rather than the indicative **gefällt**; **habe** rather the indicative **hat**; **sei** rather than **ist**. This use of the subjunctive is a very effective signaling device.

12.2,2 A further use of the subjunctive I is found in exhortations and instructions. **Er stehe fest!** 'Let him stand firm.' Such instructions are especially common in technical writing: **Man gebrauche eine Metallplatte.** 'One should use a metal plate.' In the first person plural the initial position of the verb helps one to identify this construction, *e.g.*, **Nehmen wir an** 'Let us assume.'

12.3 Pronunciation The combination **th** is used to spell [t] in words taken over from Greek and in some proper names: **Thermometer, Theorie, Goethe.**

The combination **ph** is used to spell [f] in words taken over from Greek: **Photograph, Philipp, Prophet.**

The umlaut vowels **ö** and **ü** may be spelled **oe** and **ue**, especially in names. The dots over the **o** and **u** are actually an abbreviated form of **e**: **Moehlenbrock, Goethe, Mueller.**

EXERCISES

A. Substitute appropriate subjunctive forms for the verbs given in brackets. The resulting statements will be indirect quotations.

1. Die Familie Moehlenbrock [haben] nur einen Sohn, aber der [gehen] schon auf die Universität.
2. Er dachte nach, worüber er morgen sprechen [können, sollen, müssen].
3. Die Kinder [sein] alle etwas musikalisch.
4. Der Student [haben] jetzt keine Zeit, denn er [müssen] gleich ins Laboratorium gehen.
5. Es [stehen] eine Frau auf der Straße und [warten] auf den Omnibus.
6. In der Nachbarschaft [werden] ein Haus gebaut.
7. Seine Schwester [sein] schon vor mehr als vier Wochen in Los Angeles angekommen.
8. Sein Bruder [verstehen] ihn nicht.
9. Er hoffte, daß es ihr gut [gehen].
10. Der Student [haben] einmal recht tüchtig gearbeitet.

B. Give the German for the English sentences. The word order will be exactly the same as that of the pattern sentences.

1. Kein Mensch fragte, ob es vielleicht regnen werde.
   A. No one asked whether she would begin.

B. Everyone was asking whether it would perhaps continue.

C. Her brother asked whether she would perhaps return.

2. Er hoffte, daß es hier etwas kühler sein werde.
   A. She hoped that it would be somewhat more interesting there.
   B. They hoped that he would fall asleep there somewhat more quickly.
   C. He hoped that she would fly there somewhat earlier.

3. Dann werde er seine Aufgabe schon erfüllen.
   A. Then he would surely interrupt his work.
   B. Now she would surely receive her money.
   C. Then he would surely insure his house.

4. Klaus wollte wissen, ob er das Examen bestanden habe.
   A. He wanted to know whether she had found a position.
   B. They wanted to know whether he had made the discovery.
   C. She wanted to know whether he had received the letter.

5. Ihr Vater habe sein Haus im Osten verkauft.
   A. His brother had begun his vacation in the South.
   B. Her family had built a house in the country.
   C. Her sister had found her pencil in the car.

6. Es gefalle ihr dort sehr.
   A. Klaus visits her but rarely.
   B. He sees her there often.
   C. They don't like it there.

C. Read the text of Lesson 3. Then, making the necessary changes to indicate continuity, put the conversation into indirect discourse:

Klaus Moehlenbrock traf Heinrich Seemann beim Mittagessen und fragte ihn, ob er sich zu ihm setzen dürfe. Heinrich nickte und sagte, daß er auch gerne mit ihm sprechen wolle. Klaus sagte, das freue ihn sehr, und fragte, ...

D. Making appropriate modifications in the text, proceed similarly with Lesson 4.

E. Questions.

1. Wie heiß war es während der „Sommerschule"? (thermometer at 100)
2. Warum saß Professor Niebuhr in der „Union"? (it was cool there)
3. Worüber dachte er nach? (about what he would say in class)
4. Wen sah er am Fenster? (Fritz and Inge)
5. Was lasen sie? (the work of a German poet)
6. Was fragte Klaus? (whether he had passed the exam)
7. Was antwortete der Professor? (that Klaus had worked diligently)
8. Was berichtete Heinrich? (that Eleanor had stayed in Los Angeles)
9. Was berichtete er über ihre Arbeit? (she was working as a secretary)
10. Wen hatte sie dort getroffen? (a young artist)

F. Translate in writing:

1. The professor wanted to know which poet Fritz and Inge were reading.
2. Heinrich told his friend that he had received a letter from his cousin.
3. She said she had not written until now because she had been working.
4. Let him take enough money to buy the house.
5. He said he wanted to travel there.
6. They promised each other to remain silent until she had passed the exam.

7. We heard that Professor Lueders was an able man and that he had been famous for years.
8. We read in the newspaper that the company was buying the land by the river.
9. He said she had written about it in her letter.
10. He reported that she had found a position as a teacher.

G. Free conversation.

Report a conversation on any subject you choose, *e.g.*, one between two students who have heard from an old friend; one between a student and a professor about the results of an examination; one describing the heat during summer school and efforts people are making to escape it.

BRIEF CONVERSATION

Eine Stellung im Buchladen

INGE: Wo ist eigentlich Hans Fischer? Wir bekommen ihn gar nicht mehr zu sehen.

FRITZ: Ich habe ihn vorgestern gefragt, ob er zu Hause sein werde und mit uns an der Mathematik arbeiten wolle.

INGE: Und was hat er dazu gesagt?

FRITZ: Das sei leider nicht möglich. Er habe keine Zeit und außerdem wisse er darüber nicht genug.

INGE: Ist das nicht etwas unfreundlich?

FRITZ: Ja, aber es tue ihm leid. Es habe ihm auch leid getan, als er das letzte Mal nicht mit uns habe gehen können. Aber er müsse sich etwas Geld verdienen. Er habe eine Stellung im Buchladen angenommen und nehme seine Bücher jeden Tag mit ins Geschäft.

INGE: Warum muß er das?

FRITZ: Ich glaube, ein Onkel von ihm ist gestorben, der ihm sonst immer geholfen hat. Aber er mag nicht davon sprechen.

LESSON 13

Eine kurze Fahrt

SUBJUNCTIVE II

USES OF THE SUBJUNCTIVE II

PRONUNCIATION

TEXT

Die Familie Schneider war schon Anfang August in ihr
neues Haus eingezogen. Kein Mensch in der Nachbarschaft
hatte geglaubt, daß ein Haus so schnell erbaut werden könnte.
Herr Schneider hätte sich nichts Besseres wünschen können.
5 Die Hitze der letzten Wochen war verschwunden, ein kühler
Regen war gefallen und hatte die ganze Gegend in ein angenehmes Grün verwandelt. Die Preise waren hinunter gegangen
und die Gehälter hinauf — wer hätte vom lieben Gott mehr
verlangen wollen?

Die Schneiders fühlten sich sehr wohl in ihrer neuen Woh- 10
nung. Die Moehlenbrocks hatten sich gut an ihre neuen
Nachbarn gewöhnt. Und zwischen Klaus und Karl hatte sich
eine nette Freundschaft entwickelt. Es schien Klaus, daß
niemand so gut Saxophon spielen könnte, wie Karl Schneider.
Und Karl spielte, als ob er mit dem Instrument geboren 15
wäre.

Am Dienstag, dem vierten August, stand Klaus im „Co-op"
und kaufte sich zehn Rollen Film. Die Sommerschule würde
in ein paar Tagen aufhören, und wenn die Ferien anfingen, wollte
er bereit sein. Am nächsten Ladentisch stand Elisabeth 20
Schneider und sah sich einige Bücher an. Klaus beobachtete
sie einen Augenblick. Er hatte sie vor ein paar Tagen kennengelernt. Wenn alle Mädchen so schön aussähen wie Elisabeth,
dann wäre das Leben ein Traum.

„Ich möchte gerne diese zehn Rollen haben," sagte Klaus 25
zum Mann, der ihn bediente [was waiting on]. „Würden Sie
so gut sein und eine Rolle in den Apparat einsetzen?" „Gerne.
Sonst noch etwas?" „Nein, danke," sagte Klaus. „Das wäre
alles." Und er trat zu Elisabeth hinüber, als sie von den
Büchern aufblickte. 30

„Freuen Sie sich auch auf die Ferien?" fragte er sie. „Ja,"
sagte Elisabeth. „Wenn nur erst das Examen vorbei wäre!
Es sollte keine Examen geben!"

„Das meine ich auch," sagte Klaus. „Aber leider läßt sich
daran nichts ändern. — Fahren Sie bald nach Hause?" „Ja, 35
wenn Karl seinen Wagen hier hätte, könnte ich gleich fahren.
Aber der Wagen muß erst geschmiert [greased] werden. Darum
kann ich erst in einer Stunde fahren."

„Wie wäre es, wenn Sie mit mir führen? Ich rufe Karl in
der Garage an. Wenn es ihm recht ist, bringe ich Sie nach 40
Hause. Dann braucht er nicht erst hierher zu fahren."

Fünf Minuten später fuhren Klaus und Elisabeth durch die
grüne Gegend. „Wenn ich früher gewußt hätte, daß Sie frei
sind," sagte Klaus, „dann hätte ich Sie schon vor einer Stunde
gebeten, mit mir zu fahren." „Aber vor einer Stunde hätten 45

Sie mich noch nicht im Laden getroffen," antwortete Elisabeth lachend.

Die Fahrt ging am Flusse entlang, und während der Fahrt erzählten sie sich, was sie in Zukunft tun wollten. „Wenn es
50 möglich wäre, möchte ich nach Deutschland reisen," sagte Elisabeth, „aber allein und ohne die jüngeren Geschwister [brothers and sisters]." Und er?

Nun, Klaus würde nach Kalifornien gehen. Er würde sich nach einer Stellung umsehen und versuchen, viel Geld zu
55 verdienen. „Hätte mein Onkel nicht eine einflußreiche [influential] Stellung bei der Flugzeugindustrie [airplane industry], so würde ich vielleicht Schwierigkeiten haben."

„Und wann würden Sie Ihren Militärdienst [military service] beginnen?" fragte Elisabeth.

60 „Ach ja! Daran hätte ich denken sollen," antwortete Klaus und wurde etwas schweigsam [silent].

Als Elisabeth vor ihrem Hause aus dem Wagen stieg, war Karl schon angekommen. „Vielleicht hätte ich doch mit ihm fahren sollen," sagte sie lachend. „Aber es war doch sehr
65 nett, daß Sie mich nach Hause gebracht haben. Auf Wiedersehen!"

IDIOMS AND VOCABULARY

der liebe Gott the good Lord
sich wohl fühlen feel well
sonst noch etwas? anything else?

ach oh, alas
als ob as if
ändern change, alter
der Anfang, ̈-e start, beginning
an-rufen, ie, u call up
auf-hören cease, stop
der Augenblick, -e moment

aus-sehen, a, e, ie appear, look
beginnen, a, o = an-fangen begin, start
bereit ready, prepared
bitten, a, e ask (a favor)
bringen, brachte, gebracht bring

darum for that reason
(das) Deutschland Germany
der Dienstag, -e Tuesday
doch after all, nevertheless
ein-setzen set in, put in, insert
erst only, not until; (at) first
die Fahrt, -en trip, ride
sich freuen auf [acc.] look forward to
fühlen [trans.] feel
geboren born
das Gehalt, ̈-er salary
sich gewöhnen an [acc.] get used to
der Gott, ̈-er God
hierher to this place, here
hinauf upward
hinüber across, over

das Leben life
letzt last
möglich possible
niemand nobody
der Preis, -e price
sonst else, otherwise
steigen, ie, (ist) ie rise, climb
der Traum, ̈-e dream
treten, a, (ist) e, tritt step, walk
sich um-sehen, a, e, ie (nach) look around (for)
verdienen earn, deserve
verlangen demand, ask for
verschwinden, a, (ist) u disappear
versuchen try
verwandeln change
der vierte fourth
die Zukunft future

GRAMMAR

13.1 Subjunctive II The subjunctive II is built on past indicative forms. If the verb whose subjunctive form is to be used is strong or is a modal auxiliary, its stem vowel, a, o or u is usually modified to ä, ö or ü. The ending -e is added in the ich, er, sie, es forms; -en in the wir, sie, Sie forms. (Note that sollen and wollen do not take an umlaut.)

13.1,1 Examples of common forms of the present subjunctive II are:

	sein	haben	werden	sehen
ich, er, sie, es	wäre	hätte	würde	sähe
wir, sie, Sie	wären	hätten	würden	sähen

	fahren	kaufen	bringen	
ich, er, sie, es	führe	kaufte	brächte	
wir, sie, Sie	führen	kauften	brächten	

	dürfen	können	mögen	müssen
ich, er, sie, es	dürfte	könnte	möchte	müßte
wir, sie, Sie	dürften	könnten	möchten	müßten
	sollen	wissen	denken	
ich, er, sie, es	sollte	wüßte	dächte	
wir, sie, Sie	sollten	wüßten	dächten	

13,1,2 The past subjunctive II corresponds to the indicative past perfect. The auxiliary is put in the subjunctive.

ich, er, sie, es hätte gesehen   wäre geblieben
wir, sie, Sie   hätten gesehen   wären geblieben

13.1,3 The future subjunctive II is made with the infinitive and **würde(n)**. In use, **würde(n)** resembles English *would*.

Die Sommerschule würde aufhören. 'The summer school would end.'
Wann würden Sie beginnen? 'When would you begin?'

13.1,4 The future perfect subjunctive II is relatively frequent. As in English, however, the future perfect indicative is relatively infrequent in occurrence; inasmuch as it is constructed like the future, it is easy to recognize and to construct:

ich werde sehen 'I will see';   **ich werde gesehen haben** 'I will have seen.'

In use the future perfect subjunctive II resembles English "would have" constructions:

Wenn er angerufen hätte, würde ich sie besucht haben. 'If he had phoned, I would have visited them.'
Wenn er angerufen hätte, würde ich geblieben sein. 'If he had phoned, I would have stayed.'

13,2 Uses of the Subjunctive II Subjunctive II forms indicate the speaker's uncertainty or lack of positive stand. With this underlying meaning they are used in a variety of constructions:

(1) To indicate indefiniteness or imprecision. Page 141, line 18, **Die Sommerschule würde in ein paar Tagen aufhören.** 'Summer school would end in a few days.'

(2) To indicate politeness. As in English, indefiniteness is often associated with politeness. Instead of saying: "I want these ten rolls [of film]," we commonly use a more gentle request, such as: "I'd like to have these ten rolls." The equivalent German form is illustrated on page 141, line 25, **Ich möchte gerne....** On page 141, line 28, **Das wäre alles,** the answer corresponds to the English "That will be all," in contrast to "That's all."

(3) In wishes that are not likely to be realized. Page 141, line 32: **Wenn nur das Examen vorbei wäre!** 'If only the examination were past.' In such wishes **nur** is almost always used.

(4) In conditions that are not likely to be realized. Page 141, line 36: **Wenn Karl seinen Wagen hier hätte, könnte ich gleich fahren.** 'If Karl had his car here, I could go at once.' (In this sentence the concluding clause begins with the verb, for the **wenn**-clause is treated as the first element from the point of view of word order. If **wenn** is omitted, the auxiliary is put in first place and the main clause is introduced by **so** or **denn.**) Page 142, line 55: **Hätte mein Onkel nicht die Stellung, so würde ich Schwierigkeiten haben.** 'If my uncle didn't have the position, I would have difficulties.'

(5) After **als ob** 'as if.' Page 141, line 15: **Karl spielte, als ob er mit dem Instrument geboren wäre.** 'Karl played as if he had been born with the instrument.'

(6) In indirect quotations. Subjunctive II forms are often used in indirect quotations when the subjunctive I forms would be the same as the indicative. Page 142, line 49: **Sie erzählten sich, was sie in Zukunft tun wollten.** 'They told each other what they wanted to do in the future.'

13.3 Pronunciation Both English and German have many words containing groups of two or more consonants, as in **Platz, Gelds,** *plots, kilts.* In German the consonants must be pronounced distinctly so that each of them can be heard. Practice:

sonst	**Zukunft**	**denkt**	**Künstler**
Werks	**Parks**	**nachts**	**Hefts**
Zweig	**schreiben**	**zwölf**	**springen**
schwarz	**Straße**	**sprechen**	**zwei**

Consonants which occur at the boundaries of compounds must also be distinctly pronounced, and a break must be made between components. Hyphens indicate the position of boundaries in the following:

Mäd-chen ein-schlafen sieb-zehn Wirk-lich-keit zurück-kehren Krank-heit ab-kühlen Deutsch-stunde

It is particularly important to divide consonant groups with **s** correctly, *e.g.,* **Diens-tag.** Such **s**-sounds are to be pronounced with the preceding material, as is **ß,** *e.g.,* **groß-artig.** Note also:

Lebens-mittel-geschäft Geschäfts-führer

EXERCISES

Rephrase the German sentences according to the forms suggested in English:

A. Present tense

1. Er hat Zeit.
   a. if he had ...

  B. if they had ...
  C. as if they had ...
  D. had we ...

2. Es ist kühl.
  A. if it were ...
  B. as if it were ...
  C. it would be ...
  D. they would be ...

3. Sie sind so gut.
  A. if you were ...
  B. as if you were ...
  C. would you be ...
  D. you would be ...

4. Karl fährt nach Hause.
  A. if he drove ...
  B. as if he drove ...
  C. would he drive ...
  D. he would drive ...

5. Der Regen hört auf.
  A. if it stopped
  B. as if it stopped
  C. it would stop

6. Er geht am Fluß entlang.
  A. if he went ...
  B. as if he went ...
  C. he would go ...
  D. would he go ...

B. Past tense. Follow the directions for exercise A.

1. Er hatte kein Geld.
  A. if he had had ...
  B. as if he had had ...
  C. he would have had ...

Lesson 13

2. Klaus sah seine Freundin.
   A. if he had seen ...
   B. as if he had seen ...
   C. had he seen ...
   D. he would have seen ...

3. Sie hatte ihn gebeten.
   A. if she had asked ...,
   B. had she asked ...
   C. she would have asked ...
   D. as if she had asked ...

4. Daran habe ich nicht gedacht.
   A. if I had thought ...
   B. had I thought ...
   C. I would have thought ...
   D. as if I had thought ...

5. Das Haus war verkauft worden.
   A. if it had been sold ...
   B. had it been sold ...
   C. it would have been sold ...
   D. as if it had been sold ...

C. Give the German for the English sentences, following the patterns of the German examples.

1. Wenn das Examen nur vorbei wäre!
   A. If only my friend were here!
   B. If he could only see her!
   C. If only it were possible!
   D. If we had only a little more money!

2. Das hätte ich tun sollen!
   A. He should have known that.
   B. We should have seen her.
   C. They should have bought it.
   D. They shouldn't have done that.

3. Wenn ich das gewußt hätte, wäre ich früher nach Hause gekommen.
   A. If we had seen that, we would have turned around earlier.
   B. If he had met her, he would have driven her home.
   C. If all girls looked as pretty as she, life would be a dream.
   D. If she had not written that letter, he would have been much happier.

4. Hätte er mir das früher gesagt, so würde ich das Geld nicht verloren haben.
   A. If they had written a letter, we would not have sold the house.
   B. If she had sent a picture, he would not have forgotten her.
   C. Had the house not been built, the view would not have been spoiled.

D. Rewrite the following sentences, substituting appropriate subjunctive II forms for the verbs given in brackets. Then translate the new sentences.

1. [Werden] Sie so gut sein und die Tür schließen?
2. Wenn nur diese Woche vorbei [sein]!
3. Wenn Karl seinen Wagen hier [haben], [können] wir gleich anfangen.
4. Wie [sein] es, wenn Sie mit mir [gehen]?
5. Ich [haben] nie geglaubt, daß so etwas geschehen [können].
6. Wir [haben] uns nichts Besseres wünschen können.
7. Wenn wir Ferien [haben], [können] wir so lange schlafen, wie wir [wollen].
8. Ich [haben] Ihre Arbeit gelesen, wenn Sie sie mir früher gebracht [haben].
9. Daran [haben] wir denken sollen.
10. [Sollen] es möglich sein, daß er das noch nicht gehört hat?
11. Vor zwei Stunden [haben] Sie uns noch in Neuyork getroffen.

E. Connect and rewrite the following sentences to express conditions not likely to be realized. Follow the patterns given in 1A—1C below.

1. Er hat viel Geld. Er kauft sich ein neues Haus.
   A. Wenn er viel Geld hätte, würde er sich ein neues Haus kaufen.
   B. Hätte er viel Geld, so würde er sich ein neues Haus kaufen.
   C. Er würde sich ein neues Haus kaufen, wenn er viel Geld hätte.

2. Er hat einen neuen Wagen. Er wird nach Los Angeles fahren.
3. Ich bin früher gereist. Ich habe nicht viele Menschen kennen gelernt.
4. Hat sein Vater eine einflußreiche Stellung? Er wird keine Schwierigkeiten haben.
5. Er fliegt zu ihr und besucht sie. Sie wird ihn auslachen.
6. Hatte Heinrich auf das Thermometer gesehen? Er ist nicht krank geworden.
7. Die Schneiders haben nicht sechs Kinder? Dann ist es bei ihnen nicht so lebhaft.
8. Der Mensch wird seine Aufgabe in der Welt schon erfüllen. Er wird seine Gedanken auf die Wirklichkeit richten.
9. Komme ich eine halbe Stunde zu spät nach Neuyork? Dann muß ich mehr als sechs Stunden auf den nächsten Zug warten.

F. Questions.

1. Wann zogen die Schneiders in ihr neues Haus ein? (beginning of August)
2. Was hatten die Nachbarn beobachtet? (the house had been built quickly)
3. Warum war die Gegend verwandelt? (there had been rain)

4. Warum kaufte sich Karl zehn Rollen Film? (summer school was to be over soon)
5. Wer war noch im Co-op? (Elisabeth)
6. Was wünschte sie? (that exams were over)
7. Mit wem wollte sie nach Hause fahren? (with Karl, if his car had been greased)
8. Wohin wollte Elisabeth gerne reisen? (to Germany)
9. Was wollte Klaus jetzt tun? (go to California)
10. Woran hätte er denken sollen? (of his military service)

G. Translate in writing.

1. We would soon begin to build, if only the future were not so uncertain.
2. He said he would call his friend on Tuesday after he had moved into the new apartment.
3. I would look forward to the trip if I felt well.
4. He thought if the salaries rose the prices would soon go up.
5. He said they had got used to the difficulties of the task.
6. If only I had a picture of her.
7. What would happen if thieves broke in?
8. Walter said that he would always think of the moment when the ride had stopped.
9. I'd like to visit either Mexico or Europe **(Europa)**, if I had enough money.
10. What would have happened if the neighbors had come in the afternoon?

H. Free conversation.

Discuss what you will do after school closes, proposing various alternatives — such as what you would do if you had money enough for a trip to Europe; if someone offered you a job at a cool lake; if you decided to stay through the summer and to work on your physics and chemistry.

BRIEF CONVERSATION

Deutsch in zehn leichten Aufgaben

WALTER KRENN *meets* HANS FISCHER *in the bookstore.*

HANS: Was wünschen Sie bitte?

WALTER: Hätten Sie vielleicht ein Buch, woraus ich schnell Deutsch lernen könnte?

HANS: Ja, gewiß. Kaufen Sie doch „Deutsch in zehn leichten Aufgaben"!

WALTER: „Deutsch in zehn leichten Aufgaben"? Das hätte ich gestern wissen sollen!

HANS: Wieso [why]?

WALTER: Ja, sehen Sie: wenn ich dies Buch gestern gefunden hätte, so würde ich heute morgen das Examen bestanden haben.

HANS: O, es ist nie zu spät. Möchten Sie das Buch haben?

WALTER: Ja gewiß. Würden Sie so freundlich sein und die Rechnung an meinen Vater schicken? —
„In zehn leichten Aufgaben...!" Hätte ich das nur gestern gewußt!

HANS: Was ist denn los, Herr Krenn? Sie tun ja, als ob alles verloren wäre.

LESSON 14

Lebhafter Betrieb

REVIEW OF NOUNS AND ADJECTIVES

NOUN DERIVATION

TEXT*

Endlich war die Sommerschule vorüber. Fritz Möller und Inge
Pfeiffer fuhren in den Park, um Tennis zu spielen. „ Wie wär's, "
hatte Inge gesagt, „ wenn wir einmal die Bücher vergäßen und uns an
die Wirklichkeit erinnerten ? " Denn sie hatten ihre Examen ohne
Schwierigkeiten bestanden. Es war wirklich eine Kleinigkeit für sie 5
gewesen. Und so hatten sie alle Bücher, Papiere, Hefte, Wörterbücher
und Klassenarbeiten in die Ecke geworfen, ihre Tennisschläger
[tennis rackets] geholt und waren in den Park gefahren.

* See Appendix 1.1.

Im Park herrschte lebhafter Betrieb. Es schien, als ob die ganze
10 Nachbarschaft zusammengekommen wäre. Studenten und Studen=
tinnen, Lehrer und Lehrerinnen, Männer und Frauen — alle schienen
die Wissenschaft vergessen zu haben, um sich hier in Freundschaft und
froher Gesellschaft von den Sorgen der Arbeit zu erholen. (Und nicht
nur die Menschen, sondern auch die Hunde.)

15 Als sie zu den Tennisplätzen kamen, machte Fritz Möller eine Ent=
deckung. Er sah, wie Klaus Moehlenbrock und seine Freundin,
Elisabeth Schneider, auf einer Bank unter den Bäumen saßen. Sie
hatten gerade ein aufregendes [exciting] Spiel hinter sich und ruhten
sich einen Augenblick aus. Aber sie saßen nicht da und lasen die
20 Zeitung. Nein, sie hielten sich die Hände und blickten sich in die Augen.

Als die beiden an ihnen vorbeigingen, grüßte Elisabeth und rief:
„ Es ist schön, daß ich Sie sehe. Es wäre nett, wenn Sie alle am
nächsten Mittwoch zu uns kämen. Wir haben eine kleine Abend=
gesellschaft zu Hause." Fritz und Inge dankten freundlich und
25 antworteten, daß sie gerne kommen würden. — „ Das ist herrlich, "
sagte Elisabeth. „Wissen Sie, mein Bruder hat ein Musikstück kom=
poniert, und er will uns etwas daraus vorspielen. Seine Verlobte
[fiancée] wird auch hier sein, und ich möchte, daß Sie sie kennenlernen."

Fritz und Inge spielten Tennis, bis sie müde wurden. Bei einbre=
30 chender Dunkelheit fingen die Leute an, ihr Abendessen vorzubereiten.
Bald brannten viele Feuer im Park, an den Wegen entlang gingen die
Lichter an und die Melodien froher Lieder klangen durch den Park.

Klaus und Elisabeth saßen noch immer am gleichen Platz, sprachen
leise mit einander und merkten nicht, wie dunkle Wolken am Himmel
35 aufzogen und die Sterne verschwanden. Sie saßen still zusammen,
blickten in die Dunkelheit und hatten frohe Gefühle im Herzen.

Und plötzlich brach der Sturm los. Der Wind fuhr durch die
Bäume und warf Zweige und Blätter auf die Erde. Väter riefen ihre
Kinder, Mütter packten die Vorräte zusammen, und Söhne löschten
40 [put out] die Feuer. Schwere Regentropfen begannen zu fallen, und
alle Menschen rannten zu ihren Autos.

Nur Klaus und Elisabeth eilten nicht. Arm in Arm gingen sie
zu ihrem Wagen zurück, und als der Regen durch die Gegend fegte
[swept], wußten sie, daß sie zu einander gehörten.

Endlich war die Sommerschule vorüber. Fritz Möller und
Inge Pfeiffer fuhren in den Park, um Tennis zu spielen. „Wie
wär's," hatte Inge gesagt, „wenn wir einmal die Bücher vergäßen und uns an die Wirklichkeit erinnerten?" Denn sie
hatten ihre Examen ohne Schwierigkeiten bestanden. Es war 5
wirklich eine Kleinigkeit für sie gewesen. Und so hatten sie
alle Bücher, Papiere, Hefte, Wörterbücher und Klassenarbeiten
in die Ecke geworfen, ihre Tennisschläger [tennis rackets]
geholt und waren in den Park gefahren.
  Im Park herrschte lebhafter Betrieb. Es schien, als ob die 10
ganze Nachbarschaft zusammengekommen wäre. Studenten
und Studentinnen, Lehrer und Lehrerinnen, Männer und
Frauen — alle schienen die Wissenschaft vergessen zu haben, um
sich hier in Freundschaft und froher Gesellschaft von den
Sorgen der Arbeit zu erholen. (Und nicht nur die Menschen, 15
sondern auch die Hunde.)
  Als sie zu den Tennisplätzen kamen, machte Fritz
Möller eine Entdeckung. Er sah, wie Klaus Moehlenbrock
und seine neue Freundin, Elisabeth Schneider, auf einer
Bank unter den Bäumen saßen. Sie hatten gerade ein auf- 20
regendes [exciting] Spiel hinter sich und ruhten sich einen
Augenblick aus. Aber sie saßen nicht da und lasen die
Zeitung. Nein, sie hielten sich die Hände und blickten sich
in die Augen.
  Als die beiden an ihnen vorbeigingen, grüßte Elisabeth und 25
rief: „Es ist schön, daß ich Sie sehe. Es wäre nett, wenn Sie
alle am nächsten Mittwoch zu uns kämen. Wir haben eine
kleine Abendgesellschaft zu Hause." Fritz und Inge dankten
freundlich und antworteten, daß sie gerne kommen würden. —
„Das ist herrlich," sagte Elisabeth. „Wissen Sie, mein Bruder 30
hat ein Musikstück komponiert, und er will uns etwas daraus
vorspielen. Seine Verlobte [fiancée] wird auch hier sein, und
ich möchte, daß Sie sie kennenlernen."
  Fritz und Inge spielten Tennis, bis sie müde wurden. Bei
einbrechender Dunkelheit fingen die Leute an, ihr Abendessen 35
vorzubereiten. Bald brannten viele Feuer im Park, an den

Wegen entlang gingen die Lichter an und die Melodien froher
Lieder klangen durch den Park.

Klaus und Elisabeth saßen noch immer am gleichen Platz,
40 sprachen leise mit einander und merkten nicht, wie dunkle
Wolken am Himmel aufzogen und die Sterne verschwanden.
Sie saßen still zusammen, blickten in die Dunkelheit und hatten
frohe Gefühle im Herzen.

Und plötzlich brach der Sturm los. Der Wind fuhr durch
45 die Bäume und warf Zweige und Blätter auf die Erde. Väter
riefen ihre Kinder, Mütter packten die Vorräte zusammen, und
Söhne löschten [put out] die Feuer. Schwere Regentropfen begannen zu fallen, und alle Menschen rannten zu ihren Autos.

Nur Klaus und Elisabeth eilten nicht. Arm in Arm gingen
50 sie zu ihrem Wagen zurück, und als der Regen durch die Gegend
fegte [swept], wußten sie, daß sie zu einander gehörten.

IDIOMS AND VOCABULARY

immer noch, noch immer   still, yet

der Arm, -e arm
sich aus-ruhen rest
das Blatt, ̈-er leaf, page, sheet
die Ecke, -n corner
die Erde, -n earth
das Feuer, – fire
freundlich friendly, kind
gehören [*dat.*] belong (to)
halten, ie, a, ä hold
herrlich magnificent, splendid
der Hund, -e dog
jener [*der-word*] that (one), the former
klingen, a, u sound, ring
komponieren compose
das Lied, -er song

los loose
mancher [*der-word*] many a
(der) Mittwoch Wednesday
müde tired
plötzlich sudden(ly)
rennen, a, (ist) a run
ruhen rest
sondern but (on the contrary)
der Stern, -e star
still quiet
der Sturm, ̈-e storm
vorbei, vorüber past, over
vorbereiten prepare
was für ein what kind of
der Wind, -e wind
zusammen-packen pack up

GRAMMAR

14.1 Review of Nouns and Adjectives The inflection of nouns was discussed in Lesson 1 to 4 and Lesson 7. We have observed that the gender, case, and number of a noun are indicated primarily by the preceding modifiers. In determining the meaning of a German sentence, it is therefore essential to observe the forms of the words which precede nouns: the **der**-words, the **ein**-words, and the adjectives. These were discussed in Lesson 8. The various patterns will be reviewed here.

14.1,1 A noun may be preceded by no modifier, *e.g.,* **Er schreibt auf Papier.** 'He is writing on paper.' Such patterns are less frequent in German than in English, for nouns referring to things generally require the article in German. Note page 155, line 1, **Endlich war die Sommerschule vorüber.** 'Summer school was finally over.'
Nouns without preceding modifiers are particularly frequent in the plural, for in neither English nor German is there a plural form for the indefinite article; contrast **Väter riefen...** 'Fathers called...' with **Ein Vater rief.** 'A father called.'

14.1,2 A noun may be preceded by a **der**-word. The **der**-word indicates the role of the following noun, *e.g.,* page 155, line 1, **die Sommerschule.** In this sentence **die** informs us that **Sommerschule** is feminine, nominative or accusative. A further examination of the sentence restricts the possible cases to the nominative, for **Sommerschule** is the subject. The singular verb and the absence of the plural ending **-n** confirm the conclusion that **Sommerschule** is singular. Similar information may be derived from other **der**-words.
Forms of **der** may be reduced to the ending alone, *e.g.,* page 155, line 10, **Im Park.** These reduced forms, or con-

tractions, are as informative as the entire word **dem,** for -**m** can only be a dative, singular, masculine or neuter ending.

14.1,3 A noun may be preceded by an **ein**-word. Again the ending indicates the role of the following noun, *e.g.*, page 155, line 32, **Seine Verlobte.** **Seine** informs one that the noun is feminine and either nominative or accusative. The verb **wird** informs one that the noun is nominative singular. The absence of the plural -**n** confirms this analysis.

14.1,4 A noun may be preceded by an adjective. Since the adjective has the ending of a **der**-word, it conveys similar information on the role of the noun, *e.g.*, page 155, line 35, **bei einbrechender Dunkelheit.** After **bei** the noun must be in the dative case, and an -**er** ending can only be dative, singular, feminine.

14.1,5 A noun may be preceded by a **der**-word and one or more adjectives, *e.g.*, page 155, line 11, **die ganze Nachbar-schaft.** Since the adjective has an -**en** ending in all forms but five (the three nominative singulars, the feminine and neuter accusative singulars) and an -**e** ending in these, information on the role of the noun must be derived from the **der**-word.

The same is true of **ein**-words, except for the three cases in which **ein**-words have no ending (the nominative singular masculine and the nominative and accusative singular neuter). In these cases, *e.g.*, page 155, line 20, **ein aufregendes Spiel,** the ending of the adjective supplies information on the role of the noun.

14.2 Noun Derivation   Many nouns and verbs in German are derived from simple words. The formations and their meanings generally follow certain patterns. Accordingly, the memorization of vocabulary can be aided by the knowledge of the most frequent formations.

14.2,1 Nouns may be derived from infinitives without the addition of a further ending:

sprechen	speak	**das Sprechen**	speaking
spielen	play	**das Spielen**	playing
fahren	drive	**das Fahren**	driving

Some of these nouns have been in use so long that they have special meanings:

essen	eat	**das Essen**	meal

14.2,2 Nouns indicating the agency of an action are derived from verbs, as in English, by adding **-er** to the stem:

arbeiten	work	**der Arbeiter**	worker
besitzen	own	**der Besitzer**	owner
führen	lead	**der Führer**	head, leader (as in
			der Geschäftsführer)

14.2,3 Feminine nouns are formed from masculine nouns by the addition of **-in**:

der Amerikaner	**die Amerikanerin**
American	female American
der Student	**die Studentin**
student	female student
der Freund	**die Freundin**
friend	girl friend

14.2,4 Diminutives and terms of affection are made by adding **-chen** or **-lein**: all such nouns are neuter and generally take an umlaut when the stem vowel is **a, o, u** or **au.**

die Bank	bench	**das Bänkchen**	little bench
die Stunde	hour	**das Stündlein**	little while
die Leute	people	**die Leutchen**	dear people

14.2,5 Various suffixes are used to form abstract nouns, *e.g.*, **-heit, -keit, -schaft, -ung.** They correspond in meaning to English -*hood*, -*ship*, -*tion*. By noting these suffixes and their meanings one can often deduce the meaning of new nouns from their stems. All words with these suffixes are feminine.

dunkel	dark	die Dunkelheit	darkness
krank	sick	die Krankheit	sickness
wirklich	real	die Wirklichkeit	reality
der Freund	friend	die Freundschaft	friendship
der Nachbar	neighbor	die Nachbarschaft	neighborhood
wissen	know	die Wissenschaft	science
beobachten	observe	die Beobachtung	observation
entdecken	discover	die Entdeckung	discovery
stellen	place	die Stellung	position

14.2,6 The technical vocabulary of German is made up in great part of compounded native elements; in this respect German is unlike English, which has borrowed such words from Latin and Greek. Some Latin and Greek borrowings are used in German, *e.g.*, **Thermométer,** but more often they are translated into German, as **Trennung** for *separation*. The components of many compounds are easy to perceive, *e.g.*, **Wörterbuch** 'dictionary'; one must become accustomed to inferring the English counterparts without looking them up in a dictionary.

die Ölindustrie	oil industry
die Flugzeugindustrie	aircraft industry
das Schlafzimmer	bedroom < sleeping room
die Ziehharmonika	accordion < pull-harmonica
das Lebensmittelgeschäft	grocery store < life-means-shop
sechzehnjährig	sixteen-year-old

14.3 Pronunciation   Review the section in the Appendix on consonants (Appendix 1,3).

EXERCISES

A. Make additional sentences on the basis of those given here, substituting the suggested words for those in heavy type and making any other changes made necessary by the substitutions.

1. Ehe der berühmte Professor **seine** [the, these] Beobachtungen gemacht hatte, schlief **der** [a, many a] junge Student ein.
2. Es war **dieser** [a, the] lange Brief, aber ich habe ihn nicht lesen können.
3. **Ihr** [the, his] letzter Roman war schrecklich.
4. Vor zwei Tagen habe ich **das** [that, his] lange Stück gesehen.
5. Die rechte Flamme war **heißer** [longer] als die linke.
6. **Das** [a, many a] alte Bett ist sehr groß.
7. **Zwölf** [the, many] kleine Mädchen liefen die Treppe hinunter.
8. Kennen Sie **ihr** [the, his] jüngstes Kind?
9. Wir gehen heute abend mit **der** [our, their] ganzen Familie.
10. Der Vetter schien **älter** [younger, bigger] als die Kusine.
11. Möchten Sie in **das** [his, our] große Zimmer einziehen?
12. **Wie viele** [which, what sort of] Vögel singen hier im Monat April?

B. Follow the directions for exercise A.

1. Hat sie ihren **Sohn** [daughter, child] hier verlassen?
2. Ich habe das Gefühl, daß ich diese **Blume** [chair, glass] kaufen sollte.
3. Der **Onkel** [aunt, girl], der hier steht, kommt aus Frankfurt.
4. Er hat den **Stein** [thing, ball] fallen lassen.

5. Der **Student** [girl student, girl], der jetzt spielt, versteht kein Wort Deutsch.
6. Da es ein kühler **Nachmittag** [night, year] war, sind wir zu Hause geblieben.
7. Meinen Sie, daß dieses **Bild** [apartment, table] besser als das da ist?
8. Ich möchte Ihnen auch das wunderbare **Haus** [river, street] zeigen.
9. Ist Ihre **Reise** [friend, woman teacher] wirklich so interessant gewesen?
10. Wie viele **Namen** [gentlemen, men] hat er da kennengelernt?
11. Meine kleine Schwester hat kein **Geld** [watch, plate] mitgebracht.

C. Replace the words in heavy type by the words in brackets.

1. Sie lasen zusammen **ein altes Buch.** [an old newspaper, a long letter, a hard exam, old books]
2. Die Leute saßen **in froher Gesellschaft** im Park. [at late dusk, in old friendship, in a (bei) heavy storm]
3. Wir haben **eine kleine Abendgesellschaft** zu Hause. [a little dog, a big car, a new picture, many new pictures]
4. **Fritz und Inge** saßen unter den Bäumen. [my younger sisters, his older brother, our best friend, their little girl]
5. Sie erinnerten sich noch lange an **diesen schönen Abend.** [that dark night, many a beautiful day, a cheerful party]
6. Wir haben **ein aufregendes Spiel** hinter uns. [a long assignment, this hot summer, an unpleasant week, many beautiful years]
7. Alle Menschen wollten sich von **den Sorgen der Arbeit** erholen. [the difficulties of the day, the trifles of reality, the hustle and bustle of life]

D. Fill in the appropriate German words.

1. Die beiden jungen Leute fuhren [into the] Park.

2. Frohe Lieder klangen [through the] Nacht.
3. Dunkle Wolken standen [in the] Himmel. *in dem*
4. Viele Feuer brannten [in the] Park. *in dem*
5. Klaus und Elisabeth gingen langsam [through the] Regen. *durch den*
6. Sie hatten ihre Bücher und Hefte [into the] Ecke geworfen. *in der*
7. Dann waren sie [into the] Nachbarschaft gefahren. *in dem*
8. Alle Menschen rannten [in the] Dunkelheit [to their] *in dem zu ihren*
   Wagen.
9. Ich möchte mich nicht [of my] Examen erinnern. *an mein*
10. Lebhafter Betrieb herrschte [on the] Straßen. *an den den*
11. Es standen viele Menschen [on the] Straße. *an dem auf den*
12. Wir fanden nichts Neues [in the] Zeitung. *in der*
13. Wann spielen Sie wieder Tennis [with my] Schwester? *mit meiner*
14. Ich mag [with them] sehr gerne in die Gegend fahren. *mit ihnen*
15. Wie viele Leute wohnen [at your place]? *bei Ihnen*
16. Sie wohnen noch immer [in the same] Haus. *in dem gleichen*
17. Die Sterne waren [behind the] Wolken der Nacht ver-
    schwunden. *hinter den die*
18. Blätter und Zweige lagen [on (auf) the] Erde. *auf der*
19. [Three weeks ago] kannte er sie noch nicht. *Vor drei Wochen*
20. Dunkle Wolken fegten [over our] Stadt. *über unsere*

E. Make nouns from the following infinitives:

verlangen   drehen   beobachten   mischen   wissen
bemerken   beginnen

F. Make nouns indicating the performer of an action from
the following infinitives:

erzählen   denken   herrschen   beobachten   versuchen
einbrechen   fliegen

G. Make feminines from the following masculines:

der Nachbar   der Lehrer   der Professor   der König
der Herr   der Freund

H. Make diminutives with **-chen** or **-lein** from the following nouns:

die Stunde der Brief die Stadt die Blume das Haus
der Raum der Platz der Tisch der Stuhl der Vogel
die Lieb(e) der Bruder

I. Make abstract nouns from the following:

with **-heit**: krank berühmt dunkel
with **-keit**: möglich schwierig tüchtig wirklich
with **-schaft**: Nachbar Freund bereit verwandt
with **-ung**: mischen rechnen verwandeln vorbereiten

J. Analyze the following compounds:

das Lebensmittelgeschäft   die Feuerversicherung
der Verkehrspolizist   die Angestelltenversicherung
der Nobelpreisträger   die Entwicklungstheorie

K. Questions.

1. Wohin fuhren Fritz und Inge? (into the park)
2. Wie erinnerten sie sich an die Wirklichkeit? (they played tennis)
3. Wen fanden sie im Park? (many people and dogs)
4. Wen sahen sie auf einer Bank? (Klaus and Elisabeth)
5. Warum wollte Elisabeth mit ihnen sprechen? (the Schneiders were having a party)
6. Was für Werke schrieb Elisabeths Bruder? (works of music)
7. Wen bringt er mit? (his fiancée)
8. Wann aßen die Leute im Park? (at dusk)
9. Was hörte man dann? (happy songs)
10. Warum fuhren die Leute schnell nach Hause? (it began to rain)

L. Translate in writing:

1. Suddenly the little child, who had been running with his dog, wanted to rest.
2. A friendly old man walked past.
3. We won't need the blue notebooks until next Friday.
4. Before the storm it was so quiet we heard the leaves fall from the trees.
5. To whom does that magnificent new house belong?
6. He thought he could drive faster than the train.
7. That beautiful new notebook probably belongs to the teacher.
8. Can you tell me what kind of dog that is?
9. His dog seemed friendly enough until the brown car came around the corner.
10. Can you tell me whether he is still writing his exam?

M. Free conversation.

Describe an afternoon in the park. Off to the right, some students are playing tennis; all the tennis courts are being used, but some young people are sitting and resting under the trees. At the other end of the park some men are playing ball. The women are sitting at tables and chatting. Many children are swimming in the pool. It seems as if the entire city has come out to enjoy the afternoon. — Describe other scenes.

LESSON 15

Wer pfeift am besten?

REVIEW OF VERBS AND SENTENCE STRUCTURE

TEXT

Am Mittwoch abend war Klaus der erste, der bei Schneiders ankam.
Elisabeth erwartete ihn schon an der Tür: „ O, es ist schön, daß du so
früh kommst. Karl ist eben zur Bahn gefahren, um Elli abzuholen. Sie
werden in kurzer Zeit hier sein. "

5 Im Wohnzimmer, das hell erleuchtet [lighted up] war, stand Philipp,
der Sechzehnjährige, und pfiff eine Melodie zwischen den Zähnen.
Helen, die Fünfzehnjährige, hatte eben ihre Ziehharmonika in den Ka=
sten gelegt, drehte sich um und grüßte Klaus mit lachendem Gesicht.
„ Wo sind denn Carolyn und Cathryn? " fragte Elisabeth. „ O, die

sind für den Abend verschwunden — schon nach oben gegangen," sagte 10
Philipp, zog die Hand aus der Tasche und begrüßte den Freund seiner
Schwester.

„ Sag mal, Klaus," fragte Elisabeth, „ hast du die Bilder mitgebracht,
die du uns zeigen wolltest ? " „ Ja. Die sind gar nicht so schlecht aus=
gefallen [turned out]. Ich habe die besten davon mitgebracht." 15
Und dann sahen sie sich die Aufnahmen [photographs] an, die Klaus
im Laufe der letzten Wochen gemacht hatte, Bilder vom Wagen und
vom Park, vom See, von den Bergen und vom Fluß, — aber eigentlich
waren es doch nur Bilder von Elisabeth.

„ Die sind ja wunderbar," sagte Frau Schneider, die eben zu ihnen 20
getreten war. „ Ihr jungen Leute, ihr habt gar keine Schwierigkeiten,
neue Motive [subjects, motifs] zu finden. "

Eben hörte man den Wagen über den Hof fahren. Frau Schneider
öffnete die Haustür. Karl trat fröhlich herein und stellte seiner Mutter
seine Braut [fiancée] vor. Klaus bekam einen furchtbaren Schrecken 25
[shock] : es war Eleanor Sanders.

„ Ah, sind Sie auch hier ? " sagte Eleanor. „ Es freut mich sehr, Sie
wiederzusehen." Karl wunderte sich etwas, daß sein Freund schon mit
seiner Braut bekannt war. Aber Heinrich Seemann, der gerade aus der
Dunkelheit ins Zimmer getreten war, wußte ihm zu erklären, daß Klaus 30
ihr schon im Frühling begegnet sei und ihr damals die Stadt gezeigt
habe.

Inzwischen war auch Vater Schneider herangetreten und hatte
Eleanor begrüßt : „ Ich habe immer gewußt, daß Karl einen Sinn für
Schönheit hat," lachte er laut. „ Aber einmal [here : sometime] 35
müßt ihr mir noch erzählen, wie ihr euch in Los Angeles getroffen habt. "

Karl wollte eben anfangen zu erzählen, als Klaus Elisabeth bei der
Hand nahm und sagte : „ Ich weiß nicht, Eleanor, ob Sie meine Ver=
lobte schon kennengelernt haben." „ Ihr habt euch verlobt ? " rief
Karl. Und Elisabeth nickte [nodded] und hob ihre Hand ans Licht. 40
„ Ja, gestern abend hat mir Klaus diesen Ring geschenkt. "

„ Von jetzt ab wird mich nichts mehr überraschen [surprise], "
sagte Herr Schneider zu seiner Frau. „ Was sagst du dazu ? "

Frau Schneider neigte [bent] den Kopf und sagte leise : „ Ich habe
für unsere jungen Leutchen nur einen guten Wunsch." „ Und der 45

wäre?" "Frau Schneider fuhr mit lauter Stimme fort: „Lebe, wie du,
wenn du stirbst, wünschen wirst, gelebt zu haben."

Die jungen Paare sahen sich schweigsam in die Augen. Philipp
steckte die Hände in die Taschen und pfiff durch die Zähne.

50 Da kamen Fritz Möller und Inge Pfeiffer durch die Tür. Fritz
hielt eine Zeitung hoch und Inge rief: „Habt ihr schon gesehen, was
heute in der Zeitung steht?" Und sie lasen die Überschrift [headline]:
‚Junger Musiker komponiert herrliche Symphonie.‘

Alle drängten sich um die Zeitung und baten Karl, aus seinem
55 Musikstück vorzuspielen. Während Karl das Saxophon aus dem Kasten
holte, setzte sich Elisabeth ans neue Klavier.

Klaus Moehlenbrock aber, der noch weiter in der Zeitung gelesen
hatte, wurde nachdenklich und trat zu Heinrich Seemann: „Ich glaube,
dies betrifft [concerns] Sie." Und er las: ‚Student der Chemie ge=
60 winnt Stipendium im Ausland [abroad]. Heinrich Seemann, einem
jungen Studenten der Chemie, ist es gelungen, ein elektro=chemisches
Verfahren zur Trennung [separation] von Zellen zu entwickeln. Er
hat ein Stipendium gewonnen, das ihm ermöglicht, an der Universität
Göttingen seine Studien in der Krebsforschung [cancer research] fort=
65 zusetzen.‘

Heinrich Seemann nickte schweigend. „Wann werden Sie hinfahren?"
fragte Klaus. — „So bald wie möglich."

IDIOMS AND VOCABULARY

es gelingt mir ... zu   I succeed in ...ing
gar kein (Auto)   no (car) at all
von jetzt ab   from now on

ab=holen   call for, get
damals = zu jener Zeit   at that
   time
drängen   press, crowd
eben   just

eigentlich   true, essential; really
erklären   explain, declare
ermöglichen   make possible
erwarten   await, expect

fort-ſeßen   continue
fröhlich = froh   joyful, merry
furchtbar = ſchrecklich   terrible
gelingen, a, (iſt) u   succeed
das Geſicht, ⸗er   face
gewinnen, a, o   win, obtain, gain
heben, o, o   lift, raise
hoch, höher, höchſt⸗   high, higher, highest
der Hof, ⸗e   court, yard
der Kopf, ⸗e   head
kurz   short, brief
der Lauf, ⸗e   course, run
laut   loud

leben   live
mal (= einmal)   please (once)
nachdenklich   thoughtful, pensive
oben   above, upstairs
öffnen   open
das Paar, ⸗e   pair, couple
ſchenken   give (as a present)
ſchlecht   inferior, bad
der See, ⸗n   lake
der Sinn, ⸗e   sense, mind
ſtecken   stick, put, place
die Stimme, ⸗n   voice
die Taſche, ⸗n   pocket
das Verfahren, –   process
der Zahn, ⸗e   tooth
ziehen, zog, gezogen   pull, draw

GRAMMAR

15.1 Review of Verbs and Sentence Structure   The forms of German verbs are closely parallel to the verb forms of English. All verbs have present and past tenses and compound forms. Since the compound forms consist of auxiliaries plus infinitives or participles, the only forms that need to be memorized are the present and past tenses and the principal parts.   Review Lessons 5, 6, and 10 through 13, and see Appendix 6.

15.1,1   You have learned that the pronoun of address and its accompanying verb forms are the same as the third person plural and its accompanying verb form, except that the pronoun is capitalized: **sie sehen** 'they see,' **Sie sehen** 'you see.' In this lesson two new pronouns appear: **du,** corresponding to *thou,* and **ihr,** corresponding to *ye;* (for a full list of the forms of these pronouns, see Appendix 4.1).   The pronouns **du** and **ihr** are used in addressing God in prayer, by members of a family and by close friends when speaking to one another, and in speaking to animals.   Observe that Klaus and Elizabeth use **du** to each other only after they have come to know each other very well. On the other hand, Eleanor uses **Sie** to Klaus (page 167, line 27). The verb ending associated with **du** is **-st**; that with **ihr, -t,** *e.g.*, **du sagst, ihr sagt** 'you say.'   For additional forms, see Appendix 6.

15.1,2 Imperatives are used which correspond to **du** and **ihr,** the former with final **-e** or no ending, the latter with **-t,** *e.g.*, **Frage! Fragt! (Fragen Sie!)**   As in English, these imperatives are not accompanied by pronouns.

15.1,3 In German the position of the verb varies according to the type of clause in which it is used.   In order to understand a sentence, it is necessary to locate the inflected, or finite, form of the verb.

15.1,4 In simple statements the verb stands in second place (see Lesson 1.4): **Er geht heute.** 'He is going today.'   This is the basic principle of German word order and is followed even when the first element is an object, an adverb, an adverbial phrase, or a clause: **Heute geht er. Spät am Abend geht er. Auch wenn es regnet, geht er.**

15.1,5 In questions without an interrogative and in commands, the verb stands first, as in English: **Gehen Sie morgen?** 'Are you going tomorrow?'   **Gehen Sie morgen!** 'Go tomorrow!)'
   Questions beginning with an interrogative have the same word order as statements: **Wann gehen Sie?** 'When are you going?' **Wer geht morgen?** 'Who is going tomorrow?'

15.1,6 In subordinate clauses, which may be introduced by relative pronouns, subordinating conjunctions, or interrogatives (see Lesson 9), the inflected verb stands at the end of the clause: **Ich weiß nicht, wer gegangen ist.** 'I don't know who has

gone.' **Ich wußte nicht, daß er gegangen war.** 'I didn't
know that he had gone.' Note, however, the double infinitive
construction in Lesson 11.2,4.

15.1,7 Infinitives and participles must stand at the end of their
clauses if the finite verb stands in first or second place.

The adverbial element (prefix) of a compound verb must
stand at the end of the clause if the verb is in the present, past,
or imperative; if a compound verb occurs in a dependent clause,
the prefix stands directly before the present or past form of the
verb.

15.1,8 Infinitives with objects are treated like full clauses in
German; consequently such infinitives follow their objects, *e.g.*,
page 166, line 3, **um Elli abzuholen** 'in order to fetch Elli.'

15.1,9 Review the rules of word order presented in Lesson 3.3.
Adverbs of time must precede those of place, *e.g.*, page 166,
line 3, **Karl ist eben zur Bahn gefahren.** 'Karl has just
driven to the train.' Indirect objects precede direct objects
when the direct object is a noun, *e.g.*, page 167, line 24, **Karl
stellte seiner Mutter seine Braut vor.** 'Karl introduced
his fiancée to his mother.' Compare, on the other hand,
Karl stellte sie seiner Mutter vor. 'Karl introduced her to
his mother.'

15.2 Pronunciation Review the sections in the Appendix
on vowels (Appendix 1.4).

EXERCISES

A. Substitute for the words in heavy type those in parentheses:

1. Habt ihr die Füllfeder **gekauft?** (look for)
2. **Nehmen** Sie diese Zeitung? (read)

3. Die fleißigsten Studenten **schrieben** die Briefe. (understand)
4. Wo werden wir ihn **treffen?** (see)
5. Mein älterer Bruder **fährt** sehr schnell. (speak)
6. Ich **schwimme** sehr gern. (sleep)
7. Er stand an der Ecke und **rief.** (yell)
8. Was **tust** du heute abend? (read)
9. Ist er schon **angekommen?** (pass by)
10. Ich habe die ganze Aufgabe **geändert.** (forget) t)
11. Dienstag ist er wieder nach Hause **gegangen.** (return)
12. Die kleinen Studenten haben sich **umgedreht.** (sit down)

B. Put the verbs in the sentences of exercise A into the following tenses:

present, past, future, present perfect, past perfect.

C. Substitute for the words in heavy type those in parentheses:

1. Wird diese Geschichte oft **erzählt?** (read, repeat, report, continue)
2. Der Herr fragte, wann der Student **einziehen** werde. (return, arrive, step in, drive into town)
3. Gestern wurde das Öl **verkauft.** (unload, find, use, bring into the house)
4. **Muß** ich ihn vom Bahnhof abholen? (may, should, can, be supposed)
5. Am Nachmittag ist das Mädchen **gerettet** worden. (find, see, call for, await, invite)
6. Er öffnete den Kasten und **holte** das Saxophon heraus. (take, pull)

D. Where feasible, put the verbs in the sentences of exercise C into the present, past, present perfect, past perfect.

E. Give the German for the English sentences, following the patterns of the German sentences.

1. Er legte das Instrument in den Kasten.
   A. They pulled the child out of the water.
   B. We showed the pictures from (out of) the book.
   C. He took **(bringen)** the box behind the house.

2. Philipp steckte beide Hände in die Taschen.
   A. Mr. Schneider needed a young man in his store.
   B. The teacher took **(bringen)** the little girl to her house.
   C. Karl broke a few twigs from the tree.

3. Wir besuchten unsere Freunde in der Stadt.
   A. Klaus met his girl friend in the store.
   B. They stepped through the door into the living room.
   C. She greeted her friend at the door.

4. Als wir ihn wiedersahen, war er viel älter geworden.
   A. When we turned around, the man had disappeared.
   B. When he called her up, she had driven on.
   C. When he arrived, he had become very ill.

F. Substitute for the words in heavy type those in parentheses:

1. **Nehmen** Sie das Buch bitte **mit**! (send back, bring along)
2. Fritz, **sprich** langsam. (read, walk)
3. Klaus und Elisabeth, **seht diese Bilder an**! (call your friends, show your papers)
4. **Ziehen** Sie doch am Montag **ein**! (return, fly there)
5. Bitte, **setzen** Sie sich! (look around, turn around)

G. Substitute **du, ihr,** or **Sie** for the pronouns printed in heavy type, making appropriate changes in the rest of the sentence.

1. Hast **du** das Buch mitgebracht?
2. Wenn **ihr** es morgen versucht, werdet **ihr** es sicher bekommen.

3. Wachen **Sie** jeden Morgen so früh auf?
4. Sind **Sie** auch gestern abend am Hause vorbeigegangen?
5. Geben **Sie** mir bitte **Ihre** Adresse.

H. Introduce each of the following sentences with: (*a*) **wann**; (*b*) **er erzählte mir**; (*c*) **er sagte mir, daß**; (*d*) **wenn er das gesagt hätte, dann**, making the necessary changes in word order and verb forms:

1. Sie fährt langsam.
2. Der Professor hat eine berühmte Entdeckung gemacht.
3. Der Student ist eingeschlafen.
4. Sie werden ihn einladen.
5. Er hat auch den Nachbar kennengelernt.
6. Du hast dich umgesehen.

I. Questions.

1. Wer kam zuerst am Mittwoch abend bei den Schneiders an? (Klaus)
2. Wohin war Karl gefahren? (train)
3. Wer pfiff eine Melodie zwischen den Zähnen? (Philipp)
4. Was wollte Klaus zeigen? (the photographs)
5. Worüber wunderte sich Karl? (that Klaus knew his fiancée)
6. Woher wußte Karl, daß Elisabeth verlobt war? (ring)
7. Was lasen alle in der Zeitung? (of the symphony)
8. Was für ein Instrument spielte Karl? (saxophone)
9. Wie kam es, daß Heinrich im Ausland studieren konnte? (fellowship)
10. Wann wollte er nach Deutschland fahren? (as soon as possible)

J. Translate in writing:

1. At that time you did not succeed in explaining the process.

2. Just when Henry wanted to call for Inge, she was already coming out.
3. After Helen had greeted Karl, she too went upstairs.
4. Since the pictures turned out very badly, we did not bring them.
5. Mrs. Schneider had just come into the room to look at the pictures.
6. Karl's father said to him: "You must tell me how you met Eleanor."
7. When Fritz came into the house, he held up a newspaper.
8. After Elisabeth had sat down, all of them crowded around the piano.
9. Henry wanted to continue with his work at (**auf**) the University of Göttingen.
10. He said almost nothing when Klaus asked him when he would travel there.

K. Free conversation.

Describe a party.   Give the names of various people as they arrive.   Discuss some of the incidents of the evening: one of the guests is a "camera bug" and has brought his latest pictures; others discuss their work at the university, giving their opinions of the professors; others pick up various instruments and play a number of pieces.   Only one couple is sitting to one side; they have not limited their activities to German in the course of the semester.

GERMAN—ENGLISH VOCABULARY

ENGLISH—GERMAN VOCABULARY

A number following an entry refers to the lesson in which the word first occurs. Words without numbers are not included in lesson vocabularies. Idioms are listed under one or more key words: *e.g.*, *Guten Abend* will be found under both *Abend* and *gut*.

A

ab-brennen, brannte ab, abgebrannt burn down, burn off

der **Abend, -e** *5* evening; **eines Abends** *10* one evening; **Guten Abend** *5* Good evening; **heute abend** *3* this evening; **abends** *4* in the evening(s)

das **Abendessen** evening meal

die **Abendgesellschaft, -en** evening party

abends *4* in the evening(s)

das **Abenteuer, —** adventure

aber *1* but

die **Abfahrt, -en** *4* departure

ab-holen *15* call for

ab-kühlen *9* cool off

ab-laden, u, a, ä *11* unload

ach *13* Oh, alas

acht *3* eight

achtzig *2* eighty

der **Agent, -en, -en** agent

die **Ahnung, -en** *8* foreboding, idea

der **Aktionär, -e** stockholder

all *1* all

allein *3* alone

als *6* when, than, as; **als ob** *13* as if

also *3* therefore

alt, älter, ältest- *1, 8* old, older, oldest (elder, eldest)

amerikanisch *8* American

an *2* [*dat.*] at, near, by, on; [*acc.*] to, up to, on; **denken an** [*acc.*] *10* think of

analysieren analyze

ander *6* other

ändern *13* change, alter

der **Anfang, -̈e** *13* beginning

an-fangen, i, a, ä *12* begin, start

angenehm *4* pleasant; **sehr angenehm!** *1* Pleased to meet you

der **Angestellte, -n, -n** employee

an-kommen, kam, ist ge-
kommen *10* arrive
an-nehmen, nahm, ge-
nommen, nimmt *10*
accept
an-rufen, ie, u *13* call up
an-schließen, o, geschlossen *11* connect
an-sehen, a, e, ie *11* look
at
anstatt [*gen.*]   instead of, in
place of
antworten [*dat.*] *5* answer
der Apparat, -e apparatus
der Appetit appetite
die Arbeit, -en *4* work
arbeiten *5* work
der Arbeiter, — *11* worker
der Arm, -e *14* arm
auch *1* also, too, even;
auch nicht *5* not ...
either
auf [*dat./acc.*] *2*, *5* up,
upon, on; auf dem Lan-
de *3* in the country; auf
(*or* in die) Ferien *8* on
vacation
auf-blicken look up
die Aufgabe, -n *9* lesson, task,
assignment

auf-hören *13* cease, stop
auf-machen open up
die Aufnahme, -n photograph
auf-regen excite
auf-schlagen, u, a, ä open
(*a book*)
auf-wachen, ist *10* wake
up
Auf Wiedersehn! *1* Good-
bye
auf-ziehen, zog, gezogen
move up
das Auge, -s, -n *7* eye
der Augenblick, -e *13* moment
der August August
aus [*dat.*] *1* out of, from
aus-fallen, fiel, ist gefallen, fällt aus turn out,
come out
aus-lachen *10* laugh at
das Ausland foreign country
sich aus-ruhen *14* rest
aus-sehen, a, e, ie *13* look,
appear
außerhalb [*gen.*] outside of
äußerst *8* extreme
die Aussicht, -en view
das Auto, -s = der Wagen, —
6 car
der Autor, -en author

B

der Badewart lifeguard
die Bahn, -en *4* (rail)road, train
bald *5* soon
der Ball, ⁒e *6* ball
die Bank, -en *4* bank
die Bank, ⁒e *6* bench
der Bankdirektor, -en bank
director
Bankerott machen go
broke
der Bankräuber, — bank rob-
ber
bauen *8* build

die Baugesellschaft, -en construction company
der Bauplatz, ⁒e lot
der Baum, ⁒e *6* tree
bedienen wait on
begegnen, ist [*dat.*] *5* meet
beginnen, a, o = an-fan-
gen *13* start, begin
begrüßen *11* greet
bei [*dat.*] *2* at, with, among,
near, by, at the house of
beide *7* both
bei-legen *10* enclose

das **Bein, -e** *7* leg
zum **Beispiel** = **z.B.** *2* for example, e.g.
bekannt *9* (well) known
bekommen, bekam, bekommen *6* get, receive
beliebt *11* popular
beobachten *9* observe
die **Beobachtung, -en** *9* observation
bereit *13* ready, prepared
der **Berg, -e** *4* mountain
berichten *12* report
berühmt *9* famous
der **Besitzer, —** *7* owner
besser, best- (*see* **gut**) *7* better, best
bestehen, bestand, bestanden *12* pass (an examination); consist, exist
bestellen *2* order, send for
zu **Besuch** *7* on (for) a visit
besuchen *7* visit
betreffen concern
der **Betrieb** hustle and bustle
das **Bett, -en** *7* bed
bezahlen *2* pay
die **Bibliothek, -en** library
das **Bild, -er** *4* picture
das **Bildchen, —** *4* little picture
billig *1* cheap

die **Biologie** biology
bis *4* to, as far as, until, till
ein bißchen *11* a bit, a little
bitte *2* please
bitten, bat, gebeten *13* ask (a favor)
das **Blatt, ⁼er** *14* leaf, page, sheet
bleiben, blieb, ist geblieben *6* stay, remain
der **Bleistift, -e** *1* (lead) pencil
blicken *12* look; **vor sich hin blicken** *12* stare
blühen bloom
die **Blume, -n** *7* flower
brauchen *2* need, use, require
braun *6* brown
die **Braut, ⁼e** fiancée
brechen, a, o, i *7* break
brennen, brannte, gebrannt *8* burn
das **Brett, -er** *11* board
der **Brief, -e** *2* letter
bringen, brachte, gebracht *11* bring
der **Bruder, ⁼** *4* brother
das **Buch, ⁼er** *1* book
buchstabieren spell

C

das **Cello, -s** cello
der **Cent, —** cent

die **Chemie** chemistry

D

da *1* there; then; in that case; since, because
dabei *9* in the process
damals *15* at that time
die **Dame, -n** lady

daneben beside it
danke! *1* Thanks!
danken [*dat.*] *3* thank
dann *1* then, in that case
daran about it

ich, er darf *3* [*see* **dürfen**] I am, he is permitted, may

darum *13* for that reason

das **das** *1* that [*demonst. pron.*]

daß *4* that [*conj.*]

das **Datum, die Daten** date

davon *12* of it

denken, dachte, gedacht [**an** *with acc.*] *4, 10* think (of)

denn [*adv.*] *3* anyway, and, tell me

denn [*conj.*] *7* for

der, die, das *1, 3, 6* the; which, who, that

die **Detektiv-Geschichte, -n** detective story

der **Detektiv-Roman, -e** detective story

deutsch *1* German

(das) **Deutsch** *1* the German language

die **Deutschstunde, -n** German class

der **Dichter, —** *12* poet

der **Dieb, -e** *11* thief

dienen *5* serve

der **Dienstag, -e** *13* Tuesday

dieser, diese, dies(es) *1, 3* this (one)

diesseits [*gen.*] this side of

das **Ding, -e** *6* thing

der **Direktor, -en** director

doch *3* nevertheless, please; Why don't you?

der **Dollar, —** dollar

dort *1* there

drängen *15* press, crowd

draußen *11* outside, out there

drehen *10* turn

drei *1* three

dreizehnt- *7* thirteenth

der **dritte** *7* the third

drüben *2* over there

dunkel *2* dark, gloomy

die **Dunkelheit** *8* darkness

das **Dunkle** *2* dark

durch [*acc.*] *2* through

dürfen, durfte, gedurft, darf *3, 7* be permitted, may

E

eben *11* just

die **Ecke, -n** *14* corner

ehe = bevor [*conj.*] *9* before

eigen *5* own [*adj.*]

eigentlich *15* true, essential, real

eilen, ist *5* hurry

einander *12* each other

ein, eine, ein *1, 2* a, an; one; **ein paar** *2* a couple, a few; **eines Abends (Tages)** *10* one evening (day)

ein-brechen, brach, (ist) gebrochen *11* break in, burglarize; approach

einflußreich influential

einige *6* a few, some

ein-laden, u, a, ä *11* invite

einmal *6* once; sometime

einsam *11* lonesome, lonely

ein-schlafen, ie, ist a, ä *10* fall asleep

ein-setzen *13* set in, put in, insert

ein-ziehen, zog, ist gezogen *7* move in

elektro-chemisch electro-chemical

elf *5* eleven

das **Ende, -s, -n** *2* end

endlich *8* in the end, at last, finally

englisch English; **auf Englisch** in English

die **Entdeckung, -en** *9* discovery

entlang *6* along; **am (Fluß) entlang** *6* along the (river)

entweder ... oder *7* either ... or

entwickeln *10* develop

erbauen construct

die **Erde** *14* earth

erfüllen *12* fulfill, complete

Ihr **ergebener** *8* yours [*literally* your devoted]

erhalten, ie, a, ä = bekommen *12* get, receive

sich **erholen** *10* recover

sich **erinnern** [*gen. or* an *with acc.*] *10* remember

erklären *15* declare, explain

erleuchten light up

ermöglichen *15* enable

erschrecken, a, ist o, i *6* become frightened

erst *13* only, not until; (at) first

der **erste** *7* first

ertragen, u, a, ä *11* put up with, bear

erwachen, ist *9* awake

erwarten *15* await, expect

erzählen *10* tell

essen, aß, gegessen, ißt *6* eat

etwas *1* some(thing), somewhat; **sonst noch etwas?** *13* anything else?

das **Examen, —** *2* examination

das **Experiment, -e** experiment

experimentieren experiment

F

fahren, u, ist a, ä *3* go (by vehicle), drive

der **Fahrer, —** driver

die **Fahrt, -en** *13* trip, ride

fallen, fiel, ist gefallen, fällt *6* fall, drop

fällen *11* fell, cut down

die **Familie, -n** *7* family

fangen, i, a, ä *6* catch

fassen *11* seize, grasp, catch

die **Feder, -n (Füllfeder, —)** *5* (fountain) pen

fegen sweep

das **Fenster, —** *1* window

die **Ferien** [*pl. only*] *8* vacation; **auf Ferien** *or* **in die Ferien** *8* on vacation

der **Fernseh-Apparat, -e** television set

der **Fernsprecher, —** telephone

fest firm, fast, steady

das **Feuer, —** *8* fire

die **Feuerwehr** fire department

der **Feuerwehrmann, die Feuerwehrleute** fireman

der **Film, -e** film

finden, a, u *5* find; **sich finden** be

finster = dunkel *12* dark, gloomy

die **Firma, die Firmen** firm

die **Flamme, -n** *8* flame

die **Flasche, -n** bottle

fleißig *6* industrious, diligent

fliegen, o, ist o *6* fly

fließen, o, ist geflossen *6* flow

die **Flöte, -n** flute

die **Flugzeugindustrie, -n** airplane industry

der **Fluß, die Flüsse** *4* river

fort-fahren, u, ist a, ä *1* continue, drive on

der Fortschritt, -e progress
fort-setzen *15* continue
die Frage, -n *5* question
fragen *2* ask
die Frau, -en *1* woman, wife, Mrs.
das Fräulein, — *1* young lady, Miss
frei *1* free
der Freitag, -e *7* Friday
sich freuen *10* be happy; **sich freuen auf** [*acc.*] *13* look forward to; **Das freut mich sehr** *3* I am very glad (about that)
der Freund, -e *1* friend
die Freundin, -nen girl friend
freundlich *14* friendly, kind
die Freundschaft, -en friendship

froh = fröhlich *7* joyful, merry
früh, früher *1, 7* early, earlier
der Frühling, -e *10* spring-(time)
fühlen *13* feel; **sich wohl fühlen** *13* feel well (good)
die Füllfeder, -n *5* fountain pen
fünf *1* five; **der fünfte** *10* the fifth; **fünfundzwanzig** *2* twenty-five; **fünfundsiebzig** *5* seventy-five; **fünfzehnjährig** fifteen-year-old; **fünfzig** *5* fifty
für [*acc.*] *2* for, in place of
furchtbar = schrecklich *15* terrible

G

ganz *2* entire, whole, altogether
das Ganze *2* whole
gar kein (Auto) *15* no (car) at all; **gar nicht(s)** *6* not (nothing) at all
die Garage, -n garage
der Garten, ⸚ *7* garden
geben, a, e, i *2, 6* give; **es gibt** *6* there is (are), **es gab** *6* there was (were)
geboren *13* born
der Gedanke, -ns, -n *12* thought
sehr geehrter (Herr) *8* dear (Sir) [*literally*] very honored (Sir)
gefallen, gefiel, gefallen, gefällt *3, 6* please; **Das gefällt mir** *3* That pleases me, I like that
das Gefühl, -e *7* feeling

gegen [*acc.*] *2* against
die Gegend, -en *11* neighborhood, region
das Gehalt, ⸚er *13* salary
gehen, ging, ist gegangen *2* go, walk; **Es geht mir gut** I am (feeling, doing) all right; **Wie geht's?** *or* **Wie geht es?** *1* How are you?
gehören [*dat.*] *14* belong (to)
der Geist, -er *7* ghost, spirit
gelb *4* yellow
das Geld, -er *2* money
gelingen, a, ist u *15* succeed; **Es gelingt mir ... zu** [*infinitive*] *15* I succeed in —ing
genug *5* enough
gerade *2* just now, just then; direct, straight (a

German-English Vocabulary 185

way); **Ich habe gerade**
4 I happen to have
gering *8* slight
gern(e) *3* gladly; **Ich
möchte gern** *3* I'd like
das **Geschäft, -e** *8* business
der **Geschäftsführer, —** man-
ager
geschehen, a, ist e, ie *6*
happen
die **Geschichte, -n** *2* story
die **Geschwister** [*pl.*] brothers
and sisters
die **Gesellschaft, -en** *4* company, party, society
das **Gesicht, -er** *15* face
gestern *6* yesterday
gesund *9* healthy
gewinnen, a, o *15* win,
gain, obtain
gewiß *3* certain
sich **gewöhnen an** [*acc.*] *13* become used to
gewöhnlich *6* usual

es gibt *6* there is (are)
der **Giebel, —** gable
gießen, o, gegossen *9* pour
das **Glas, ⁼er** *7* glass
glauben *5* believe, think
gleich [*adj.*] *9* same, equal
gleich [*adv.*] *3* immediately
das **Glück** *11* luck, happiness
glücklich *10* lucky, happy
der **Gott, ⁼er** *13* god; **der
liebe Gott** *13* the good
Lord
grau *1* gray
groß *6* great, large, big,
tall
großartig *11* magnificent
grün *5* green
grüßen *5* greet
gut, besser, best- *1* good,
better, best; well, O.K.;
**Guten Abend (Morgen,
Tag)!** *1, 3, 5* Good evening (morning, day)!

H

das **Haar, -e** *3* hair
haben, hatte, gehabt, hat
1 have
halb *5* half **(um) halb
fünf (Uhr)** *5* (at) four-
thirty (o'clock)
halten, ie, a, ä *14* hold
die **Hand, ⁼e** *6* hand
die **Handelskammer** Cham-
ber of Commerce
das **Haus, ⁼er** *4* house; **nach
Hause** *3* home(ward);
zu Hause *3* at home
die **Haustür, -en** front door
heben, o, o *15* lift, raise
das **Heft, -e** *2* notebook
heilen *9* heal
heiraten *12* marry
heiß *4* hot

heißen, ie, ei *1* be called
helfen, a, o, i [*dat.*] *3* help
hell *8* bright, light
her *15* hither, here [*toward
the speaker*]
heran-treten, a, ist e, tritt
step up
heraus out
herein in
herein-treten, a, ist e, tritt
step in
der **Herr, -n, -en** *1* gentleman,
master, Mr.
herrlich *14* magnificent,
splendid
herrschen *11* rule, prevail
das **Herz, -ens, -en** *7* heart
heute *3* today; **heute
abend (mittag, morgen)**

3, 5 this evening (noon, morning)
hier *1* here
hierher *13* to this place
hiermit herewith
der Himmel, — *12* heaven(s)
hin *12* to that place [*away from the speaker*]
vor sich hin blicken *12* stare
hinauf *13* upward
hinüber *13* across
hinunter *7* down (downward)
hin und her *6* to and fro
hin-fahren, u, ist a, ä travel to a place

hin-fliegen, o, ist o *10* fly to a place
hinter [*dat./acc.*] *2, 9* behind
hinunter-gehen, ging, ist gegangen go down
die Hitze *4* heat
hoch, höher, höchst- *15* high, higher, highest
der Hof, ̈e *15* yard, court
hoffen *10* hope
holen *4* go and get, fetch
hören *1* hear
der Hund, -e *14* dog
hundert *4* hundred

I

immer *3* always; immer kälter *9* colder and colder; immer noch (*or* noch immer) *14* still, yet
in[*dat.*] *1* in, within; [*acc.*] into

der Ingenieur, -e engineer
das Instrument, -e instrument
interessant *5* interesting
inzwischen meanwhile

J

ja *1* yes; indeed; to be sure
das Jahr, -e *6* year
jeder, jede, jedes *2* each, every
jedesmal every time
jener, jene, jenes *14* that (one), the former

jenseits [*gen.*] on the other side of
jetzt *1* now
jung, jünger, jüngst *1* young, younger, youngest
der Juni June

K

ich, er kann *2* I, he can [*see* können]
der Kasten, ̈ *8* chest, box, crate
kaufen *2* buy
kaum *11* hardly
kein, keine, kein *1, 4* not

any, no; gar kein (Auto) *15* no (car) at all
kennen, kannte, gekannt *2* know (a person)
kennen-lernen *11* get to know, meet
das Kind, -er *6* child

German-English Vocabulary   187

das **Kino, -s** *3* movies
die **Klasse, -n** *1* class
die **Klassenarbeit, -en** exercises done in class
das **Klavier, -e** piano
klein *6* little (in size)
die **Kleinigkeit, -en** *11* trifle, little thing
Kleinigkeit! *11* Nothing to it!
die **Klima-Anlage, -n** air conditioning
klingen, a, u *14* sound, ring
kommen, kam, ist gekommen *1* come
komponieren compose

können, konnte, gekonnt, kann *2, 8, 9* can, be able to
der **Kopf, ⁓e** *15* head
kosten *5* cost
krank *3* sick
das **Krankenhaus, ⁓er** hospital
die **Krankheit, -en** *10* sickness, illness
der **Krebs, -e** cancer
die **Krebsforschung, -en** cancer research
die **Küche, -n** *7* kitchen
kühl *6* cool
der **Künstler, —** *12* artist
der **Kurs, -e** course
kurz *15* short, brief
die **Kusine, -n** *3* (female) cousin

L

das **Laboratorium, die Laboratorien** laboratory
lächeln smile
lachen *6* laugh
der **Laden, -** *5* store
das **Land, ⁓er** *3* land, country
lang, länger, längst- *2* long, longer, longest; **lang(e)** [*adv.*] *7* a long time; **vier Tage lang** *7* for four days
langsam *8* slow
längst *12* long ago
lassen, ließ, gelassen, läßt *9* let, leave, permit
der **Lauf, ⁓e** *15* course, run
laufen, ie, ist au, äu run
laut *15* loud
leben *10* live
das **Leben** *13* life
das **Lebensmittelgeschäft, -e** grocery store
lebhaft lively
leer empty, vacant
legen *5* lay, put, place
der **Lehrer, —** *1* [*man*] teacher

die **Lehrerin, -nen** *1* [*woman*] teacher
leicht *11* light, easy
Das tut mir leid *3* I am sorry about that
leider *2* unfortunately
leihen, ie, ie *8* lend
leise *12* soft, quiet, in a low voice
lernen *1* learn
lesen, a, e, ie *2, 6* read
letzt- *13* last [*adj.*]
die **Leute** [*pl. only*] *5* people
das **Licht, -er** *5* light
lieb *10* dear; **der liebe Gott** *13* the good Lord
die **Liebe** *2* love
lieben love
lieblich lovely
das **Lied, -er** *14* song
liegen, a, e *6* lie (repose)
link- *8* left
los *14* loose
los-brechen, a, ist o, i break loose
löschen put out

M

machen　*2* make, do

das Mädchen, — *1* girl

der Mai　May

man　*6* one, 'they, you'

mancher, manche, manches　*14* [*variously*] many, many a

manchmal　*7* sometimes

der Mann, ⸚er　*2* man, husband

die Medizin　medicine

mehr　*8* (any) more, (any) longer [*see* viel]

nicht mehr　*5* not any more

mehrere　*9* several

mein, meine, mein　*1* my

meinen　*4* mean, have an opinion, think

meist　*8* most [*see* viel]

die Melodie, -n　melody

der Mensch, -en, -en　*3* human being

merken　*9* notice

das Meteor, -e　meteor

der Militärdienst　military service

die Minute, -n　*1* minute

mischen　*9* mix

mit [*dat.*]　*3* with; [*adv.*] along

mit-bringen, brachte, gebracht　bring along

der Mittag, -e　*5* noon

mit-teilen　*10* inform, notify

mitten　in the middle of

der Mittwoch,　*14* Wednesday

modern　modern

mögen, mochte, gemocht, mag　*2, 11* may, like to; ich möchte gern(e)　*3* I'd like to

möglich　*13* possible

der Monat, -e　*7* month

morgen　*3* tomorrow

der Morgen　*3* morning; Guten Morgen!　*1* Good morning; heute morgen　*3* this morning

das Motiv, -e　subject, motif

müde　*14* tired

die Musik　music

der Musiker, —　musician

das Musikinstrument, -e　musical instrument

das Musikstück, -e　piece of music

müssen, mußte, gemußt, muß　*2* must, have to

die Mutter, ⸚　*3* mother

N

nach [*dat.*]　*3* after, toward, to; according to; nach Hause　*3* home(ward)

der Nachbar, -n　*11* neighbor

die Nachbarschaft　neighborhood

nachdem [*conj. only*]　*9* after

nach-denken, dachte, gedacht　*12* consider, think over

nachdenklich　thoughtful

der Nachmittag, -e　*6* afternoon; am Nachmittag　*6* in the afternoon

nächst　*6* next [*see* nahe]

die Nacht, ⸚e　*7* night

nachts　*7* at night

nah(e), näher, nächst-　*6, 9* near, nearer, nearest

der Name, -ns, -n　*11* name;

Wie ist Ihr Name? *2* What is your name?

nämlich *8* namely, you know (see)

natürlich *4* natural; of course

neben [*dat./acc.*] *2, 7* beside, next to

nehmen, nahm, genommen, nimmt *5* take

neigen bend

nein *1* no

nett *4* nice, fine

neu *5* new

neugierig *8* curious, inquisitive

nicht *1* not; **nicht mehr** *5* not any more; **auch**

nicht *5* not either; **gar nicht** *6* not at all; **noch nicht** *1* not yet

nichts *5* nothing; **gar nichts** *6* nothing at all

nicken nod

nie(mals) *3* never

niemand *13* nobody

der **Nobelpreis, -e** Nobel prize

noch *1* still, yet; **noch immer** *or* **immer noch** *14* still, yet; **noch nicht** *1* not yet; **sonst noch etwas?** *13* anything else?

nun *1* now; well

nur *1* only

O

ob *10* if, whether

oben *15* above, upstairs

oder *1* or

öffnen *15* open

oft *4* often

ohne [*acc.*] *2* without

das **Öl, -e** *9* oil

die **Ölindustrie** oil industry

der **Onkel, —** *7* uncle

das **Opfer, —** *9* victim, sacrifice

der **Osten** *3* east

P

das **Paar, -e** *15* pair, couple; **ein paar** *6* a couple, a few; **vor ein paar Tagen** *9* a few days ago

packen *14* pack

die **Packung, -en** pack

das **Papier, -e** *1* paper

der **Papierkorb, ⸚e** wastebasket

der **Park, -s** *6* park

die **Pause, -n** *11* pause, intermission

die **Person, -en** *2* person

die **Pfanne, -n** pan

pfeifen, pfiff, gepfiffen whistle

die **Physik** *1* physics

die **Physikstunde, -n** *1* physics class

die **Pille, -n** pill

planen plan

der **Platz, ⸚e** *7* place, room; seat

plötzlich *14* suddenly

die **Polizei** police

der **Polizist, -en, -en** policeman

der **Präsident, -en, -en** president

der **Preis, -e** *13* price

der **Professor, -en** *1* professor

R

der **Raum, ⸚e** *8* room, space
rechnen *5* figure
die **Rechnung, -en** *2* bill
recht *8* right (hand), correct, quite, all right
der **Regen** *4* rain
der **Regentropfen, —** raindrop
regnen *12* rain
die **Reise, -n** *3* trip
reisen, ist *5* travel
rennen, rannte, ist gerannt *14* run

das **Resultat, -e** result
die **Retorte, -n** retort
retten *8* rescue, save
richten [an, auf *with acc.***]** *12* direct (to, at)
der **Ring, -e** ring
die **Rolle, -n** roll
der **Roman, -e** *8* novel
rot *1* red
rufen, ie, u *6* call
ruhen *14* rest; **sich ausruhen** *14* rest

S

die **Sache, -n** *2* thing
sagen *1* say
das **Saxophon, -e** saxophone
Es ist schade *4* It is too bad
der **Schatten, —** shade
der **Scheck, -e** check
scheinen, ie, ie *6* shine, seem
schenken *15* give, present
schicken *2* send
schlafen, ie, a, ä *6* sleep
das **Schlafzimmer, —** *7* bedroom
schlagen, u, a, ä *6* strike, beat
schlecht *15* bad, inferior
schließen, o, geschlossen *7* close, shut
schlucken swallow
schmieren grease
der **Schnee** *4* snow
schnell *5* fast
der **Schnupfen** cold
schon *1* already; surely
schön *1* pretty
die **Schönheit, -en** *15* beauty
der **Schrecken, —** shock, fright

schrecklich = furchtbar *8* terrible
schreiben, ie, ie *2* write
das **Schreibpapier, -e** writing paper
schreien, ie, ie *6* scream, yell
die **Schule, -n** *12* school
schwarz *3* black
schweigen, ie, ie *8* be silent
schweigsam quiet, silent
schwer *8* heavy, hard, difficult
die **Schwester, -n** *3* sister
die **Schwierigkeit, -en** *7* difficulty
schwimmen, a, ist o *6* swim
sechs *2* six
sechzehnjährig sixteen-year-old
der **See, -n** *15* lake
sehen, a, e, ie *2, 6* see
sehr *4* very; **sehr angenehm** *1* pleased to meet you
sein, seine, sein *2* his

sein, war, ist gewesen, ist *1, 5, 6* be

seit [*dat.*] *3* since [*time*]

die Seite, -n *8* page, side

die Sekretärin, -nen secretary

selten *6* seldom, rare

setzen *3* set, place

sich setzen *10* sit down

sich *5* himself, herself, itself, themselves; each other

sicher *2* sure

sieben *5* seven

siebzehn *2* seventeen

singen, a, u *7* sing

der Sinn, -e *15* sense, mind

sitzen, saß, gesessen *6* sit

so *1* so, thus, in this way; then

so (schön) wie *1, 8* as (pretty) as

sobald *9* as soon as

der Sohn, ⸚e *7* son

solcher, solche, solches *4* such

sollen *2, 7* ought to; be said to

der Sommer, — *3* summer

die Sommerschule, -n summer school

sondern *14* but (on the contrary)

die Sonne, -n *4* sun

der Sonntag Sunday

sonst *13* else, otherwise; sonst noch etwas? *13* anything else?

die Sorge, -n *11* care, sorrow

spät *4* late

das Spiel, -e *10* play, game

spielen *6* play

der Spieler, — player

die Sprache, -n language

sprechen, a, o, i *1* speak

springen, a, ist u *6* jump

die Stadt, ⸚e *2* city, town

stark *5* strong

die Stärke, -n strength

statt, anstatt *4* instead of, in place of

stecken *15* stick, put, place

stehen, stand, gestanden *6* stand; Es steht in der Zeitung (im Buch) *6* It says in the paper (book); stehen-bleiben, blieb stehen, ist stehengeblieben stop; remain standing

steigen, ie, ist ie *13* rise, climb

steil steep

der Stein, -e *6* stone

stellen *7* set, put, place

die Stellung, -en *10* position, situation, job

sterben, a, ist o, i *6* die

der Stern, -e *14* star

still *14* quiet

die Stimme, -n *15* voice

das Stipendium, die Stipendien stipend

der Stoff, -e substance, material

stolpern, ist stumble

die Straße, -n *5* street

das Stück, -e *8* piece

der Student, -en, -en *6* student

die Studentin, -nen [*girl*] student

studieren *1* study

das Studium, die Studien study

der Stuhl, ⸚e *7* chair

stumm = schweigend *12* silent, mute

die Stunde, -n *1* hour, class

der Sturm, ⸚e *14* storm

die Substanz, -en substance

suchen *2* seek, look for

der Süden *6* south

der Südwesten southwest

die Symphonie, -n symphony

T

die Tafel, -n blackboard
der Tag, -e *4* day; **Guten Tag!** *3* Hello; **vor ein paar Tagen** *9* a few days ago
die Tante, -n *7* aunt
die Tasche, -n *15* pocket
das Telefon, -e telephone
das Telefonbuch, ¨er telephone book
    telefonieren *5* telephone
das Telegramm, -e *3* telegram
der Teller, — *7* plate
das Tennis tennis
der Tennisplatz, ¨e tennis court
der Tennisschläger, — tennis racket
    teuer *1* expensive
das Tier, -e *2* animal
das Thermometer, — thermometer

der Tisch, -e *5* table
die Tochter, ¨ *7* daughter
der Topf, ¨e pot
der Traum, ¨e *13* dream
    träumen *1* dream
    traurig *10* sad
    treffen, traf, getroffen, trifft *6* meet
die Trennung, -en separation
die Treppe, -n *7* stairs
    treten, a, ist e, tritt *13* step, walk
    trinken, a, u *11* drink
    trotz *(gen.)* *4* in spite of
die Trompete, -n trumpet
    tüchtig *12* able, capable, excellent
    tun, tat, getan *1* do; **Das tut mir leid** *3* I am sorry about that
die Tür, -en *1* door
das Türmchen, — little tower

U

    über [*dat./acc.*] *2, 5* over, above, across, concerning, about
    überraschen surprise
die Überschrift, -en headline
    übersetzen translate
    übrigens *11* by the way
die Uhr, -en *3* clock, watch, o'clock; **um (zehn) Uhr** *1* at (ten) o'clock; **(um)- halb fünf (Uhr)** *5* (at) four-thirty (o'clock)
    um [*acc.*] *2* around, about, for; [*with time*] *1* at [*see* Uhr]
    um [*conj.*] ... zu *6* in order to
sich um-drehen *10* turn around

sich um-sehen, a, e, ie (nach) *13* look around (for)
die Umwelt environs
    un- [*prefix*] *6* un-, dis-, in-
    unangenehm unpleasant
    und *1* and
der Unfall, ¨e accident
die Union Student Union building
die Universität,-en *2* university
    unser, unsere, unser *1* our
    unter [*dat./acc.*] *2, 5* under, below, among; lower
    unterbrechen, a, o, i *12* interrupt
    unterhalb [*gen.*] below
die Unterschrift, -en signature
die Ursache, -n cause

V

der **Vater, ⸚** *2* father
verderben, a, (ist) o, i *11* spoil, perish
verdienen *13* earn, deserve
das **Verfahren, —** *15* process
vergehen, verging, ist vergangen *11* pass (time), go away, go by
vergessen, vergaß, vergessen, vergißt *10* forget
das **Vergnügen, —** *4* pleasure, fun
verkaufen *10* sell
der **Verkäufer, —** sales clerk
der **Verkehr** *5* traffic
verlangen *13* demand, ask for
verlassen, verließ, verlassen, verläßt *7* abandon, leave
verleben spend (time)
sich **verlieben in** [*acc.*] *10* fall in love with
sich **verloben** get engaged
die **Verlobte, -n** fiancée
verschwinden, a, ist u *13* disappear
versichern *8* insure
versprechen, a, o, i *12* promise
verstehen, verstand, verstanden *6* understand
versuchen *13* try
verwandeln = ändern *13* change

der **Verwandte, -n, -n** *7* relative
Verzeihen Sie! *5* Pardon me
der **Vetter, -n** *7* (male) cousin
viel, mehr, meist- *4, 8* much, more, most
vielleicht *4* perhaps
vier *1* four; **vier Wochen** *10* a month; **der vierte** *13* fourth
vierzehn *7* fourteen; **vierzehn Tage** *7* two weeks
der **Vogel, ⸚** *7* bird
voll *7* full
von [*dat.*] *3* from, of, about
vor [*dat./acc.*] *2, 5* before, ago; **vor ein paar Tagen** *9* a few days ago; **vor sich hin blicken** *12* stare
vorbei *5* over, past, by
vorbei-gehen, ging, ist gegangen *10* pass, go by
vor-bereiten *14* prepare
vorgestern = vorzwei Tagen *8* day before yesterday
der **Vorrat, ⸚e** *11* supply, provision
vorsichtig careful
vor-spielen play (for someone)
vor-stellen *11* present, introduce; imagine; **sich vorstellen** *11* introduce oneself; imagine
vorüber = vorbei *14* past, over

W

der **Wagen, —** *6* car
wahr *4* true
während [*gen.*] *4* during; [*conj.*] *9* while
wann *2* when
warnen *8* warn

warten [**auf** *with acc.*] *5* wait (for)
warum *3* why
was *1, 3* what; **was für ein** what kind of
das **Wasser, ⸚** [*or* —] *6* water

der **Wasserdruck** water pressure
die **Wasserleitung, -en** water pipes
der **Weg, -e** *2* way
wegen [*gen.*] *4* on account of
weil *9* because
weiß *1* white
weit, weiter, weitest *3* far, farther, farthest; **weiter** *3* further, on
welcher, welche, welches *2, 9* which, that, what, who
die **Welt, -en** *2* world
wenn *7* if, when (whenever)
wer *2, 9* who; whoever, (he) who
werden, wurde, ist geworden, wird *4* become, get
werfen, a, o, i *6* throw
das **Werk, -e** *12* work [*esp. of art*]
wertvoll *8* valuable
wie *1* as, how, like; **so (schön) wie** *1* as pretty as; **Wie ist Ihr Name?** *2* What is your name?
wieder *4* again
wiederholen *5* repeat, review
wieder-sehen, a, e, ie see again; **Auf Wiederseh(e)n!** *1* Good-bye
wieso how (so)
wieviel, wie viele *7* how much, how many
ich, er will *3* I, he want(s) [*see* **wollen**]

der **Wind, -e** *14* wind
wird *4* [*see* **werden**]
wirklich *3* really
die **Wirklichkeit, -en** *12* reality
wissen, wußte, gewußt, weiß *6* know (a fact)
die **Wissenschaft, -en** *9* science
wissenschaftlich scientific
wo *1* where
die **Woche, -n** *3* week
woher from what, from where
wohin whereto
wohl *4* well, indeed, in fact, probably, no doubt; **sich wohl fühlen** *13* feel well (good)
wohnen *4* live, dwell, reside
die **Wohnung, -en** *7* place to live, apartment
das **Wohnzimmer, —** living room
die **Wolke, -n** *12* cloud
wollen, wollte, gewollt, will *4* want to
womit *5* with what, how
woran about what
das **Wort, -e** *or* ¨er *2* word
das **Wörterbuch,** ¨er dictionary
worüber about what
wunderbar *4* wonderful
sich **wundern über** [*acc.*] *8* be surprised at
der **Wunsch,** ¨e *8* wish
wünschen *2* wish

Z

der **Zahn,** ¨e *15* tooth
zehn *1* ten; **zehntausend** ten thousand
das **Zeichen, —** *10* sign, token;
zum Zeichen as a sign
zeigen *4* show
die **Zeit, -en** *4* time
die **Zeitung, -en** *6* newspaper

die **Zelle, -n** cell

ziehen, zog, gezogen *15* pull, draw

die **Ziehharmonika** accordion

das **Zimmer, —** *7* room

zu *1* too; [*dat.*] to; **zu Besuch** *7* on (for) a visit; **zum Zeichen** as a sign; **zu Hause** *3* at home; **zuerst** *12* (at) first

der **Zug, ⁓e** *4* train

die **Zukunft** *13* future

zu-machen close

zurück *10* back

zurück-gehen, ging, ist gegangen go back

zurück-kehren = zurück-kommen *10* return

zurück-schicken *10* send back

zusammen *6* together

zusammen-kommen, kam, ist gekommen get together, assemble

zusammen-packen pack together

zuviel = zu viel *12* too much

zwanzig *4* twenty

zwei *2* two

zweimal *3* two times

der **Zweig, -e** *7* twig, branch

der **zweite** *7* second

der **Zwilling, -e** twin

zwischen [*dat./acc.*] *2, 6* between, among

zwölf *2* twelve

A

a, an   ein, eine, ein
abandon   verlassen, verließ, verlassen, verläßt
able   tüchtig
be able   können, konnte, gekonnt, kann
about   von [dat.]; über, um [acc.]
above   über [dat./acc.]; oben [adv.]
accept   an-nehmen, nahm, genommen, nimmt
according to   nach [dat.]
on account of   wegen [gen.]
across   über [dat./acc.]; hinüber [adv.]
a few   einige
after [prep.]   nach [dat.]; [conj.] nachdem
afternoon   der Nachmittag, -e
again   wieder
against   gegen [acc.]
ago   vor [dat.]
alas   ach
alone   allein
along   entlang; mit
all   all   all right   gut, recht
already   schon
also   auch
alter   ändern
altogether   ganz
always   immer
I am   ich bin [see sein]

I am permitted   ich darf
I am sorry   Das tut mir leid
American   amerikanisch
among   bei [dat.]; unter, zwischen [dat./acc.]
and   und; denn
animal   das Tier, -e
answer   antworten
(any)more   mehr
anything else?   Sonst noch etwas?
anyway   denn
not any   kein, keine, kein
apartment   die Wohnung,-en
appear   aus-sehen, a, e, ie
How are you?   Wie geht es? Wie geht's?
arm   der Arm, -e
around   um [acc.]
arrive   an-kommen, a, ist o
artist   der Künstler, —
as   als, wie;   as (pretty) as   so (schön) wie
as if   als ob
as far as   bis
as soon as   so bald
ask   (information) fragen; (a favor) bitten, bat, gebeten
ask for   verlangen
assignment   die Aufgabe, -n
at   bei [dat.]; an [dat./acc.]; um [acc.]
at first   (zu)erst

at **home** zu Hause
at **night** nachts
at **last** endlich
at **that time** damals

at **the house of** bei [*dat.*]
aunt die Tante, -n
await erwarten
awake erwachen, ist

B

back zurück
bad schlecht
It is too bad Es ist schade
ball der Ball, ⸚e
bank die Bank, -en
be sein, war, ist gewesen, ist
I am sorry Das tut mir leid
How are you? Wie geht es? Wie geht's?
be able to können, konnte, gekonnt, kann
be called heißen, ie, ei
be said to sollen
be silent schweigen, ie, ie
bear ertragen, u, a, ä
beat schlagen, u, a, ä
beauty die Schönheit, -en
because weil
become werden, u, ist o, i
become frightened erschrecken, erschrak, ist erschrocken, erschrickt
become used to sich gewöhnen an [*acc.*]
bed das Bett, -en
bedroom das Schlafzimmer, —
before vor [*dat./acc.*]; [*conj.*] ehe
begin an-fangen, i, a, ä; beginnen, a, o
beginning der Anfang, ⸚e
behind hinter [*dat./acc.*]
believe glauben
belong (to) gehören [*dat.*]

below unter [*dat./acc.*]; unterhalb [*gen.*]
bench die Bank, ⸚e
beside neben [*dat./acc.*]
best best-
better besser
between zwischen, unter [*dat./acc.*]
big groß
bill die Rechnung, -en
bird der Vogel, ⸚
a bit ein bißchen
black schwarz
blackboard die Tafel, -n
board das Brett, -er
book das Buch, ⸚er
born geboren
both beide
branch der Zweig, -e
break brechen, a, o, i; **break in** ein-brechen, a, o, i
brief kurz
bright hell
bring bringen, brachte, gebracht
brother der Bruder, ⸚
brown braun
build bauen
burglarize ein-brechen, a, o, i
burn brennen, brannte, gebrannt
but aber, doch; (on the contrary) sondern
business das Geschäft, -e
buy kaufen
by bei, von [*dat.*]; vorbei
by the way übrigens

C

call   rufen, ie, u
call for   ab-holen
call up   an-rufen, ie, u
be called   heißen, ie, ei
can, be able to   können, konnte, gekonnt, kann
capable   tüchtig
car   der Wagen, —; das Auto, -s
care   die Sorge, -n
in that case   da; dann
catch   fangen, i, a, ä; fassen
cease   auf-hören
certain   gewiß
chair   der Stuhl, ⁻e
change   ändern; verwandeln
cheap   billig
chest   (box) der Kasten, ⁻
child   das Kind, -er
city   die Stadt, ⁻e
class   die Klasse, -n; die Stunde, -n
climb   steigen, ie, ist ie
clock   die Uhr, -en
close   schließen, o, geschlossen; zu-machen
cloud   die Wolke, -n
colder and colder   immer kälter
come   kommen, kam, ist gekommen

company   die Gesellschaft, -en
complete   [adj.] erfüllen
concerning   über [acc.]
connect   an-schließen, o, geschlossen
consider   nach-denken, dachte, gedacht
consist   bestehen, bestand, bestanden
continue   fort-fahren, u, ist a, ä; fort-setzen
cool   kühl; cool off   ab-kühlen
corner   die Ecke, -n
correct   recht
cost   kosten
country   das Land, ⁻er
couple   das Paar, -e; a couple (few)   ein paar
course   der Lauf, ⁻e
of course   natürlich
court   der Hof, ⁻e
cousin   [male] der Vetter, -n; [female] die Kusine, -n
crate   der Kasten, ⁻
crowd   drängen
curious   neugierig
cut down   fällen

D

dark   dunkel; finster
dark   das Dunkle
darkness   die Dunkelheit
daughter   die Tochter, ⁻
day   der Tag, -e; good day! (Hello!)   Guten Tag!
a few days ago   vor ein paar Tagen
day before yesterday   vorgestern
one day   eines Tages
dear   lieb
Dear Sir   Sehr geehrter Herr!

declare   erklären
demand   verlangen
departure   die Abfahrt, -en
deserve   verdienen
develop   entwickeln
die   sterben, a, ist o, i
difficult   schwer
difficulty   die Schwierigkeit, -en
diligent   fleißig
direct   [adj.] gerade; direct (at) richten [auf acc.]
dis-   un-

disappear verschwinden, a, ist u
discovery die Entdeckung, -en
do tun, tat, getan; machen; **I am doing (feeling) fine** Es geht mir gut
dog der Hund, -e
door die Tür, -en
no doubt wohl

downward hinunter
draw ziehen, zog, gezogen
dream träumen; der Traum, ̈-e
drink trinken, a, u
drive fahren, u, ist a, ä
drop [*intrans.*] fallen, ie, ist a, ä
during während [*gen.*]
dwell wohnen

E

each jeder, jede, jedes; **each other** einander; sich
early früh; **earlier** früher
earn verdienen
earth die Erde
east der Osten
easy leicht
eat essen, aß, gegessen, ißt
eight acht
eighty achtzig
either ... or entweder ... oder
elder, eldest älter, ältest-
eleven elf
else sonst; **anything else?** sonst noch etwas?
enable ermöglichen
enclose bei-legen
end das Ende, -n
in the end endlich
English englisch; **in English** auf Englisch
enough genug

entire ganz
equal gleich
essential eigentlich
even auch
evening der Abend, -e; **good evening** Guten Abend! **in the evening** abends; **one evening** eines Abends; **this evening** heute Abend
every jeder, jede, jedes
examination das Examen, —
for example (e.g.) zum Beispiel (z.B.)
excellent tüchtig
exist bestehen, bestand, bestanden
expect erwarten
expensive teuer
explain erklären
extreme äußerst
eye das Auge, -n

F

face das Gesicht, -er
in fact wohl
fall fallen, fiel, ist a, ä
fall in love with sich verlieben in [*acc.*]
family die Familie, -n
famous berühmt
far weit
fast schnell

father der Vater, ̈
feel fühlen **feel good (or well)** sich wohl fühlen **I am feeling (doing) all right** Es geht mir gut
feeling das Gefühl, -e
fell fällen
fetch holen
a few einige; ein paar; **a few**

days ago vor ein paar Tagen

fiancée die Verlobte

figure rechnen

the fifth der fünfte

fifty fünfzig

finally endlich

find finden, a, u

fine nett

first, at first erst, zuerst; **the first** der erste

five fünf

flame die Flamme, -n

flow fließen, o, ist geflossen

flower die Blume, -n

fly fliegen, o, ist o; **fly to a place** hin-fliegen, o, ist o

for [*prep.*] für, um [*acc.*]; [*conj.*] denn; **for a visit** zu Besuch

for example (e.g.) zum Beispiel (z.B.)

for four days vier Tage lang

for that reason darum

foreboding die Ahnung, -en

forget vergessen, vergaß, vergessen, vergißt

the former jener, jene, jenes

look forward to sich freuen auf [*acc.*]

fountain pen die Füllfeder, -n

four vier

fourteen vierzehn

(at) four-thirty (o'clock) (um) halb fünf (Uhr)

the fourth der vierte

free frei

Friday der Freitag, -e

friend der Freund, -e

friendly freundlich

become frightened erschrecken, erschrak, ist erschrocken, erschrickt

from aus, von [*dat.*]

fulfill erfüllen

full voll

fun das Vergnügen, —

further (on) weiter

future die Zukunft

G

gain gewinnen, a, o

garden der Garten, ⸚

game das Spiel, -e

gentleman der Herr, -n, -en

German deutsch **the German language** (das) Deutsch; **in German** auf Deutsch

get bekommen, bekam, bekommen; erhalten, ie, a, ä; werden, u, ist o, i

get to know kennen-lernen

ghost der Geist, -er

girl das Mädchen, —

give geben, a, e, i **give** (as a present) schenken

gladly gern(e); **I am very glad** Das freut mich sehr

glass das Glas, ⸚er

gloomy finster, dunkel

go (on foot) gehen, ging, ist gegangen; (by vehicle) fahren, fuhr, ist gefahren, fährt

go and get holen

go by [*time*], **pass** vergehen, ging, ist vergangen; **go by** vorbeigehen, ging, ist gegangen

god der Gott, ⸚er

good gut; **Good evening** (morning, day)! Guten Abend (Morgen, Tag)! **good-bye** Auf Wiederseh(e)n! **the good Lord** der liebe Gott

grasp fassen

gray grau

great groß

green grün

greet grüßen, begrüßen

H

hair das Haar, -e
half halb
Hand die Hand, ⁼e
happen geschehen, a, ist e, ie;
 I happen to have Ich habe
 gerade
happiness das Glück
happy glücklich; be happy
 sich freuen
hard (difficult) schwer
hardly kaum
have haben, hatte, gehabt, hat
have an opinion meinen; have
 (something done) lassen, ließ,
 gelassen, läßt; have to müssen, mußte, gemußt, muß
head der Kopf, ⁼e
heal heilen
healthy gesund
hear hören
heart das Herz, -ens, -en
heat die Hitze
heaven(s) der Himmel, —
heavy schwer
Hello! Guten Tag!
help helfen, a, o, i [dat.]

here hier; (toward the speaker)
 her
herself sich
he who wer
high hoch, höher, höchst-
himself sich
his sein, seine, sein
hither her
hold halten, ie, a, ä
at home zu Hause
home (ward) nach Hause
hope hoffen
hot heiß
hour die Stunde, -n
house das Haus, ⁼er at the
 house of bei [dat.]
how wie, womit; How are you?
 Wie geht's? Wie geht es?
how many, how much wie
 viele, wie viel
human being der Mensch, -en,
 -en
hundred hundert
hurry eilen, ist
husband der Mann, ⁼er

I

idea die Ahnung, -en
if wenn; (whether) ob
ill krank
illness die Krankheit, -en
imagine sich vor-stellen
immediately gleich
in in [dat./acc.]
in- un-
in fact wohl
in order to um zu
in place of für [acc.]; (an)statt
 [gen.]
in spite of trotz [gen.]
in that case da, dann

in the country auf dem Lande
in the end endlich
in the process dabei
in this way so
indeed wohl
industrious fleißig
inferior schlecht
inform mit-teilen
inquisitive neugierig
insert ein-setzen
insure versichern
instead of (an)statt [gen.]
interesting interessant
intermission die Pause, -n

interrupt unterbrechen, a, o, i
into in [*acc.*]
introduce vor-stellen; **intro-** duce oneself sich vor-stellen
invite ein-laden, u, a, ä
itself sich

J

job die Stellung, -en
joyful froh, fröhlich
jump springen, a, ist u

just eben; **just now, just then** gerade

K

kind freundlich
kitchen die Küche, -n
know (a fact) wissen, wußte, gewußt, weiß; **know** (a person) kennen, kannte, gekannt; **you know** nämlich; **get to know** kennen-lernen; **known** bekannt

L

young lady das Fräulein
lake der See, -n
land das Land, ⁻er
laugh lachen; **laugh at** auslachen
large groß, größer, größt
last [*adj.*] letzt-
at last endlich
late spät
lay legen
lead pencil der Bleistift, -e
leaf das Blatt, ⁻er
learn lernen
leave lassen, ließ, gelassen, läßt; verlassen, ie, a, ä
left link-
leg das Bein, -e
lend leihen, ie, ie
lesson die Aufgabe, -n
let lassen, ließ, gelassen, läßt
letter der Brief, -e
lie (repose) liegen, a, e
life das Leben
lift heben, o, o
light (*in color*) hell; **light** (*in weight; not difficult*) leicht

light das Licht, -er
like wie
like to mögen, mochte, gemocht, mag; **I'd like** ich möchte gern; **I like that** Das gefällt mir
little (*in size*) klein
a little (bit) ein bißchen
little thing die Kleinigkeit, -en
live leben
lonely, lonesome einsam
long lang, länger, längst-; **long ago** längst; **a long time** lang(e); **(any) longer** mehr
look blicken
look (appear) aus-sehen, a, e, ie
look around (for) sich um-sehen, a, e, ie nach [*dat.*]
look at an-sehen, a, e, ie
look for suchen
look forward to sich freuen auf [*acc.*]
loose los
break loose los-brechen, a, o, i
the good Lord der liebe Gott
(a) lot, much viel

loud laut
love die Liebe; **fall in love with** sich verlieben in [*acc.*]
in a low voice leise

lower unter
luck das Glück
lucky glücklich

M

magnificent großartig, herrlich
make machen; tun, tat, getan
man der Mann, ̈-er
many a mancher, manche, manches
marry heiraten
master der Herr, -n, -en
I may, am permitted ich darf [*see* dürfen]
may, like to mögen, mochte, gemocht, mag
mean, have an opinion meinen
meet begegnen, ist; kennenlernen; treffen, a, o, i; **pleased to meet you** Sehr angenehm!
merry froh, fröhlich
mind der Sinn, -e
minute die Minute, -n
Miss (das) Fräulein, —
mix mischen
moment der Augenblick, -e

money das Geld, -er
month der Monat, -e; vier Wochen
more mehr [*see* viel]
morning der Morgen, —; **Good morning** Guten Morgen! **this morning** heute morgen
most meist [*see* viel]
mother die Mutter, ̈-
mountain der Berg, -e
move in ein-ziehen, zog, ist gezogen
movies das Kino, -s
Mr. der Herr, -n, -en
Mrs. (die) Frau, -en
much viel, mehr, meist-
must, have to müssen, mußte, gemußt, muß
mute stumm
my mein, meine, mein

N

name der Name, -ns, -n
What is your name? Wie ist Ihr Name?
namely nämlich
natural natürlich
near an, bei [*dat.*]; nah(e), näher, nächst-
need brauchen
neighbor der Nachbar, -(e)n
neighborhood die Nachbarschaft, -en
never nie(mals)
nevertheless doch

new neu
newspaper die Zeitung, -en
next nächst- [*see* nahe]
next to neben [*dat./acc.*]
nice nett
night die Nacht, ̈-e; **at night** nachts
no nein
no [*adj.*] = **not any** kein, keine, kein
no (car) at all gar kein (Auto)
nobody niemand
no doubt wohl

noon der Mittag, -e; **this noon** heute mittag
not nicht
not any kein, keine, kein; **not any more** nicht mehr; **not at all** gar kein; **not . . . either** auch nicht; **not until** erst; **not yet** noch nicht

notebook das Heft, -e
nothing nichts; **nothing at all** gar nichts; **nothing to it** Kleinigkeit!
notice merken
notify mit-teilen
novel der Roman, -e
now jetzt, nun

O

observe beobachten
observation die Beobachtung, -en
obtain gewinnen, a, o
occasionally manchmal
o'clock Uhr; **at (ten) o'clock** um (zehn) Uhr; **(at) four-thirty (o'clock)** (um) halb fünf (Uhr)
of von [*dat.*]; [*usually gen. of the noun*]
of course natürlich
of it davon
often oft
oh, o ach!
oil das Öl, -e
o.k. gut
old alt, älter, ältest-
on an [*dat./acc.*]
(up)on auf [*dat./acc.*]
on, further weiter; **on account of** wegen [*gen.*]; **on vacation** auf (in die) Ferien; **on a visit** zu Besuch

once einmal
one, 'they, you' man
one ein, eine, ein
only nur; erst
open öffnen; auf-machen, auf-schlagen, u, a, ä [*book*]
have an opinion meinen
or oder
in order to um . . . zu
other ander
otherwise sonst
ought to sollen
our unser, unsere, unser
out of aus [*dat.*]
outside draußen
outside of außerhalb [*gen.*]
out there draußen
over (above) über. [*dat./acc.*]
over (past) vorbei, vorüber
over there drüben
own eigen
owner der Besitzer, —
order – bestellen

P

pack packen
page das Blatt, ¨er; die Seite, -n
pair das Paar, -e
paper das Papier, -e
Pardon me Verzeihen Sie!
park der Park, -s
party die Gesellschaft, -en

pass (an examination) bestehen, bestand, bestanden; **pass (by)** vorbei-gehen, ging, ist gegangen; **pass (time), go by** vergehen, verging, ist vergangen
past vorbei, vorüber
pause die Pause, -n

pay bezahlen
pen die Feder, -n; (Füllfeder)
pencil der Bleistift, -e
people die Leute [*pl.*]
perhaps vielleicht
perish verderben, a, ist o, i
permit lassen, ließ, gelassen, läßt; **be permitted** dürfen, durfte, gedurft, darf
person die Person, -en
physics die Physik
physics class die Physikstunde, -n
picture das Bild, -er
piece das Stück, -e
place der Platz, ¨e; **place (to live)** die Wohnung, -en; **to that place** hin; **to this place** (hier)her
place legen, setzen, stecken, stellen
plate der Teller, —
play das Spiel, -e
play spielen
pleasant angenehm
please bitte; doch
please gefallen, ie, a, ä; **Pleased to meet you!** Sehr angenehm!
That pleases me Das gefällt mir
pleasure das Vergnügen, —
pocket die Tasche, -n
popular beliebt
poet der Dichter, —
position die Stellung, -en
possible möglich
pour gießen, o, gegossen
prepare vor-bereiten
prepared bereit
present (give) schenken; **present (introduce)** vor-stellen
press, crowd drängen
pretty schön
prevail herrschen
price der Preis, -e
probably wohl
process das Verfahren, —
professor der Professor, -en
promise versprechen, a, o, i
provision der Vorrat, ¨e
pull ziehen, zog, gezogen
put legen, setzen, stecken, stellen; **put in** ein-setzen; **put up with** ertragen, u, a, ä

Q

question die Frage, -n
question fragen
quiet leise, still
quite recht

R

(rail)road die Bahn, -en
rain der Regen
rain regnen
raise heben, o, o
rare selten
read lesen, a, e, ie
ready bereit
reality die Wirklichkeit, -en
really wirklich, eigentlich
receive bekommen, a, o; erhalten, ie, a, ä
recover sich erholen
red rot
region die Gegend, -en
relative der Verwandte, -n, -n
remain bleiben, ie, ist ie
remember sich erinnern [*gen. or an with acc.*]
repeat wiederholen
report berichten
require brauchen
rescue retten

reside wohnen
rest ruhen, sich aus-ruhen
return zurück-kommen, kam, ist o; zurück-kehren, ist
review wiederholen
ride die Fahrt, -en
right (hand) recht
ring klingen, a, u

rise steigen, ie, ist ie
river der Fluß, die Flüsse
room der Raum, ⁼e; der Platz, ⁼e; das Zimmer, —
rule herrschen
run rennen, rannte, ist gerannt
run der Lauf, ⁼e

S

sacrifice das Opfer, —
sad traurig
be said to sollen
salary das Gehalt, ⁼er
same gleich
save retten
say sagen; **It says in the paper** (book) Es steht in der Zeitung (im Buch)
school die Schule, -n
science die Wissenschaft, -en
scream schreien, ie, ie
seat der Platz, ⁼e
the second der zweite
see sehen, a, e, ie; **you see** nämlich
seek suchen
seem scheinen, ie, ie
seize fassen
seldom selten
sell verkaufen
send schicken; **send back** zurück-schicken
sense der Sinn, -e
serve dienen
set setzen, stellen; **set in** einsetzen
seven sieben
seventeen siebzehn
seventy-five fünfundsiebzig
several mehrere
sheet das Blatt, ⁼er
shine scheinen, ie, ie
short kurz
show zeigen

shut schließen, o, geschlossen
sick krank
sickness die Krankheit, -en
side die Seite, -n
sign das Zeichen, —
silent stumm; **be silent** schweigen, ie, ie
since [*prep.*] seit [*dat.*]; **since** [*conj.*] da
sing singen, a, u
sister die Schwester, -n
sit sitzen
sit down sich setzen
situation (job) die Stellung, -en
six sechs
sleep schlafen, ie, a, ä
slight gering
slow langsam
snow der Schnee
so so
society die Gesellschaft, -en
soft (voiced) leise
some einige
some(thing), **somewhat** etwas
sometimes manchmal
son der Sohn, ⁼e
song das Lied, -er
soon bald; **as soon as** so bald wie
sorrow die Sorge, -n
I am sorry Das tut mir leid
sound klingen, a, u
south der Süden
space der Raum, ⁼e; der Platz, ⁼e
speak sprechen, a, o, i

spell buchstabieren
in spite of trotz [*gen.*]
spirit der Geist, -er
splendid herrlich
spoil verderben, a, ist o, i
spring (springtime) der Frühling
stairs die Treppe, -n
stand stehen, stand, gestanden
star der Stern, -e
stare vor sich hin blicken
start beginnen, a, o; an-fangen, i, a, ä
stay bleiben, ie, ist ie
step treten, a, ist, e, tritt
stick stecken
still (yet) noch; immer noch; noch immer
stone der Stein, -e
stop auf-hören
store der Laden, ⁓
storm der Sturm, ⁓e
story die Geschichte, -n

straight(way) gerade
street die Straße, -n
strike schlagen, u, a, ä
strong stark
student der Student, -en, -en; **girl student** die Studentin, -nen
study studieren
succeed gelingen, a, ist u; **I succeed in** es gelingt mir zu [*plus infinitive*]
such solcher, solche, solches
suddenly plötzlich
summer der Sommer, —
sun die Sonne, -n
supply der Vorrat, ⁓e
sure sicher; **to be sure** ja
surely doch; schon
be surprised at sich wundern über [*acc.*]
swim schwimmen, a, ist o

T

table der Tisch, -e
take nehmen, nahm, genommen, nimmt
tall groß, größer, größt
task die Aufgabe, -n
teacher (*man*) der Lehrer, —
teacher (*woman*) die Lehrerin, -nen
telegram das Telegramm, -e
telephone das Telefon, -e; der Fernsprecher, —
telephone telefonieren
tell erzählen; sagen
ten zehn
terrible furchtbar; schrecklich
than als
thank danken [*dat.*]
thanks! danke!
that das; daß; der, die, das; welcher, welche, welches; **that one** jener, jene, jenes
the der, die, das

themselves sich
then da, dann, so
there da, dort
there is (are) es gibt; **there was (were)** es gab
therefore also
'they, you', one man
thief der Dieb, -e
thing das Ding, -e; die Sache, -n
think denken, dachte, gedacht; meinen; glauben; **think of** denken, dachte, gedacht an [*acc.*]; **think over** nach-denken, dachte, gedacht
the third der dritte
thirteenth dreizehnt-
this dieser, diese, dieses; **this evening** (noon, morning) heute abend (mittag, morgen); **in this way** so
thought der Gedanke, -ns, -n

three drei
through durch [*acc.*]
throw werfen, a, o, i
thus so
till bis
time die Zeit, -en; **at that time** damals
tired müde
to zu, nach [*dat.*]; an, bis [*acc.*]
to be sure ja
to that place hin
to this place her
to and fro hin und her
today heute
together zusammen
token das Zeichen, —
tomorrow morgen
too (also) auch
too (excessive) zu
it is too bad Es ist schade
too many zu viele; **too much** zu viel, zu viele
tooth der Zahn, ¨e

toward nach [*dat.*]
town die Stadt, ¨e
traffic der Verkehr
train der Zug, ¨e; die Bahn, -en
translate übersetzen
travel reisen, ist
tree der Baum, ¨e
trifle die Kleinigkeit, -en
trip die Fahrt, -en; die Reise, -n
true wahr, eigentlich
try versuchen
Tuesday der Dienstag, -e
turn drehen
turn around (sich) um-drehen
twelve zwölf
twenty zwanzig
twenty-five fünfundzwanzig
twice zweimal
twig der Zweig, -e
two zwei; **two weeks** vierzehn Tage; **two times** zweimal

U

un- un-
uncle der Onkel
under unter [*dat./acc.*]
understand verstehen, verstand, verstanden
unfortunately leider
university die Universität, -en
unload ab-laden, u, a, ä
until bis; **not until** erst

up, upon auf [*dat./acc.*]; heran
upward hinauf
up to an [*acc.*]
upstairs oben
use brauchen
become used to sich gewöhnen an [*acc.*]
usual gewöhnlich

V

vacation die Ferien [*pl.*]; **on vacation** auf (in die) Ferien
valuable wertvoll
very sehr

victim das Opfer, —
visit besuchen
voice die Stimme, -n

W

wait for warten auf [*acc.*]
wake up auf-wachen, ist
walk gehen, ging, ist gegangen; treten, a, ist, e, tritt
want wollen, wünschen
warn warnen
watch die Uhr, -en
water das Wasser, (-)
way der Weg, -e; **by the way** übrigens; **in this way** so
Wednesday der Mittwoch, -e
week die Woche, -n; **two weeks** vierzehn Tage
well [*interj.*] nun
well gut, wohl
well-known bekannt
what welcher, welche, welches
What is your Name? Wie ist Ihr Name?
when als
when? wann
when(ever) wenn
where wo
whether ob
which der, die, das; welcher, welche, welches

while während
white weiß
who wer; der, die, das; welcher, welche, welches
whoever, (he) who wer
whole ganz; das Ganze
why warum
wife die Frau, -en
win gewinnen, a, o
wind der Wind, -e
window das Fenster, —
wish der Wunsch, -̈e
wish wünschen
with mit, bei [*dat.*]
within in [*dat.*]
with what womit
without ohne [*acc.*]
woman die Frau, -en
wonderful wunderbar
word das Wort, -̈er *or* -e
work arbeiten
work die Arbeit, -en; [*esp. work of art*] das Werk, -e
worker der Arbeiter, —
world die Welt, -en
write schreiben, ie, ie

Y

yard der Hof, -̈e
year das Jahr, -e
yell schreien, ie, ie
yellow gelb
yes ja
yesterday gestern; **day before yesterday** vorgestern
yet noch; immer noch *or* noch

immer; **not yet** noch nicht
you know, you see nämlich
'you, they', one man
young jung, jünger, jüngst-
young lady das Fräulein; die Dame, -n
yours [*in close of letters*] ihr ergebener

APPENDIX

APPENDIX

THE GERMAN ALPHABET, SOUNDS, AND PUNCTUATION

THE NOUN

DER-WORDS, *EIN*-WORDS, AND ADJECTIVES

PRONOUNS

NUMERALS AND DATES

THE VERB

1. The German Alphabet, Sounds, and Punctuation

1.1 The Alphabet The same alphabet is used in German and in English. In some German printed matter, an older form of letters called Fraktur, or Gothic, more curved and ornate than the common English type faces, is used; in contemporary books this type is very infrequent. The texts in Lessons 14 and 15 have been printed in Fraktur. As is clear from these lessons, one can read Fraktur type as readily as he can read an English book printed in black-letter type.

There is also a special German script in handwriting, but this is no longer in general use.

Roman		"Fraktur"		German Script		Pronunciation
a	A	a	𝔄	*a*	*A*	[a:]
b	B	b	𝔅	*b*	*B*	[be:]
c	C	c	ℭ		*C*	[tse:]
d	D	d	𝔇	*d*	*D*	[de:]
e	E	e	𝔈		*E*	[e:]
f	F	f	𝔉	*f*	*F*	[ef]
g	G	g	𝔊	*g*	*G*	[ge:]
h	H	h	ℌ	*h*	*H*	[ha:]
i	I	i	ℑ	*i*	*I*	[i:]
j	J	j	ℑ	*j*	*J*	[yot]
k	K	f	𝔎	*k*	*K*	[ka:]
l	L	l	𝔏	*l*	*L*	[el]
m	M	m	𝔐	*m*	*M*	[em]
n	N	n	𝔑	*n*	*N*	[en]
o	O	o	𝔒	*o*	*O*	[o:]
p	P	p	𝔓	*p*	*P*	[pe:]
q	Q	q	𝔔	*q*	*Q*	[ku:]
r	R	r	𝔑	*r*	*R*	[er]

Roman		"Fraktur"		German Script		Pronunciation
s	S	ſ	S			[es]
t	T	t	T			[te:]
u	U	u	U			[u:]
v	V	v	B			[fau]
w	W	w	W			[ve:]
x	X	x	X			[iks]
y	Y	ŋ	Y			[ipsilon]
z	Z	ʒ	Z			[tset]
ä	Ä	ä	A			
ö	Ö	ö	O			
ü	Ü	ü	U			
ß		ß				
ch		ch				
sch		ſch				
ck		ck				
final s		s				
tz		tz				
st		ſt				

The German alphabet contains four modified letters in addition to the 26 ordinary letters of the alphabet: ß, a form of double **s** used primarily after long vowels and diphthongs and ä, ö, and ü, the so-called umlaut vowels. Other special forms are used in the German script and, to a certain extent, in Fraktur for the further elements given above.

The German names of the ordinary letters of the alphabet are approximately the same as the English names, but are of course pronounced with the German values of the vowels; indications of pronunciation given in brackets in the right-hand column are the same as those used in the lessons and later in the Appendix.

1.2 General Rules of German Pronunciation
In approaching another language it is as important to know the characteristic manner of pronouncing one's own language as it is to know the essentials of accurate pronunciation of the new language. One's best guide is always a competent speaker, whose pronunciation must be followed as closely as possible.

Americans speak in a very relaxed way. We drawl most of our vowels; we do not pronounce our [p t k] clearly, especially when they end a word. It is difficult, for example, for us to distinguish between such words as *tap*, *tat* and *tak* unless we can see the mouth of the speaker pronouncing them or unless we have enough context to guess the proper word. Furthermore, syllables upon which a chief accent does not fall are almost completely unstressed. In order to learn to speak German properly, therefore, we must adopt a completely different set of speech habits.

German distinguishes between a set of short vowels and a set of long vowels, not only in name. The primary difference between the pronunciation of **Stadt** 'city' and **Staat** 'state' is that the vowel in **Stadt** is short; its duration is about half that of the vowel in **Staat.** The German short vowels present one of the chief problems in pronouncing German. *We must speed up our speech tempo when we speak German, paying special attention to making the short vowels really short.*

We must also place somewhat heavier stresses on unstressed syllables than we do in English.

In the following discussion, the letters in heavy type refer to spelling symbols *e.g.*; **lieb,** the letters in brackets refer to actual sounds, *e.g.*, [li:p].

1.3 The German consonants In general, the German consonants are like the English consonants and will cause little difficulty in pronunciation. German spelling, on the other hand, is more consistent than that of English. For this reason the consonants are discussed here in accordance with the way they are pronounced rather than the way they are written.

German [p b m] are like English [p b m]:

Papier	paper	**braun**	brown	**mein**	my
Park	park	**Boot**	boat	**Maus**	mouse

German [t d n] are like English [t d n], except that the tip of the tongue must be farther forward in pronouncing the German sounds so that it touches the edge of the upper teeth; in this respect German resembles Spanish more than it does English.

Tee	tea	**da**	there	**Name**	name
hat	has	**direkt**	direct	**in**	in

German [k g ŋ] are like English [k g ŋ]. Note that **ng** in German is always pronounced like the **ng** in **young,** never like that in **younger :**

kein	no	**gestern**	yesterday	**jung**	young
kalt	cold	**Gold**	gold	**lang**	long

At the ends of words (or of syllables before **t s**) **b d g** are pronounced [p t k]:

lieb	dear	**Tod**	death	**mag**	may
liebte	loved	**und**	and	**sagt**	says

German [f s š] are like English [f s š (sh)]. The symbol **v** is often used to spell [f]. An **s** indicates an [s] only when it is final, or in a final consonant group; medially, [s] is spelled **ss** or **ß.** The spelling for [š] is **sch,** except as indicated below:

Fenster window	**Haus** house	**schon** already
vier four	**links** to the left	**Schuh** shoe

At the beginnings of words, **sp** and **st** are pronounced [šp] and [št]:

sprechen speak	**Stadt** city
spät late	**stehen** stand

German [v z ž] are like English [v z ž]. [v] is spelled with **w;** [z] is spelled with **s** and occurs only initially and medially; [ž], the first consonant in *azure,* is characteristically found in words borrowed from other languages and is spelled with **g** or **j:**

wir we	**sie** she	**Garage** garage
wie how	**lesen** read	**Journal** journal

A sound that occurs only rarely in English is the consonant of **ich** and **ach.** This sound may be used in English as the initial consonant of words like *huge* and *hue;* some speakers use it in the pronunciation of the Scottish *loch.* To learn to make it, pronounce with as much friction as possible the initial consonant of *hue;* say **ee,** [i:] before this, and then bring the two sounds, the **ee** and the **h,** together. When you do, you will have the pronunciation of the word **ich** 'I.' You will find that the **ch**-sound is produced by means of friction between the tongue and the roof of the mouth. The initial consonant of *think* is similarly made, but with friction between the front part of the tongue and the teeth.

ich I **riechen** smell

When this sound is made after the vowels [a o u], the friction will be produced even farther back in the mouth, but your tongue will automatically make the shift:

noch still **Buch** book

The **-ig** suffix has the consonant of **ich**:

König king   **fleißig** diligent

The two consonant combinations [pf] and [ts] are not difficult to pronounce, but American speakers must be aware that the consonants are pronounced almost simultaneously. There is no trace of a vowel between the [p] and the [f], the [t] and the [s]. [ts] is spelled with z or tz:

Pfennig penny   **Zeit** time
Pfeife   pipe   **Fritz** Fred

The consonants **k** and **g** are pronounced when they occur before **n**:

Knie knee   **begegnen** meet

German [h] is pronounced like English [h], and it too occurs only initially. After vowels, h is often used to indicate the length of the vowel, as in **Schuh, ihn.**

helfen help   **heute** today

German [j] is pronounced like the initial consonant of English **yet**:

ja yes   **jener** that one

German [l] is pronounced like the English [l] used at the beginning of a word. Speakers of American English must avoid the **oo**-like l which they may use at the ends of words; the German [l] is always **ee**-like.

billig cheap   **bellen** bark

German **r** is pronounced variously by different German speakers. According to the accepted pronunciation, it is trilled with the tip of the tongue. (Children often make this sound when they imitate a motor.) We use one type of this **r** in words like *water, button*; note how in *button* the **t** made by having the tongue flip rapidly against the front part of the roof of the mouth.

The other type of German **r** is made by friction between the back of the tongue and the uvula (the free-hanging end of the back of the roof of the mouth). We do not use this sound in English.

It will be best for you to learn the **r**-sound of your teacher.

waren were   **rot** red   **Fritz** Fred

After vowels, the **r** is often merely a glide:

hier here   **teuer** expensive   **wieder** again

1.4 The German vowels   In making the German vowels it is important to be aware that our English vowels are virtually all diphthongs. For example, when we say *bee* the vowel starts out like the corresponding German (and Italian, French, etc.) vowel, but then the tongue is raised and the vowel ends with a consonant something like the initial sound of **yet**. In German, such glides are not found.

Moreover, the German vowel system is much simpler than is that of English. In German there are basically five tongue positions; since before **t** our glides are as short as anywhere, we may indicate the basic German vowels with the following words (the triangular arrangement indicates the relative positions of the tongue):

beet   *boot*

bate   *boat*

bot

From these you can learn the German long vowels [i: e: a: o: u:] if you take care to avoid any diphthongal glides.

biet' offer   **gut** good   **ihn** him   **tun** do

Beet bed   **Boot** boat   **See** lake   **Sohn** son

bat asked   **lahm** lame

The short vowels, as mentioned above, are pronounced with the tongue position of the long vowels, but are about half their length.

bitt' ask   **und** and   **ist** is   **Sturm** storm
   Bett bed   **Sonne** sun   **es** it   **offen** open
      hat has   **Lamm** lamb

Besides these five pairs of long and short vowels, German has two pairs of vowels that are produced with the tongue position of [i: e:], but are made with rounded lips. In pronouncing [i: e:] the lips are spread, as in a smile; but in pronouncing these two others pairs, they are rounded as in a pout. These vowels are written **ü** and **ö** and are called *umlaut vowels*.

Long: **Tür** door   **grün** green
      König king   **hören** hear

Short: **Stück** piece   **jünger** younger
       können can   **zwölf** twelve

There is another umlaut vowel, **ä,** but this is generally pronounced like **e:**

Mädchen girl   **Länder** countries

In unstressed syllables there is a further vowel, spelled **e,** that is pronounced [ə], like the last vowel of *sofa:*

bitte please   **Liebe** love

Besides these fifteen vowels, German has three diphthongs [ai oi au].

ein a, an   **neu** new   **Frau** woman
Preis prize   **träumen** dream   **aus** out

1.5 The German Sentence Melody In German, as in any language, the inflections of the voice, or intonation patterns, are of prime importance for conveying the exact meaning of sentences. Every sentence has one of a possible variety of these inflections that indicate the meaning of the sentence as a whole. For example, in English "I saw her" has a drop in pitch at the end; this drop gives the notion of finality. On the other hand, in "I saw her, (but she said no)" the pitch does not fall before the comma, and we get the impression of something to follow. We may illustrate the two patterns as follows:

<pre>
        saw   saw her,
   I   I
        her.
</pre>

These inflections, you must learn from the beginning. You can most readily do so by observing the intonation patterns of German speakers.

The usual German sentence pattern is like that of English. For example, in **Hier ist die Klasse** the pitch is relatively low during the first part of the sentence, rises on **Klas-**, and then falls. We may illustrate this pattern as follows:

<pre>
                  Klas-   Eng-
   Hier ist die   Jetzt lernen wir
                  se.   lisch.
</pre>

The melody of questions requiring the answer "yes" or "no" does not have the fall at the end. We may illustrate it as follows:

<pre>
          hier?   Freund?
    Ist er   Ist das nicht Ihr
</pre>

There are other sentence melodies in addition to those illustrated. Most of them vary with the mood and intention of the speaker. You can best learn them by imitating the intonation of German spoken in sequence.

1.6 Different Varieties of German German, like other languages, varies from area to area. If you model your speech on that of a careful speaker, your pronunciation will be acceptable, even if it differs in some respects from that described here. As you know from the varieties of American English, it would require a long description to give some idea of the differences between the speech of various areas of a country.

1.7 Capitalization With the following exceptions, capitalization in German is like that in English. All German nouns are capitalized: **der Vater** 'the father,' **der Junge** 'the boy.' **Sie** 'you' and **Ihr** 'your' are written with capitals, *e.g.*, **Haben Sie Ihr Buch mitgebracht?** 'Did you bring your book along?' Note that **ich** 'I' is not capitalized. Note further that adjectives denoting nationality are not capitalized: **ein amerikanisches Kind** 'an American child.'

1.8 Punctuation The most important difference between punctuation in German and that of English is that the semicolon is rarely used in German. Commas, on the other hand, are used much more than in English and must be placed before any new clause. **Ist dies das Buch, das Sie mitgebracht haben?** 'Is this the book that you brought along?'

Exclamation points are used after salutations in letters and after imperatives in German. **Bringen Sie mir das Buch!** 'Bring me the book.'

1.9 Syllabication Syllable division is much simpler in German than in English. The rules are: Single consonants between vowels are put with the following vowel: **Va-ter, ge-hen;** since **ß, sch, ch** represent single sounds, they follow this rule: **hei-ßen, wa-schen, rie-chen.** If two or more consonants occur between vowels, the last alone is put with the following vowel: **El-tern, Freun-de, Mor-gen.**

Compounds words, however, are divided in accordance with their simple elements: **Deutsch-stunde, wirk-lich, Gesell-schaft, fünf-und-sieb-zig.**

2. The Noun Forms of words are listed in the following sections according to paradigms for the purpose of providing a survey. The lexical meanings may be found in the glossary; the grammatical meanings in the pertinent lessons. In the sections on nouns, adjectives, and pronouns, *Sg* stands for *Singular*, *Pl* for *Plural*, *N* for *Nominative*, *A* for *Accusative*, *D* for *Dative*, *G* for *Genitive*.

Sg N	der Vater	⎰ die Mutter	⎰ das Fenster	
A	den Vater			
D	dem Vater	der Mutter	dem Fenster	
G	des Vaters	der Mutter	des Fensters	

Pl N	⎱ die Väter	⎰ die Mütter	⎰ die Fenster	
A				
D	den Vätern	den Müttern	den Fenstern	
G	der Väter	der Mütter	der Fenster	

Sg N	der Sohn	⎰ die Stadt	⎰ das Jahr	
A	den Sohn			
D	dem Sohn	der Stadt	dem Jahr	
G	des Sohns	der Stadt	des Jahrs	

Pl N	⎱ die Söhne	⎰ die Städte	⎰ die Jahre	
A				
D	den Söhnen	den Städten	den Jahren	
G	der Söhne	der Städte	der Jahre	

Sg N	der Mann	⎰ das Haus	
A	den Mann		
D	dem Mann	dem Haus	
G	des Manns	des Hauses	

Pl N	⎱ die Männer	⎰ die Häuser	
A			
D	den Männern	den Häusern	
G	der Männer	der Häuser	

Sg N	⎱ der Student	⎰ die Bank	⎰ die Lehrerin	
A	⎰ den Studenten			
D	dem Studenten	der Bank	der Lehrerin	
G	des Studenten	der Bank	der Lehrerin	

Pl N	⎱ die Studenten	⎰ die Banken	⎰ die Lehrerinnen	
A				
D	den Studenten	den Banken	den Lehrerinnen	
G	der Studenten	der Banken	der Lehrerinnen	

Irregular Nouns

Sg N	der Herr			
	der Name	das Auge	das Herz	das Kino
A	den Herrn			
	den Namen			
D	dem Herrn	dem Auge	dem Herzen	dem Kino
	dem Namen			
G	des Herrn	des Auges	des Herzens	des Kinos
	des Namens			

Pl N	die Herren			
A	die Namen	die Augen	die Herzen	die Kinos
D	den Herren	den Augen	den Herzen	den Kinos
	den Namen			
G	der Herren	der Augen	der Herzen	der Kinos
	der Namen			

3. der-words, ein-words, and Adjectives

Sg N	dieser gute Vater	diese gute Mutter	dieses gute Kind
A	diesen guten Vater	diese gute Mutter	dieses gute Kind
D	diesem guten Vater	dieser guten Mutter	diesem guten Kind
G	dieses guten Vaters	dieser guten Mutter	dieses guten Kinds

Pl N	diese guten Väter	diese guten Mütter	diese guten Kinder
A	diese guten Väter	diese guten Mütter	diese guten Kinder
D	diesen guten Vätern	diesen guten Müttern	diesen guten Kindern
G	dieser guten Väter	dieser guten Mütter	dieser guten Kinder

Sg N kein jung**er** Vater
           keine junge Mutter   kein jung**es** Kind
  A keinen jungen Vater
           keine junge Mutter   kein jung**es** Kind
  D keinem jungen Vater
           keiner jungen Mutter   keinem jungen Kind
  G keines jungen Vaters
           keiner jungen Mutter   keines jungen Kinds

Pl N ⎱ keine jungen Väter
  A ⎰   keine jungen Mütter   keine jungen Kinder
  D keinen jungen Vätern
           keinen jungen Müttern keinen jungen Kindern
  G keiner jungen Väter
           keiner jungen Mütter   keiner jungen Kinder

Sg N ⎱ starker Verkehr
  A ⎰ starken Verkehr   große Schwierigkeit   langes Haar
  D starkem Verkehr großer Schwierigkeit   langem Haar
  G stark**en** Verkehrs großer Schwierigkeit   lang**en** Haars

Pl N ⎱
  A ⎰ starke Weine   große Schwierigkeiten lange Haare
  D starken Weinen   großen Schwierigkeiten langen Haaren
  G starker Weine   großer Schwierigkeiten langer Haare

4. Pronouns

4.1 Personal Pronouns; Reflexives

	N					
Sg N	ich	du	Sie	er	sie	es
A	mich	dich	Sie	ihn	sie	es
D	mir	dir	Ihnen	ihm	ihr	ihm

Pl N	wir	ihr	Sie		sie
A	uns	euch	Sie		sie
D	uns	euch	Ihnen		ihnen

Sg/Pl A, D   sich   sich

4.2 Interrogatives

Sg/Pl N	wer	was
A	wen	was
D	wem	—
G	wessen	—

4.3 The relative pronoun <u>der</u>, <u>die</u>, <u>das</u>

Sg N	der	}	}
A	den	} die	} das
D	dem	der	dem
G	dessen	deren	dessen

Pl N	}
A	} die
D	denen
G	deren

5. Numerals and Dates

5.1 Cardinal Numerals

0 null			
1 eins	11 elf		100 (ein) hundert
2 zwei	12 zwölf	20 zwanzig	200 zweihundert
3 drei	13 dreizehn	30 dreißig	300 dreihundert
4 vier	14 vierzehn	40 vierzig	400 vierhundert
5 fünf	15 fünfzehn	50 fünfzig	500 fünfhundert
6 sechs	16 sechzehn	60 sechzig	600 sechshundert
7 sieben	17 sieb(en)zehn	70 siebzig	700 siebenhundert
8 acht	18 achtzehn	80 achtzig	800 achthundert
9 neun	19 neunzehn	90 neunzig	900 neunhundert
10 zehn			1000 tausend

1 000 000 **eine Million**   1 000 000 000 **eine Milliarde**

1 000 000 000 000 **eine Billion**

21 **einundzwanzig** 43 **dreiundvierzig** 95 **fünfundneunzig**
106 **hundert(und)sechs** 264 **zweihundertvierundsechzig**

5.2 Ordinal Numerals

The suffix **-te** is added to the cardinal numerals up to 19,
-ste is added from 20 on.

der, die, das **erste**	sechste	elfte	zwanzigste
zweite	sieb(en)te	zwölfte	dreißigste, etc.
dritte	**achte**	dreizehnte, etc.	
vierte	neunte		hundertste
fünfte	zehnte		tausendste

5.3 The suffix **-ns** is added to ordinal numerals to make adverbs:

> **erstens** firstly
> **zweitens** secondly
> **zehntens** tenthly

-l is added to ordinals to make fractions; but note **halb** 'half':

> **Drittel** third **Viertel** fourth **Zehntel** tenth

5.4 To give the day of the month one uses ordinals, *e.g.*, **Heute ist der dreizehnte August.** 'Today is the thirteenth of August.'

The names of the months are masculine. They are:

Januar	April	Juli	Oktober
Februar	Mai	August	November
März	Juni	September	Dezember

The names of the days of the week are masculine. They are:

Sonntag	Mittwoch
Montag	Donnerstag
Dienstag	Freitag
Sonnabend/Samstag	

6. The Verb

6.1 Auxiliary Verbs

Infinitive	sein	haben	werden
Pres Ptc	seiend	habend	werdend
Past Ptc	gewesen	gehabt	geworden

Pres	Indic	Subj	Indic	Subj	Indic	Subj
ich	bin	sei	habe	habe	werde	werde
er, sie, es	ist	sei	hat	habe	wird	werde
du	bist	seiest	hast	habest	wirst	werdest
wir, sie, Sie	sind	seien	haben	haben	werden	werden
ihr	seid	seiet	habt	habet	werdet	werdet

Past						
ich	war	wäre	hatte	hätte	wurde	würde
er, sie, es	war	wäre	hatte	hätte	wurde	würde
du	warst	wärest	hattest	hättest	wurdest	würdest
wir, sie, Sie	waren	wären	hatten	hätten	wurden	würden
ihr	wart	wäret	hattet	hättet	wurdet	würdet

Imperative

(du)	sei	habe	werde
(ihr)	seid	habt	werdet
	seien Sie	haben Sie	werden Sie

6.2 Weak Verbs and Strong Verbs

Infinitive	fragen	fahren
Pres Ptc	fragend	fahrend
Past Ptc	gefragt	gefahren

Pres	*Indic*	*Subj*	*Indic*	*Subj*
ich	frage	frage	fahre	fahre
er	fragt	frage	fährt	fahre
du	fragst	fragest	fährst	fahrest
wir, sie	fragen	fragen	fahren	fahren
ihr	fragt	fraget	fahrt	fahret

Past				
ich, er	fragte	fragte	fuhr	führe
du	fragtest	fragtest	fuhrst	führest
wir, sie	fragten	fragten	fuhren	führen
ihr	fragtet	fragest	fuhrt	führet

Pres Perfect		*Subj Past I*
ich	habe gefragt	habe gefragt
er	hat gefragt	habe gefragt
du	hast gefragt	habest gefragt
wir, sie	haben gefragt	haben gefragt
ihr	habt gefragt	habet gefragt

Pres Perfect		*Subj Past I*
ich	bin gefahren	sei gefahren
er	ist gefahren	sei gefahren
du	bist gefahren	seiest gefahren
wir, sie	sind gefahren	seien gefahren
ihr	seid gefahren	seiet gefahren

Past Perfect		*Subj Past II*
ich, er	hatte gefragt	hätte gefragt
du	hattest gefragt	hättest gefragt
wir, sie	hatten gefragt	hätten gefragt
ihr	hattet gefragt	hättet gefragt

Past Perfect		Subj Past II
ich, er	war gefahren	wäre gefahren
du	warst gefahren	wärest gefahren
wir, sie	waren gefahren	wären gefahren
ihr	wart gefahren	wäret gefahren

Future		Subj Fut I
ich	werde fragen	werde fragen
er	wird fragen	werde fragen
du	wirst fragen	werdest fragen
wir, sie	werden fragen	werden fragen
ihr	werdet fragen	werdet fragen

Future		Subj Fut II
ich	werde fahren	würde fahren
er	wird fahren	würde fahren
du	wirst fahren	würdest fahren
wir, sie	werden fahren	würden fahren
ihr	werdet fahren	würdet fahren

Future Perfect

ich werde gefragt haben	ich werde gefahren sein

Future Perfect Subj I	Future Perfect Subj II
ich werde gefragt haben	ich würde gefahren sein

6.3 Reflexive Verbs

	Pres Indic	Past Indic
ich	erinnere mich	erinnerte mich
er	erinnert sich	erinnerte sich
du	erinnerst dich	erinnertest dich
wir	erinnern uns	erinnerten uns
sie	erinnern sich	erinnerten sich
ihr	erinnert euch	erinnertet euch

6.4 Modals (Present Tense) and <u>wissen</u>

	dürfen	können	mögen	müssen	sollen	wollen	wissen
ich, er	darf	kann	mag	muß	soll	will	weiß
du	darfst	kannst	magst	mußt	sollst	willst	weißt
wir, sie	dürfen	können	mögen	müssen	sollen	wollen	wissen
ihr	dürft	könnt	mögt	müßt	sollt	wollt	wißt

6.5 Passive Forms

Infinitive	gefragt werden
Pres Ptc	gefragt werdend
Past Ptc	gefragt worden

	Pres Indic	*Past Indic*
ich	werde gefragt	wurde gefragt
er	wird gefragt	wurde gefragt
du	wirst gefragt	wurdest gefragt
wir, sie	werden gefragt	wurden gefragt
ihr	werdet gefragt	wurdet gefragt

Pres Perf	ich bin gefragt worden
Past Perf	ich war gefragt worden
Future	ich werde gefragt werden
Fut Perf	ich werde gefragt worden sein

INDEX

INDEX

Numbers within entries refer to the Grammar sections of lessons unless otherwise specified; *e.g.*, 10.2.1 refers to Lesson 10, section 2, subsection 1 of the Grammar discussion. References to subdivisions of the Appendix are preceded by "Appendix." For definitions and examples of grammatical terms, see the Preface to the Student.

235